Connecticut by Bicycle
Fifty Great Scenic Routes

Frederick John Lamp

The Farmington Valley Greenway near the Massachusetts border

Cover and book designed by: Bruce Waters
Type set in Myriad Pro

ISBN: 978-0-7643-3794-9
Printed in China

Schiffer Books are available at special discounts for bulk purchases for sales promotions or premiums. Special editions, including personalized covers, corporate imprints, and excerpts can be created in large quantities for special needs. For more information contact the publisher:

Published by Schiffer Publishing Ltd.
4880 Lower Valley Road
Atglen, PA 19310
Phone: (610) 593-1777; Fax: (610) 593-2002
E-mail: Info@schifferbooks.com

For the largest selection of fine reference books on this and related subjects, please visit our website at **www.schifferbooks.com**
We are always looking for people to write books on new and related subjects. If you have an idea for a book please contact us at the above address.

This book may be purchased from the publisher.
Include $5.00 for shipping.
Please try your bookstore first.
You may write for a free catalog.

In Europe, Schiffer books are distributed by
Bushwood Books
6 Marksbury Ave.
Kew Gardens
Surrey TW9 4JF England
Phone: 44 (0) 20 8392 8585; Fax: 44 (0) 20 8392 9876
E-mail: info@bushwoodbooks.co.uk
Website: www.bushwoodbooks.co.uk

Contents

North-Central 123
The Farmington and Connecticut River Valleys

Northwest 153
Litchfield Hills, the Upper Housatonic to the Berkshires

Southwest 183
From Long Island Sound to Candlewood and Black Rock Lakes

Introduction

In April 1886, a 43-year-old French immigrant to the United States by the name of Pierre Lallement rode a two-wheeled contraption that he'd just made, beginning in Ansonia and ending at the Green in New Haven, Connecticut. He had just invented the bicycle, and the first bicycle patent was awarded in New Haven. Born in France at Pont à Mousson in 1843, he had emigrated to the United States in July 1865 at the age of 22, and came to live in Ansonia. He died in Boston in 1891. A bronze plaque commemorating Lallement and his invention lies in the brick pathway leading to the Green from the corner of Chapel and College Streets.

Shortly after I came to Connecticut in 2004, I organized a group bike ride, starting in New Haven and riding down the coast through West Haven and Milford. I decided that a convenient and recognizable place to start would be the New Haven Green and that the corner of Chapel and College would be the most logical place to meet. As we gathered at the entrance to the Green, I looked down, and to my immense surprise, there was the plaque commemorating the very first bicycle ride—ever, anywhere. It was one of those "Can you believe this?" moments, and quite an auspicious way to begin.

This guide is intended for touring Connecticut by bicycle, and the emphasis is on sightseeing. All the routes can be done on a road bicycle, although some would be more comfortable on a hybrid, especially on dirt and gravel roads; mountain bikes are not needed although they will also be OK to use. The routes are chosen for their scenic value, which means that frequently they are good open biking routes, avoiding the heavily trafficked highways, but, most importantly, there are interesting things to see on the way. Although serious bicycle trainers will want to just keep pumping through to the end, I recommend looking at things on the way, which means turning your head as you ride, and stopping to see some of the wonderful sights. There is nothing like a bike ride to see the sights that you would often miss speeding, or even just cruising, in a motor vehicle. These routes go through picturesque villages, farmland, and forests, and by expansive lakes, rivers, ponds, harbors, and the Long Island Sound that forms the entire southern coast of the state. Sometimes there are cafes and restaurants along the way, sometimes not, but always there are glorious sites for sitting down and enjoying a lunch—at the peak of a mountain, by a bubbling brook, or dangling your legs off a wooden wharf—the name "Connecticut" originates from the Mohegan word *quinnitukqut*, meaning "place of the long tidal river."

On the historical aspects of the descriptions in this book, I am indebted to Patricia E. Kane, Friends of American Arts Curator of American Decorative Arts at the Yale University Art Gallery, for her careful reading of the text and her advice. Riders would benefit from some advance reading, such as *Connecticut: An Explorer's Guide* by Barnett D. Laschever and Andi Marie Cantele (Woodstock, Vermont: Countryman, 2009), *Off the Beaten Path: Connecticut*, by Joan and Tom Bross (Guilford, Connecticut: Globe Pequot, 2009), and for deeper perspective, *Connecticut*, written by the Federal Writers Project of the WPA (Boston: Houghton Mifflin, 1938).

Take along a little camera that you can throw into your back pocket. There are recent digital cameras that have high power and still are easily portable. I carry a small Coolpix with 5.1 megapixels—all the photographs in this book have been taken with this, handheld, without a tripod.

Before each ride, photocopy the map in this book along with the cue sheet to carry on the ride. Enlarge them if you can, so that the details can be seen easily at a glance. It would be a good idea also to bring more detailed maps of the area, as directions on cue sheets can be a little misleading because the writer may assume things that you don't (Is that actually a right turn or a forward? Is this really an intersection or a Y with an immediate right? Was that a dead end or just a name change? A bridge to me may be a culvert to you.). Also, frequently there are no road signs posted, or there is one name on the right and another name on the left. In

Connecticut, road names change as soon as they cross a town jurisdiction line. I frequently barrel forward on a new road when the original road actually bent to the left or right, and find myself hopelessly lost if I haven't brought a map.

A note on maps: this is not an exact science, and no two maps are the same. In fact, sometimes they are shockingly different: one shows a road, the other does not; on one the road goes to the northeast, on the other it goes to the northwest; one shows that two roads connect, the other shows that they do not; one shows a continuous road, the other indicates a gap with dead ends; on one, two roads merge, on the other they abut at a ninety-degree angle; one shows a lake, the other does not; the mileage scale is frequently way off; the map shows a through street at an intersection, but, in fact, it's a dogleg; and so on. The most inaccurate maps are those from websites on biking trails. The maps in this book are likely to be fairly accurate for the tested bike route itself, but other routes and landmarks are simply cobbled from the available maps, and are only as reliable as the originals.

Schedule a whole day for these rides and not a day when you have to be back at five for an appointment (unless you start out at the crack of dawn). You will be tired at the end of the ride—but that's a good thing. I like to sit in a hot tub afterwards and listen to music, and think about how I've just redistributed my weight.

Don't think you have to have an outfit to bicycle. You don't need a bicycle jersey, or bicycle shoes, or a fancy water backpack, as useful as these items may be (the jerseys expel moisture better than cotton, the shoes fit into stirrups or clips, and the water backpack makes drinking on the run easier). The early bicyclists rode in coats and ties (the women in petticoats and heels) and they won competitions at incredible speeds even on their iron "bone shakers." The world of competitive bicyclists today tends to have a follow-the-leader mentality, and sports clothing manufacturers and retailers have benefited from this. You do need a helmet and bicycle shorts with good padding, however, if you intend to do these rides. Otherwise, a T-shirt and sneakers will do. Be sure to bring water bottles full.

Connecticut is a great state for bicycle riding. It has all sorts of terrain, from the absolutely flat right along the coastline to extremely hilly in the northwest as it reaches the Berkshires. The hill ranges, in general, run vaguely north to south, so most of the routes in this book have been designed as north-south ovals or rectangles, to save the rider from having to do too many roller coasters on the east-west routes. Lots of rivers meander from the north to the south, all emptying eventually into the Long Island Sound: The Connecticut River, The Housatonic River, The Farmington River, The Quinebaug River, Mystic River, and many more. The entire stretch of the Long Island Sound is good for bicycling as it meanders in and out of coves and peninsulas. Hundreds of lakes and reservoirs dot the state,

some, unfortunately entirely surrounded by private homes, but many bordering on state parks and smaller picnic grounds and beaches. Remember that entrance to state parks is free for bicyclists. There are still many miles of dirt road and only the occasional car. While traffic can be heavy along the coast and also in the southwest with its attraction for the New York second-home crowd, many areas in the north still have those quiet tobacco roads, and even outside of New Haven there are lonely routes wandering through forests and along lakes.

We hope it stays this way. We can even hope it gets better. New housing developments are everywhere threatening to turn the entire southern half of the state into one enormous suburbia, and this can only be regulated by state legislation, where Connecticut is really behind, compared to some other states. The state has made a start by identifying good bicycle routes. And there is a good commitment to continuing the construction of bicycle and hiking paths along former railroad tracks and canals. The East Coast Greenway is still somewhat of a dream, but it actually exists for quite a few miles. Let's complete those routes. State, city, and local governments need to think about bicyclists when they construct new roads, providing for comfortable shoulders, and bike lanes when possible. City streets are the most dangerous, yet this is where it's needed the most—where we really need to move from motoring to bicycling. Many people do not bicycle because they are afraid, and government needs to provide safe routes.

In cities, bicycling would benefit if the legislature would set traffic regulations for bicycles that recognize their difference from motor vehicles in terms of safety and speed—somewhere in-between a motor vehicle and a pedestrian. Many people ride bicycles to work or simply to get to nearby destinations, and this kind of cycling would be greatly encouraged if cyclists had a different set of rules enabling them to beat the traffic. Most cyclists ignore the traffic laws for this reason; officers of the law mercifully often look the other way; but new, reasonable laws for bicycling should be enacted.

The rides in this book are targeted toward a mid-level ridership—those who aren't quite ready for the Centennial ride, not really training for the Tour de France, but have some experience riding, are interested in some substantial exercise after a week in the office swivel chair, and want something more challenging than a leisurely few miles. But those speed demons lunching on an energy bar will find many of the rides here equally invigorating, and the maps can be used to combine rides to create lengths of 80-100 miles or more. For the more leisurely set, the maps show ways to find shortcuts, creating 15, 20, or 30-mile rides. Some may want simply to follow a single stretch of any one route that seems the most interesting, and turn around at any place to return back to the starting point. Remember, if you cut across a circular or rectangular route at the middle, you are not cutting the route in half because although you're saving the mileage to the top of the route and back, you're adding the route across the middle, so you're really only cutting about one-fourth to one-third. Remember also that east-west shortcuts are likely to take you up and down the ridges.

Many of the rides in this book are drawn from two sources: the Connecticut Bicycle Map and the Southwest Connecticut Bicycle Route. The first is produced by The Department of Transportation of the State of Connecticut, and it provides a good state map in color, with bike rides classified as "Recommended Routes," "Cross State Routes," and "Loop Ride Routes." Four loops are given with cue sheets—all these are included in this book, somewhat modified. There are special maps indicating river crossings. And the main map shows state parks and forests, hiking trails, Indian tribal land, park and ride lots, and points of interest throughout the state. Many of the rides in this book follow the yellow "Recommended Routes," combining them as possible. The second source is a more detailed map of the coastline from New Haven to Greenwich and the New York border, produced by the East Coast Greenway Alliance in Wakefield, Rhode Island. It traces a route along the coastline, eastbound and westbound, and is intended to be part of the larger East Coast Greenway connecting the Entire Eastern Seaboard from Maine to Florida. In this book these rides are modified with deviations in one direction that take the rider down to the waterside as much as possible, which results in longer but more interesting rides.

When I came to Connecticut in 2004 I was surprised to find that there were no books on bike routes in the state for more experienced riders. There are, however several other sources that should be consulted as a supplement to this book. *Short Bike Rides in Connecticut* by Edwin Mullen and Jane Griffith is a good introduction with thirty-two suggested routes distributed evenly throughout the state, and for more "combination rides," linking two or three of the basic rides. This is where I got my start. The book provides a good narrative to each ride with comments on the interesting sights, black and white photos, good data on the rides, and maps of each route, which are simple, but sometimes difficult to follow because they do not provide the cross streets or sometimes distort the details of the route. The book also does not provide cue sheets, so the rider has to follow the map, which doesn't have enough detailed and accurate information, or carefully read the text, which is more detailed, but difficult to do while you're riding. I frequently got lost.

Another useful book is *The Official Rails-to-Trails Conservancy Guidebook* for Connecticut, Rhode Island, Massachusetts, Vermont, New Hampshire, and Maine (in other words, the whole of New England). This is a great source for the many, many bicycle, pedestrian, and bridle trails throughout the state, mostly transformed from old railway lines. These routes vary from 2 or 3 miles to some longer interstate trails. Many are still unfinished, and some are too rough for a road bike or even a hybrid. The format of the book is the same as *Short Bike Rides*, although it has more information about such things as wheelchair access, places to find food, restrooms, seasonal schedules, access and parking, and places to rent bikes. My one reservation about the book, again, is that the maps are extremely simple (although a little better than the previous book) and not always accurate in noting what portions of the route are passable or impassable by bicycle.

Bicycle: the History, by David V. Herlihy, was published by Yale University in 2006. It gives the history of the invention of the velocipede and ultimately the true bicycle, by Lallement. With a lively narrative and lots of great illustrations of early bicycles and posters and news clippings of some curious and wonderful events, it makes great reading for anyone. One insight that I came away with is that motorists and pedestrians have always been vying with great antagonism for the right-of-way with bicyclists, and it will probably ever be so. All the more the need for education on both sides.

Backroad Bicycling in Connecticut, by Andi Marie Cantele (Woodstock, Vermont: Countryman, 2007), is an excellent guide especially for shorter rides of several miles, including dirt trails, but also including some longer road rides. The introduction is a good survey on bicycling safety, supplies, and rules of the trail. The book targets an extremely broad ridership, with its range of distances from four to sixty-one miles, and includes thirty-two rides, some for road bikes and others requiring mountain bikes, so it is limited for any one level of rider. The maps outline principally the main route, making it difficult to deviate, and there are, strictly speaking, no cue sheets, but, rather a more narrative list of turns with mileage, also giving descriptions, which makes it a little unwieldy to use in the saddle. Nevertheless, it covers the state, and is a well-informed tour guide.

Best Bike Rides in New England, by Paul Thomas and updated by Paul Angiolillo (Globe Pequot, 1998), covers all of New England in forty-four routes, with some rides in northeastern Connecticut for mid-level to competitive cyclists. But its emphasis is further north. Each ride profile rates the level of difficulty, and gives information on interesting sights and places to eat or rest, as well as detailed directions with mileage and a map.

There are numerous bicycle clubs throughout the state, and some of these post bicycle routes and cue sheets on the Internet. Sound Cyclists Bicycle Club is in the southwest. Southern Connecticut Cycle Club is based in New Haven. Yankee Peddlers operates out of Farmington in the north central. Healthy Gears combines biking with nutritional counseling. Travelers Bike Club offers Wednesday night rides starting at 6 P.M. over courses of 10 to 25 miles around the greater Hartford area. Other smaller groups exist, and some rides are organized by bicycle shops, such as the Devil's Gear in New Haven. Elm City Cycling's bike tours are offered as part of the annual Arts & Ideas Festival in June, centered on the Green, and they conclude with the New Haven Century. Nearly a hundred riders may turn up, from novices to experienced racers. All rides leave from the New Haven Green and lead to the waterside or the hills.

One of the most helpful websites is www.wecyclect.org, the website of the Central Connecticut Bicycle Alliance. Their goals are promoting bicycling and human powered transportation, working to improve the bicycling environment, and educating motor vehicle operators and bicyclists about their respective rights and responsibilities. The section on Bicycle Health, Safety & the Environment has detailed information on Connecticut Bicycle Statutes, Rail-Trails and Safe Communities, Health Benefits of Bicycling, How Not to Get Hit by Cars, Bicycle Commuter Tips, Advocacy & Education Groups, and Federal, State, & Regional Organizations. Advocacy Highlights gives current news on bicycling legislation and other legal action on the federal and local level. The Events Calendar and Bike Everywhere sections list a number of local rides. Connecticut Law on Bicycling, researched and written by CCBA Board Member Ben Bare, pulls together every law enacted covering bicycling in the state.

There is a great website that has hundreds of bike routes of all lengths from less than 35 miles to more than 50 miles submitted by hundreds of bikers—www.ctbikeroutes.org. This website has been developed as a service to the cycling community and is free. You can search and find detailed information on over 250 bike routes, most of which are located entirely in Connecticut, with some rides, though, venturing into the adjoining states of Rhode Island, Massachusetts or New York. Ride lengths range from 25-100 miles; most are 30-40 miles. You can refine your search to focus on terrain from level to very hilly, and you can search specific regions and towns. Don Shildneck, Doug McKain, and Rich Lenoce conceived, developed, and implemented the project. The website solicits new bike routes from its visitors, and welcomes feedback from riders.

The Internet also is a good source for information on the rails-to-trails, often with good color photographs and descriptions of the routes, with maps. The Rails-to-Trails Conservancy (RTC) has just established a partnership with Google Maps to indicate recommended bike routes from one direction to another, like the service that has long been available to motorists. Go to the website www.railstotrails.org. Users can type in their starting point and destination to receive directions as a cue sheet and as a map with the route highlighted. Like the motorists' maps, these indicate the most direct route (which may be a busy highway like Route 1), but not necessarily the most pleasant or scenic route. RTC has also provided its rails-to-trails maps to Google to be included in their service. These were previously not indicated on Google maps. Unfortunately, many of these rails-to-trails maps are not kept up-to-date, indicating detours that are no longer necessary because the trail has been extended. More often, the source will indicate a long trail when, in fact, portions of the trail have not been completed and are impassable. Sometimes it is not clear whether the trail described is a projection or a current reality. So the rider needs to carry along a good map to find out where to go when the trail ends at an old, bumpy set of railroad ties or a muddy swamp. Connecticut Rails-to-Trails may be found on the website www.traillink.com. Those suitable for a road bike or hybrid are the following:

Airline State Park Trail—South: Hartford, Middlesex, New London, Windham Counties. 22.40 miles
Charter Oak Greenway: Hartford County. 9.80 miles
Derby Greenway: New Haven County. 1.70 miles
Farmington Canal Heritage Trail: Hartford, New Haven Counties. 40 miles
Farmington River Trail: Hartford County. 8 miles
Housatonic Rail-Trail – Trumbull (Pequannock Valley Greenway): Fairfield County. 3.40 miles
Middlebury Greenway: New Haven County. 4.40 miles
Putnam River Trail: Windham County. 2 miles
Quinebaug River Trail: Windham County. 4 miles
Railroad Ramble: Litchfield County. 1.70 miles
Stratton Brook State Park Trail: Hartford County. 2 miles
Vernon Rails-to-Trails: Tolland County. 4 miles
Windsor Locks Canal State Park Trail: Hartford County. 4.50 miles

We hope that many more bicycle trails will be opened, existing trails extended and connected, and undeveloped trails made passable for bicyclists. Some wonderful possibilities exist. One of the rails-to-trails routes with the greatest potential is the Air Line State Park Trail, but it is finished with crushed stone only from East Hampton to a few miles short of Willimantic. North of Willimantic, the trail is paved for a few miles, but then it disintegrates into dirt and gravel, which would be serviceable for bicyclists if it were not for the equestrian use that chops up the surface, making it impossible for all but mountain bikes (even though the publicity offers bicycle use). This makes it clear that a bridle path cannot double as a bicycle trail. But much of the support for that trail comes from equestrians, so this is probably not going to change. The trail would ultimately lead all the way to Provenance if it were developed. On the other hand, there has been great progress on the Farmington Canal Heritage Trail, which now can be taken into Massachusetts all the way to Northampton. We still need to see the central portion completed, from Plantsville to Farmington, as this is a big gap that must be traversed on unpleasant roads. The East Coast Greenway from the New York border to New Haven is meant to be actually green, and to connect with the Farmington Canal Heritage Trail. Currently, it is a street route through some rather gritty urban sections. The dream is to follow alongside the Merritt Parkway, where one short portion has already been completed—the bridge over the Housatonic River. Funding has just been received for the Norwalk River Valley Trail, which will extend 27 miles from Calf Pasture Beach in Norwalk through the Norwalk River Valley to Danbury, incorporating existing trails in Norwalk, Ridgefield, and Wilton. As of this writing, a one-mile heads north from the Maritime Aquarium in Norwalk. Look for these new bicycle trails to come, and press for continued developments on the existing trails.

The cue sheets in this book are meant to be as concise as possible so that when you are hurtling down a hillside at 35 mph on your bicycle you can, quickly as possible, see the next turn at the mileage indicated. You don't have a lot of time to read interesting narrative en route (that's in the descriptions of the rides). The names of the streets and roads are kept as brief as possible, eliminating the word "Street" or "Road" unless it would be confusing to do so (for example, "New Haven" is a road as well as a city; and "Hulls Hill" would be the name of the hill, as well as a road; "Water" would suggest the waterside rather than a street by this name). Words are abbreviated to one or two letters for quick recognition. Landmarks indicated are limited to those that are relatively permanent—such things as red lights, stop signs, and stores can be here one day and gone the next, so they are not used here.

Guide to Notations:

N = north
S = south
W = west
E = east

L = left
R = right
F = forward
BL = bear left (branch)
BR = bear right
SL = sharp left
SR = sharp right
L-R = dogleg left, then right
R-L = dogleg right, then left

Y = fork in the road
X = intersection

Rules of the Road

Cyclists must abide by the same rules and regulations as motorists, and are obligated by law to obey all traffic signals. Traffic summonses may be issued to cyclists for running stop signs and red lights or riding on the wrong side of the road. Cyclists ride with the traffic on the right (not against it, on the left, as pedestrians walk). Cyclists must stop at all marked intersections.

At all intersections, with or without stop signs, cyclists should yell "car left" or "car right" to other cyclists if cars are approaching from either of those directions. One thing that cannot be stressed enough is riding single file, especially in high traffic areas and on narrow roads. During cycling tours, stay to the right and ride single file.

Before making a left turn, first check traffic to see if any cars are coming, then fully extend your left arm and point in that direction. Signal well in advance of the actual turn, and then position your bike so that traffic can move around you. When making a right turn, fully extend your right arm and point in the intended direction. Some cyclists signal a right turn by holding their left arm out with the forearm pointing up. Either way is correct. You should signal well in advance of the actual turn, and then use both hands to steer through the turn.

If there is debris or a hazard in the road, fully extend your arm and point to the hazard. Sometimes moving your arm while pointing draws more attention to the debris. Potholes, branches, glass, sand, storm drains, etc. should all be called out verbally as a courtesy to riders in the rear. When slowing or stopping, fully extend your arm down and out with the palm of your hand facing those who might be behind you. Call out "slowing" or "stopping" while displaying your hand signal to forewarn riders behind that you are slowing or stopping. When passing, call up to the rider you are passing and announce, "passing left" or simply, "on your left." Check that you are not cutting off another rider and only pass on the left, leaving about three feet of clearance. If you are being passed, continue straight, do not turn and look back.

Sharing the road: The bicyclist has the same right to a lane that the motorist has. Courtesy by anyone operating a slow vehicle suggests yielding space on the lane by moving to the right, and this is encouraged for bicyclists, so that the vehicle behind can pass. But when there is danger on the right, including debris or parked cars where a driver's door may open unexpectedly, the bicyclist should not move over, but should claim the lane. By moving over, bicyclists endanger themselves—many bicyclists have been injured and killed by car doors opening in front of them. Furthermore, when bicyclists move over, motor vehicle drivers frequently take the full lane, endangering the bicyclist from the left—bicyclists have also been injured and killed by vehicles passing and scraping them.

When riding in a group, if a car is approaching from behind, call out to the riders ahead of you, "car back." This warning should be passed along by each rider to the front of the group until there is no one left to warn. On hearing this warning, form a single file and, if there is no danger on the right, move to the right. When a car is approaching from ahead, call out to the riders behind you, "car up." This warning should be passed along by each rider to the back of the group until there is no one left to warn. On hearing this warning, form a single file.

Sidewalks versus streets: Just as cars are not permitted to drive down the sidewalk, neither are bicycles. In some cities, where congestion is heavy and there is no bicycle lane, the police will overlook bicyclists on the sidewalk. In fact, in New Haven, one frequently sees bicycle patrolmen, themselves, riding on the sidewalk. So the bicyclist may use discretion, but under no circumstances, should a bicyclist charge down a sidewalk at a speed faster than a running pedestrian. We recommend following the law and rightfully claiming the streets.

View of New Haven from East Rock Park

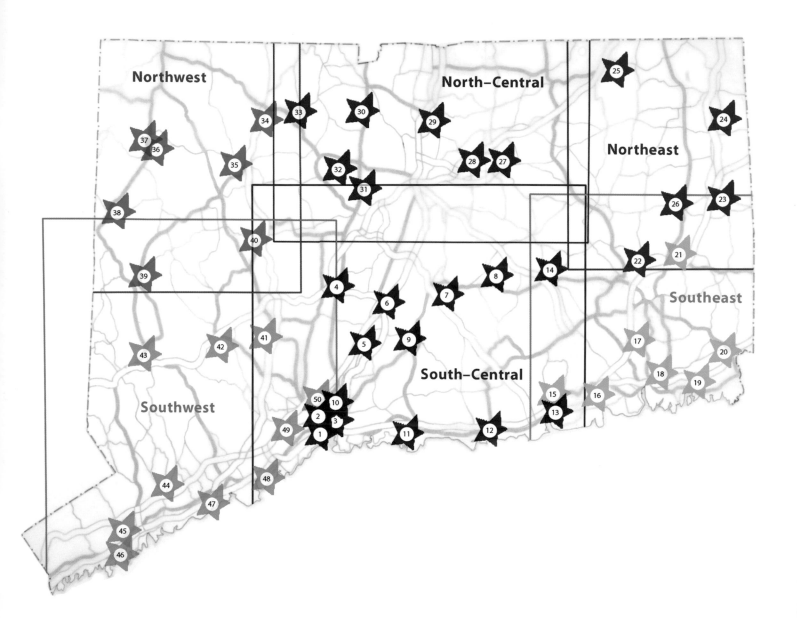

Northwest

North-Central

Northeast

Southwest

South-Central

Southeast

South-Central

Yale – New Haven – The Quinnipiac and the Lower Connecticut Rivers

Smith-Hubble Wildlife Sanctuary, Milford

[1] East Coast Greenway: New Haven – Milford

Meeting place: New Haven Green, SW corner by the plaque honoring the inventor of the bicycle, at Chapel & College
Length: 40 miles
Lunch: There are several small cafes and beer gardens. Or bring lunch to enjoy at the Wildlife Refuge.
Sights: Long Island Sound, beaches, harbors, historic churches and homes, beach houses, Silver Sands State Park, Connecticut Audubon Coastal Center, Charles E. Wheeler wildlife area, Smith-Hubble wildlife sanctuary.
Challenge: easy; generally flat, mostly paved streets with little traffic, and a few short gravel paths.

This ride follows (with some deviations for a better view) the easternmost stretch of the "East Coast Greenway Trail" from the New York border to New Haven, where it connects with the Farmington Canal Greenway Trail. This section is one magnificent view after another. Take time every once in awhile to walk out a couple of the many piers over the water or to sit on a sunny beach. Returning eastward we simply follow every through street that goes along the waterside. A detailed map of this section of the East Coast Greenway may be found at the website: http://greenway.org.

We start at the beautiful New Haven Green at the corner of Chapel and College, at the site of the bronze plaque honoring the acknowledged inventor of the bicycle, Pierre Lallement. Here we have a view of the formidable nineteenth-century fortress that flanks the entrance to the Old Campus of Yale University at Phelps Gate. We head south on Chapel and East Street to the harbor, following Long Wharf Drive, which gives a beautiful view across the New Haven harbor to the east shore and the lighthouse. After negotiating some well-traveled streets across the Kimberly Avenue Bridge and Main Street into West Haven, we pass by the Green and the magnificent Congregational Church built in 1859, and then down Savin Avenue to Savin Rock. We follow the coast on Ocean Avenue, Route 162, and Merwin Avenue, and then Buckingham takes us back to Route 162 into the heart of old Milford. A right on Prospect Street leads to the grand Congregational Church of 1823, designed by David Hoadley (who also designed the United Church Of Christ, Congregational, on the New Haven Green in 1813), and the gold domed Town Hall on the little Wepawaug River and West River Street leading to Broad.

Lafayette and Rogers take us down to the waterside and East Broadway to Surf, then heading directly west on Meadowside straight through Milford Point Road all the way to the end at the Smith-Hubble Wildlife Sanctuary and the Connecticut Audubon Coastal Center with its displays on marsh life. This is the high point of the trip, with magnificent views across the marshes and lakes on the one side which can be seen from the top of a lookout tower. A boardwalk takes us out to the grassy border of the Long Island Sound on the other side.

The route back east takes us down every through street that follows along the coastline, sometimes zigzagging around residential areas (no dead end streets). Generally these streets are one-way eastbound, and there is almost no traffic. At the end of Milford Point Road and East Broadway, we pass by a paved path through Walnut Beach Park, and Silver Sands State Park, with its long boardwalk over the marshes to the sea. Following the coastline back to Milford, and circling through the residential area of Golden Hill, we pass three seventeenth- and eighteenth-century houses on High Street that are open to the public: local Native American artifacts are displayed in the Eells-Stow House of 1700. Further up Hellwig Street, at a charming area of outdoor cafes and beer gardens, a picturesque footbridge crosses the inner Milford Harbor to Wilcox Park. Now we zigzag by every coastal street past Welch's Point to the beach at the entrance to Milford Harbor, with a wide stretch of sand, then Bayview Beach and Pond Point Beach to Pond Point. From here we circle back to the main road, and then back down to the water side on Yale Avenue to the cliffs far above the water, giving a magnificent view along Morningside Drive. At Woodmont, we round the bend at Merwin Point with its grand homes and private beaches. The point itself is a rocky outcropping that is a delightful stopping place to climb out to the end for a view of the coastline.

Route 162 and Ocean Avenue lead us back to the sandy beach past Savin Rock on a part-paved, part-gravel path, which is worth a visit just to sit on this promontory of rock shelves and view the Long Island Sound. Ride slowly and cautiously along this path, as it is sometimes packed with pedestrians who are oblivious to the bicycle icon stamped on the pavement. The path leads to Beach Street and 1st Avenue and a right on Kimberly over the bridge leads us back by Howard, Spring, Union (past Union Station), State, and Chapel Streets to the New Haven Green.

First Church of Christ, "Center Church on-the-Green," 1812-1814, New Haven

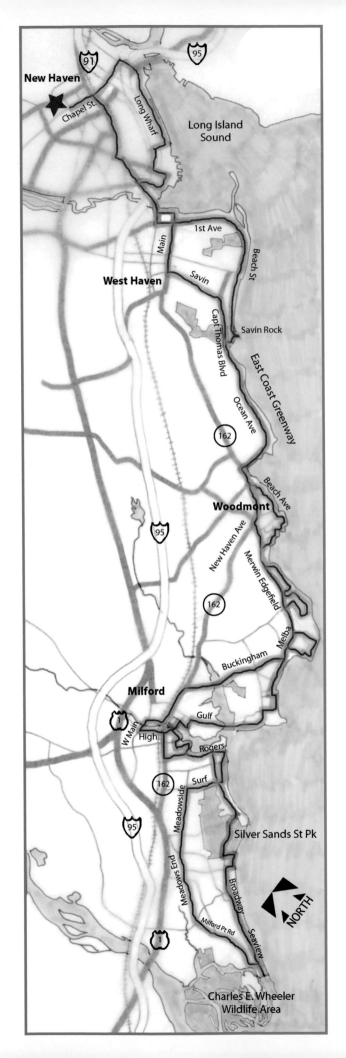

1. East Coast Greenway: New Haven – Milford
Meet: New Haven Green at Chapel & College

(Route deviates both ways from official Greenway)

00.00	L	Chapel St. under I-91
01.00	R	East St. → Long Wharf under I-95 to end
02.50	L	Sargent Dr → 5th
02.80	L	Howard over I-95 2 bl
03.00	R	Sea St. → E. T. Grasso Blvd.
03.46	L	Kimberly under I-95, over bridge to 1st L.
04.07	L	Water St. around curve
04.24	F	Main past W. Haven Green
05.00	L	Savin to end
05.87	L	Capt. Thomas Blvd. → Ocean Av to circle
08.60	L	Rte 162 (New Haven Av) to Robert Treat Nursery on L.
09.45	L	Merwin → Edgefield → Melba to just before steep short hill
12.60	R	Buckingham to end
13.05	L	Rte 162 (New Haven Av)
13.60	R	Prospect under RR to 1st X.
13.85	BL	W. Main (toward Superior Court) over small bridge to 1st L.
13.95	L	W. River St
14.26	R	Rte 162 (Broad)
14.65	L	Greens End
14.69	L	Rte 162
14.73	R	Lafayette → Rogers
15.45	R	E. Broadway
15.88	R	Surf → Robert Treat
16.34	L	Meadowside → Meadows End → Milford Point Rd
19.46	R	Milford Point Rd. into Audubon Center
19.85		Return on Milford Point Rd
20.25	F	Seaview → Broadway → E. Broadway
21.70	R	Viscount 1 bl to end
21.75	L	drive into carpark to end of pavement
21.98	L	paved path to end to 1st R.
22.15	R	pavement thru Walnut Beach Pk onto gravel path to end
22.55	R	Silver Sands St. Pk to end at water
22.83	L	E. Broadway to 1st X.
23.40	R	Shell to end
23.65	R	Seaside 1 bl to end
23.68	L	Trumbull to end
23.90	L	Rogers to first R.
24.47	R	Merwin Pl. around L. to Pond St. to end
24.74	R	Green 1 bl to end
24.83	R	High 1 bl
24.91	L	Helwig → Factory Ln to footbridge on R.
25.10	R	(dismount to cross foot bridge)
25.14	R	thru Wilcox Pk onto Shippard Ln
25.35	R	Harborside around L. to Bedford to end
25.63	R	Gulf (across bridge) → Welch's Point
26.95	R	Deerfield to end at waterside
27.10	L	Field Ct to end
27.22	L	Oakland 1 bl
27.25	R	Bayshore → Warren → Melba
27.97	R	Platt to end
28.20	L	Morehouse 1/2 bl to 1st R.
28.22	R	Virginia 2 bl to end
28.30	L	Point Beach Dr
28.50	L	Atwater to end
28.83	R	Edgefield
29.20	R	Yale to end
29.32	R	Ridgewood
29.55	L	Little Pond 1 bl to end
29.62	L	Morningside to end
30.04	L	Norwood 1 bl to end
30.10	F	Ridgewood 1/2 bl to end
30.15	R	Edgefield 1 bl to 1st R.
30.23	R	South Av 1 bl to end
30.25	L	Hillside to end
30.70	R	Edgefield to 1st R.
31.03	BR	Abigail 1 bl & BR, then L. to end
31.23	R	Mark
31.25	L	Kings Hwy 1 bl to 1st R.
31.32	R	Beach Av—90° curves around coastline
32.28	L	Spencer 1 bl to end
32.31	R	Hawley 1 bl to end
32.36	L	Anderson 1 bl to 1st X.
32.40	R	Rte 162 (New Haven Av) to circle
32.66	BR	Ocean Av
34.80	R	pedestrian walkway to end
35.88	F	Beach St. → 1st Av
37.75	R	Kimberly over bridge & under I-95 to end
38.80	BL	Howard
38.84	R	Spring → Union → State St
39.80	L	Chapel St
40.10	R	at College St. into New Haven Green

[2] New Haven – Bethany – East Rock

Meeting place: New Haven Green at Chapel & College Streets
Length: 25 miles
Lunch: There are some small cafes and snack shops at the halfway point at Whitney and Mount Carmel. Or bring lunch to enjoy at East Rock.
Sights: Yale University, West River, Edgewood Park, West Rock, East Rock Park, Sleeping Giant State Park, forests, lakes, communities of North Haven and New Haven.
Challenge: easy; paved roads with light to moderate traffic and a few hills.

This is a short and sweet little ride beginning in the city at the fortress that is called Yale University and meandering along rural roads, lakes, and quiet residential communities. The route is modified from Rides 26 and 27 in Mullen and Griffith, *Short Bike Rides*.

Starting at the Green in New Haven, we head out Chapel Street passing Yale's Old Campus, the Yale University Art Gallery, the Center for British Art (all the Yale museums are free admission), Yale Repertory Theatre, the School of Architecture's Paul Rudolf building (1963), and the School of Art. The Art Gallery is a block and a half long, consisting of the elaborately carved, stone, Gothic Street Hall (1864-1866) by P. B. Wright, the towering hulk of Egerton Swartwout's neo-Romanesque/Italian Renaissance Old Art Gallery (1928), and the modern, minimalist building by Louis Kahn (1953), his first major commission. The metalclad Center for British Art was Kahn's last commission (1977), so the two facing buildings bookend the career of this controversial architect. Even more controversial was Paul Rudolf and his brutalist-style, of which the monumental building at Chapel and York, in ribbed, bush-hammered concrete, is a premier example.

Chapel takes us to the corner of Ella Grasso Blvd. . and the winding drive down through Edgewood Park, along the West River and grassy fields, all the way to Whalley, which we cross to Fitch. Left on Blake, we soon enter Valley Street and get a view of the magnificent vertical cliff sides of the West Rock Ridge. At the end, Pond Lily Avenue takes us left to a right on Route 69, otherwise known as the Litchfield Turnpike. This takes us for several miles on a gentle incline past various lakes, following the West River, and then through forested countryside past lakes on Downs Road, which becomes Brooks and then Westwoods Road. A right on the similarly named West Woods Road takes us east across the West Rock plateau and then plunges all the way

to Whitney Avenue and the Farmington Canal Trail, where there are some small shops to get a bite to eat.

Continuing across Whitney on Mount Carmel, we pass the Sleeping Giant State Park (with great hiking trails, where, if you have time, a hike up to the tower would be rewarding) on the left, and on the right the charming little Jonathan Dickerman House built in 1792, open to the public on weekend afternoons, and worth a stop to see the period furnishings and the garden of folk medicine herbs. Here we head south on New Road along the campus of Quinnipiac College, alongside a couple of ponds, and then follow Ives and Broadway to Ridge Road. This aptly named road goes several miles along the top of a ridge through elegant neighborhoods of homes built in the 1930s and 40s, all the way to East Rock Park. Here we take the park drive all the way to the top where a breathtaking view awaits us, stretching all the way through the towns of New Haven, West Haven, and Fair Haven to the New Haven harbor and the Long Island Sound. Descending from the mountain on hairpin turns, we enter New Haven by Orange Street along Edgerton Park, and then make our way back to the Green by way of Grove and Temple streets.

With time to spare, get a good look at the three wonderful early nineteenth-century churches on the Green (Church of Christ, Center Church, and Episcopalian), and enjoy the peace of this historic place. With more time to spare, enter through the forbidding brown stone Phelps Gate facing the Green on College Street, and take a leisurely walk through the Old Campus of Yale University to High Street, which is lined with one magnificent building after another, from neo-Gothic to ultra modern. The oldest building on the Yale campus is the brick Connecticut Hall of 1750, the only building left of The Old Brick Row. Surrounding it are Gothic-style buildings dating to the mid and late nineteenth century.

School of Architecture, 1963, Paul Rudolph, architect, Yale University, Chapel & York Streets

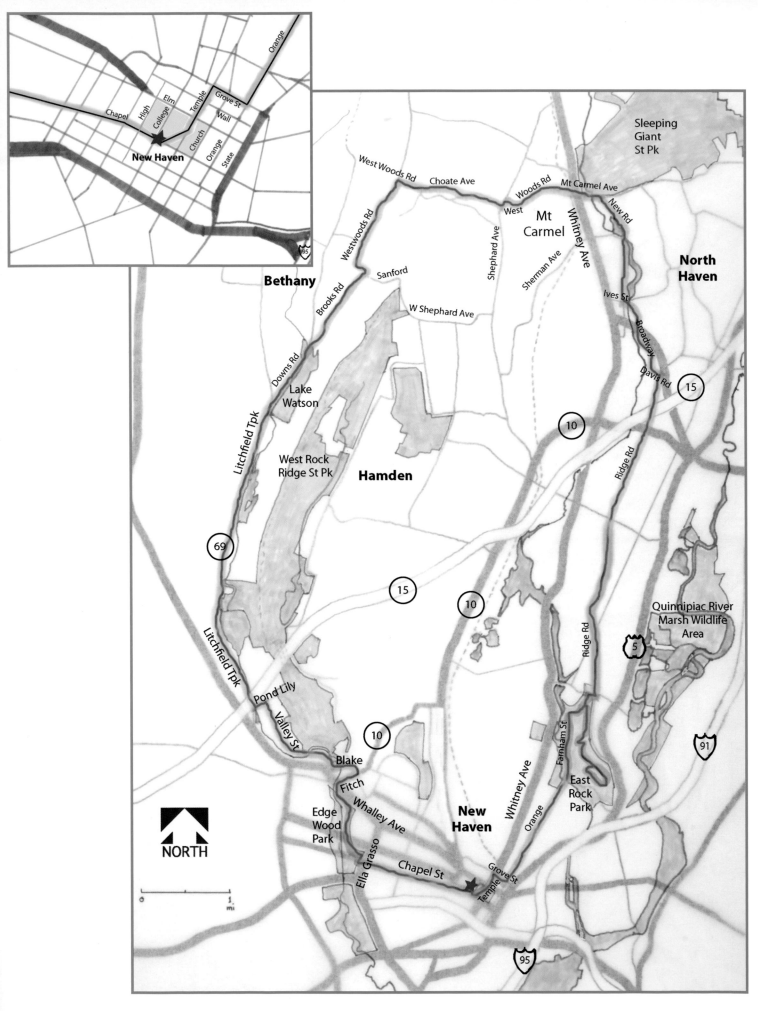

New Haven

Chapel
High
Elm
College
Temple
Grove St
Wall
Church
Orange
State
Orange

95

West Woods Rd
Choate Ave
Woods Rd
Mt Carmel Ave
New Rd

Sleeping
Giant
St Pk

Westwoods Rd

Mt
Carmel

West

Whitney Ave

**North
Haven**

Bethany

Brooks Rd
Sanford

Shephard Ave
Sherman Ave

Ives St

Broadway

W Shephard Ave

Davis Rd

Downs Rd

15

Lake
Watson

10

Litchfield Tpk

West Rock
Ridge St Pk

Hamden

Ridge Rd

69

15

10

Litchfield Tpk

Ridge Rd

Quinnipiac River
Marsh Wildlife
Area

5

Pond Lily

Valley St

10

91

Blake

Fitch

Whalley Ave

Farnham St

Edge
Wood
Park

Whitney Ave

East
Rock
Park

Ella Grasso

Chapel St

Grove St

Orange

**New
Haven**

Temple

NORTH

0   1.
           mi

95

2. New Haven – Bethany – East Rock
Meet: New Haven Green at Chapel & College Sts

00.00	R	Chapel to Ella Grasso Blvd..
01.22	BR	into Edgewood
		Park drive downhill
02.13	F	Fitch (across Whalley)
02.43	L	Blake
02.80	R	Valley to end
04.05	L	Pond Lily
04.18	R	Whalley → Lichfield Tnpk
		(Rte 69) past Lake Dawson
		to 1st R.
07.42	BR	Downs past Lake Watrous
to 1st R.		
08.45	R	Brooks → Westwoods to 1st R.
10.83	R	West Woods to 1st R.
		(keep straight)
11.10	F	Choate
11.66	F	West Woods (continues)
		w dogleg L-R at Shepard
		(12.10 mi.) to Whitney
		(Rte 10)
13.10	F	(with dogleg R-L) on
		Mount Carmel to 1st R.
13.35	R	New Rd. (into
		Quinnipiac College)
14.63	L	Ives to bend
14.70	R	Broadway → Davis Rd
15.63	R	Ridge past Bassett
		Park & downhill
19.30	R	Davis St. to immediate L
19.38	L	Farnham into East Rock Park
19.45	L	to East Rock at the top and return
22.05	L	Farnham
23.00	R	Orange
24.35	R	Grove
24.50	L	Temple to pass 2nd church
		on Green
24.80	R	diagonal path through Green
24.90		finish at Chapel & College

East Rock Park from Orange Street, New Haven

[3] Farmington Canal Greenway Trail (South): New Haven – Plantsville

Meeting place: New Haven Green, SW corner at Chapel and College Streets
Length: 13 miles
Lunch: There are several small cafes along the trail, and restaurants in Cheshire.
Sights: Yale University, town Greens, historic churches and houses, woods, streams, Canal Lock 12
Challenge: easy; generally flat, all paved, some traffic on roads, no traffic on trail, but some strollers, joggers, and skaters.

The lower two thirds of this ride follows the paved path that was once the towpath for the Farmington Canal and then the railroad track for Amtrak/CSXT. Eventually this bike path will be continuous from the New Haven harbor to Massachusetts. But as of this writing, there are still sections unfinished, necessitating some detours on the roads. Be sure to check for updates on construction. The trail is almost completely straight and flat, and goes through quiet wooded areas, following the old canal, and sometimes dipping into residential and commercial areas. Weekends, especially in the spring and early summer, the path can be packed with strollers, dogs, and children, but during the week it can be smooth sailing. A detailed map of this section of the East Coast Greenway may be found at the website: http://greenway.org.

We begin at the New Haven Green and catch the trail a few blocks away on Hillhouse Avenue (as of this writing, it doesn't yet continue south to the harbor). From here it's smooth sailing for 15 miles on the paved path all the way to Cheshire. The newly completed section through Hamden goes through some colorful if shabby old neighborhoods, and on a Sunday morning, some spirited gospel music pours forth from several tiny Black churches right beside the path. Further along the way there is the beautifully restored Canal Lock 12, with a museum and an old lockmaster's house that is now a private home. This section of the path ends at Cornwall Avenue, where it runs up against an old industrial section that bordered the former railroad, where some intransigence appears to have blocked the continuation of the route, but we hope this will soon be resolved. Here, we parallel the canal path on local roads, Willow, Main, and Peck/Canal/Atwater as far as the village of Plantsville on West Main, where there are some funky little cafes, an unusual nineteenth-century Gothic Congregational Church on West Main, the Henry Kilton house on Route 10 built between 1748 in 1760, and lots of antique shops.

This is the end of the line, where we turn back south. But it is also the beginning of the next finished section of the Farmington Canal Greenway Trail, so for the really hearty, the ride could continue north.

Turning south, we follow Route 10 for 6 miles back to Cheshire, with lots of traffic but a good shoulder for most of the way. The Cheshire Green, with its classical white Congregational Church, built in 1826, offers a pristine New England moment. Just after the Green, we cross over on Cornwall Avenue to meet the trailhead again for the trip south on the canal path. Ten miles later, just before the bridge over Connolly Street and under the Wilbur Cross Parkway (Route 15) at Dixwell, we exit the Farmington Canal Greenway and try another scenic route back that takes us through a beautiful residential area, through the woods of East Rock Park with a grand view of Lake Whitney, and then back by the bike lane of Orange Avenue, Humphrey, and Whitney, to Temple Street, and into the Green. Here we encounter two early nineteenth-century Congregational churches—the United Church on the Green (North Church, built by David Hoadley in 1814) and the Center Church on the Green (built by Ithiel Towne in 1812-1814)—and a third stone Gothic church, Trinity Episcopal Church on the Green, also designed by Ithiel Town, opened in 1816. We cut a diagonal through the Green to our starting point. Here is Yale University's old campus, just through Phelps Gate in the center of College Street, a serene setting of nineteenth-century stone Gothic fortresses and bronze statues to past heroes. With some time left, the Center Church offers some highlights: The Crypt (with stones dating from 1687), the Waterford crystal chandelier, the Fisk Pipe Organ, and Tiffany stained glass windows.

Canal Lock 12 Historic Park, Farmington Canal Greenway

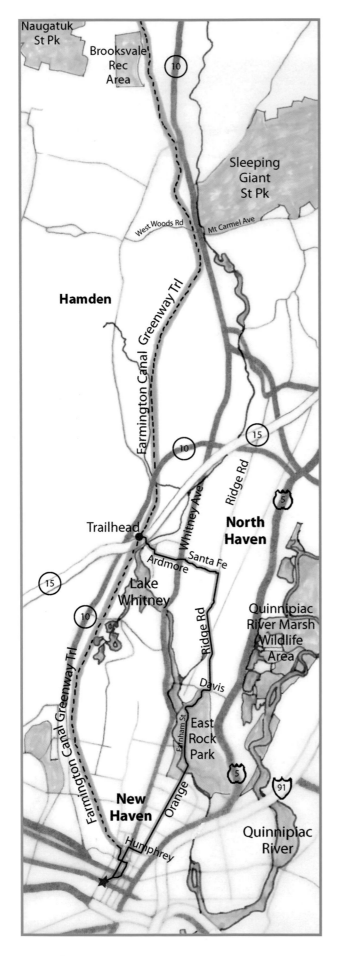

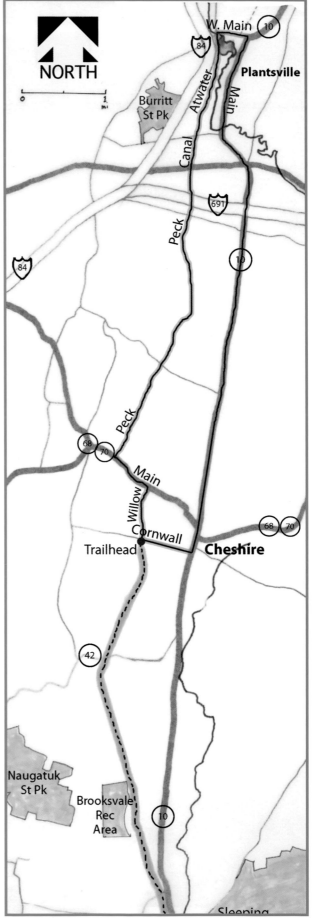

3. Farmington Canal Greenway Trail (South):
New Haven – Plantsville
Meet: New Haven Green, SW corner, Chapel & College Streets

00.00		Cross Green diagonally to NE corner
00.25	BL	Church St—2 bl
00.40	L	Grove—to 2nd R
00.45	R	Hillhouse—1/2 bl over bridge
00.55	L	onto Farmington Canal Greenway Trail—to end at Cornwall Av
14.30	R	Cornwall—1/4 bl
14.31	L	Willow—2 bl
15.11	L	Main → West to 4th R
15.66	R	Peck → Canal → Atwater to end
20.90	R	W. Main to center of Plantsville
21.33	R	Rte 10 (Main) to Cheshire, pass Green
27.53	R	Cornwall to trailhead on left
28.12	L	Farmington Canal Greenway Trail to exit just before Rte 15 underpass
37.82	L	Connolly → Elgin to end
38.16	R	Greenway—1/4 bl
38.17	L	Ardmore → Santa Fe (dogleg L-R at Whitney) to end
38.88	R	Ridge
40.26	R	Davis
40.34	L	Farnham (East Rock Park)
41.35	R	Orange
42.19	R	Humphrey
42.39	L	Whitney → Temple
43.10	R	(path across Green at 1st church)
43.24		to start at Chapel & College

The Cheshire Green, with the First Congregational, United Church of Christ, 1826

[4] Farmington Canal Greenway Trail (Central): Plantsville – Farmington
(unfinished section between trailheads)

Meeting Place: Plantsville Trailhead (I-91 to Rte 691 west to Rte 10 north to left on West Main St, Plantsville—right on Summer St to Trailhead Parking)
Length: 30 miles
Lunch: There are many cafes and restaurants in Farmington.
Sights: Shade Swamp State Wildlife Area, Farmington River, Farmington Valley Greenway, the town of Farmington, historic homes and churches.
Challenge: easy; generally flat, short paved bicycle trail, and some streets with traffic.

This is the middle section of the Farmington Canal Greenway Trail—or, that is, it will be, whenever the Trail is finished. At the time of this writing this bike route is only a detour on the roads alongside the old abandoned railroad for the most part, connecting from the very short paved section of the Trail at Plantsville to the beginning of the northern section at Farmington. Some of these roads are heavily traveled, without a wide shoulder in some sections, so the route is less pleasant through some busy commercial and industrial areas. These industries fronting the old railroad are now the impediment to the completion of the Greenway Trail, and we hope they will soon resolve their issues with the State. But there is one major treat—and that is the small town of Farmington close to the northern end of this section. The ride is worth doing simply for connecting the dots of the future Farmington Canal Greenway Trail and seeing the old railroad which we cross periodically. A detailed map of this section of the East Coast Greenway may be found at the website: http://greenway.org.

The ride begins in the little town of Plantsville, where the paved trail has become a delightful little town park with strollers and green shoulders—for only two miles. Then we need to take Curtiss Street to Route 10 and north by way of Route 177 as far as the Plainville Industrial Park, where Northwest Drive takes us to Robertson Airport. A left on Johnson Avenue to Hyde Road takes us to New Britain Avenue where we pass the Shade Swamp State Wildlife Area and the Indian Burial Grounds on the right just before we meet the northern section of the Trail at Red Oak Hill Road (on the right, not the left, which is the similarly named Farmington River Trail that heads to the northwest). We take the Trail only to the trailhead parking lot at Brickyard Road, just for a taste of it (the northern section of the Trail is described elsewhere).

At the parking lot, a right takes us south on Brickyard to Route 4 East, across the scenic Farmington River to the incredibly charming town of Farmington. A circle around the edge of the town on High, Mountain, Reservoir, Diamond Glen, Winchell Smith, and Garden takes us past beautiful historic sites open to the public such as the Stanley-Whitman House, a beautiful period-furnished Connecticut saltbox built around 1709; the Hill-Instead House, a magnificent 1901 plantation-style mansion with sweeping views of the rolling hillsides; Riverside Cemetery, where a brown sandstone monument, erected in 1840, honors the Native American Tunxis, and a gravestone where it said that knocking can be heard; and the lovely Farmington River bubbling over rocks. Back where we began on Route 4, we head straight south through the center of town on Route 10, passing the First Church of Christ Congregational built in 1771 in the very simple but elegant colonial style. The church became a hub of the Underground Railroad in the early nineteenth century, and housed the slaves of the *Amistad* during the first civil rights case in the United States held in New Haven, which is commemorated by Amistad Hall. Other attractions here are Miss Porter's School established in 1843 (where Jackie Bouvier Kennedy Onassis attended), and row after row of beautiful, well-maintained eighteenth and nineteenth-century homes.

Route 10 can take us all the way back to Plantsville, but a more pleasant route is to continue straight on Cooke Street where Route 10 (Main Street) branches to the right. At the end, a left on Route 372 and a right on Route 72 takes us over Highway 84 and then south on the more bucolic rural roads of Ledge, Shuttle Meadow, and Flanders back to meet Route 10 briefly where we take Curtiss to Hart and Kane Streets to the Trail leading south back to Plantsville. A few antique shops here are worth a visit before returning home.

The First Church of Christ Congregational, Farmington, 1771

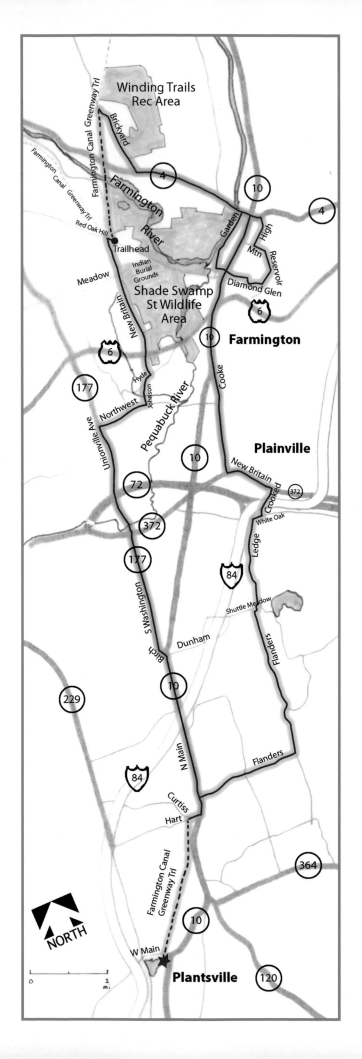

Winding Trails
Rec Area

Farmington Canal Greenway Trl

Brickyard

④

⑩

④

Farmington Canal Greenway Trl

Farmington Canal Greenway Trl

Red Oak Hill

Farmington River

Garden

Mtn

High

Reservoir

Diamond Glen

Trailhead

Meadow

Indian Burial Grounds

Shade Swamp St Wildlife Area

New Britain

⑥

⑩

Farmington

⑥

Hyde

Johnson

Cooke

⑩

177

Northwest

Unionville Ave

Pequabuck River

⑩

Plainville

New Britain

Crooked

372

72

White Oak

Ledge

372

84

177

Shuttle Meadow

Dunham

S Washington

Flanders

Birch

229

⑩

N Main

84

Flanders

Curtiss

Hart

364

Farmington Canal Greenway Trl

NORTH

⑩

229

0   1
mi.

W Main

★

Plantsville

120

28

4. Farmington Canal Greenway Trail
(Central): Plantsville – Farmington (unfinished)
Meet: Plantsville Trailhead (I-91 to Rte 691 W.
to Rte 10 N. to L on W. Main St, Plantsville—R.
on Summer St. to Trailhead Parking)

00.00	F	trailhead, Farmington Canal Greenway to end
01.95	R	Hart/Kane → Curtiss to end
02.12	L	N. Main (Rte 10)
04.72	L	Rte 177
04.95	R	Rte 177 (Birch → South Washington → Unionville Av)
07.90	R	Northwest
08.60	L	Johnson
08.85	R	Hyde to 1st L.
09.00	L	New Britain
11.00	R	Red Oak Hill to trailhead at immediate L.
11.05	L	(trailhead, Farmington Canal Greenway) to Greenway parking at Brickyard Rd
12.90	R	Brickyard Rd. to end
13.95	L	Rte 4 across Rte 10 to 1st R.
15.85	R	High to end
16.25	L	Mountain Rd
16.50	R	Reservoir Rd
16.90	R	Diamond Glen
17.50	R	Rte 10 to immediate L.
17.52	L	Winchell Smith Dr. 1 bl to end
17.56	R	Garden St. to end
18.48	R	Rte. 4 to 1st X.
18.58	L	Rte 10 (Main)
20.86	BL	Cooke at "Y" to end
22.28	L	Rte 372 (New Britain)
22.92	R	Crooked St. (to Rte 72) across bridge over Rte 72 to end
23.32	R	White Oak/Woodford to overpass
23.40	L	Ledge to 1st R.
24.74	R	Shuttle Meadow to 1st L.
24.90	L	Flanders Rd
27.00	R	Flanders St. to end
28.45	L	Rte 10
28.68	R	Curtiss to Y.
28.84	F	Hart/Kane to immediate L.
28.86	L	(trailhead, Farmington Canal Greenway)
30.76		end at trailhead on W. Main St, Plantsville

The Farmington River at Unionville

[5] North Haven – Middletown

Meeting Place: Wilbur Cross Pkwy (Rte 15) to Exit 65, west to Rte 150, parking at Masonicare, Ashlar Center, Wallingford
Length: 45 miles
Lunch: There are several cafes and restaurants in Middletown at the halfway point. Or bring lunch to enjoy at Wesleyan or by the river.
Sights: Historic homes and towns, state parks, farms, cows and horses, Wesleyan University, Connecticut River.
Challenge: easy; mostly flat with a few rolling hills and paved roads with light to moderate traffic.

For a very long stretch, the route begins and ends following just beside the Wilbur Cross Parkway (Route 15) but you'd never know it because of the woods lining the Quinnipiac River State Park. Abundant parking at Exit 65 is the advantage of starting here.

Following the Quinnipiac River north on Route 150 we detour around much of the town of Meriden by way of Routes 71 and 70. On Oregon road we pass the lovely Hanover Pond covered with a net of tiny green vegetation amongst which the swans glide. This is worth a stop at the parking overlook. Just at the bridge across the creek leading to Hanover Pond, with its bright red iron footbridge, a biking and hiking path leads about a mile and a half along a creek and through the woods, making a nice diversion. At the end of Oregon, Main Street takes us directly through town, and then Colony, Britannia, and Westfield lead us to the open country with pleasant horse farms. Six miles down the road, and a couple of name changes, we arrive at Route 3, into Middletown, and around Wesleyan University, with its abundant lawns and stately buildings. Some of the most interesting are the Victorian houses that now serve the University. Cross, Church, and Pleasant Streets take us in a straight line down to the mighty Connecticut River, where a waterside park with a monument to Christoforo Columbo makes a good rest stop by the Wesleyan Boat Club.

A pedestrian tunnel under the highway leads directly to Route 66, the major thoroughfare through Middletown, with no shoulder, and speeding traffic. It would be good to fortify ourselves at one of the charming outdoor cafes in the center of town. Shortly, and mercifully, down the hill westward out of town, we turn south on the lightly traveled Route 157 and follow the route signs for seven miles, with many turns and many different names, passing the picnic area of Wadsworth Falls State Park, to the road's end. Along the short stretch of Route 68 West, the major attraction is the TILCON Mining Company, with its mountains of asphalt, all chopped out of the mutilated ridge behind all the scaffolding, chutes, and loading docks. One is dwarfed standing beside the immense gravel peak resembling a pyramid at Giza.

Just beyond, Branford Road takes us south past big green cattle pastures to Route 17, and Route 22 brings us back over I-91 and the Wilbur Cross Parkway through the town of North Haven. North on the very wooded Hartford Turnpike, we parallel the Parkway past the Quinnipiac River State Park all the way back to the starting point where the name becomes Masonic Road briefly and then Route 150 again.

Hanover Pond, Oregon Road, Meriden

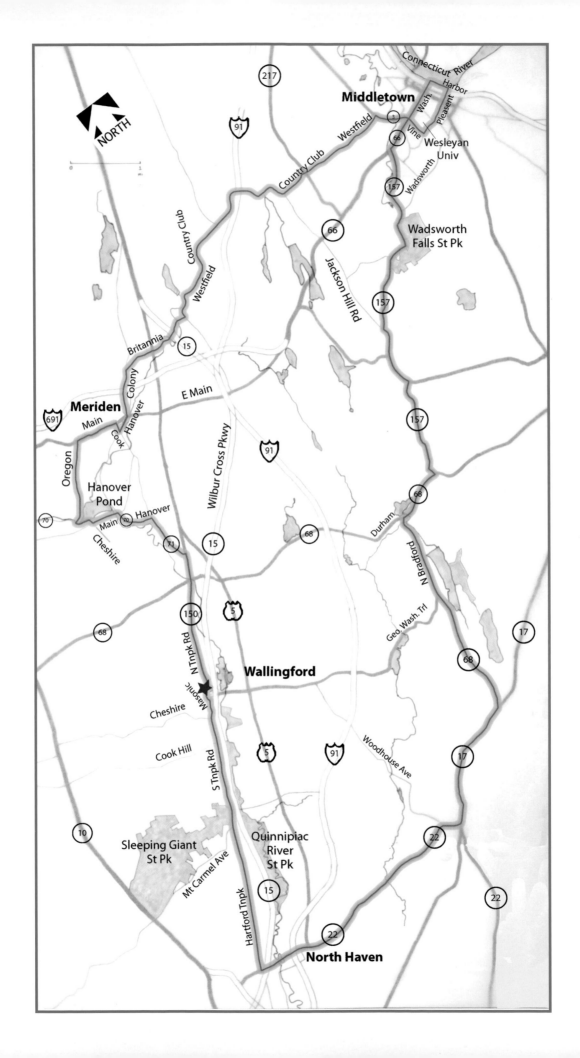

NORTH

Connecticut River

Harbor

Middletown

Wash

Pleasent

Westfield

Vine

Wesleyan Univ

Country Club

Wadsworth

Wadsworth Falls St Pk

Jackson Hill Rd

Country Club

Westfield

Britannia

Colony

E Main

Meriden

Main

Hanover

Cook

Oregon

Hanover Pond

Main

Hanover

Cheshire

Wilbur Cross Pkwy

Durham

N Bradford

Geo. Wash. Trl

N Tnpk Rd

Wallingford

Masonic

Cheshire

Cook Hill

Woodhouse Ave

Sleeping Giant St Pk

Mt Carmel Ave

Quinnipiac River St Pk

S Tnpk Rd

Hartford Tnpk

North Haven

5. North Haven – Middletown
Meet: Wilbur Cross Pkwy (Rte 15) to Exit 65, west to Rte 150, parking at Masonicare, Ashlar Center, Wallingford

00.00	N	Rte 150 (N. Tnpk Rd) to just before stone railroad overpass
02.55	L	Rte 71 (Old Colony Rd)
03.52	L	Hanover (Rte 70) to 2nd L.
04.25	L	Main (Rte 70) to 1st X.
04.75	R	Cheshire/River Rd. (Rte 70) to 2nd R.
05.15	R	Oregon to end
06.84	R	Main to end of two-way
07.60	R	Cook to 1st L.
07.75	L	Hanover to end
08.00	L	Colony under Rte 691 to 1st X.
08.95	R	Britannia to end
10.45	L	Westfield Rd. → Country Club Rd. (over I-91) → Westfield St. to end
16.60	R	Rte 3 (cross Rte 66) → Vine 1 bl
17.00	L	Cross → Church to end
18.30	L	Pleasant to end
18.60	L	Harbor Dr
18.65	F	thru riverside park path
18.96	L	pedestrian tunnel under Rte 9 and carry bike up stairs
19.00	L	DeKoven Dr
19.07	L	Washington (Rte 66) west thru Middletown
20.48	L	Rte 157 (many turns, many street names) to end
27.34	R	Rte 68 (Wallingford Rd) to 1st L.
28.32	L	N. Branford to end
32.40	R	Rte 17
34.77	R	Rte 22 W over I-91 and Rte 15
39.33	R	Hartford Tnpk → S. Turnpike Rd
44.35	L	Masonic
44.80	L	return to parking

TILCON Mining Company, Route 68, Wallingford Road

[6] Meriden – Wethersfield

Meeting Place: Meriden, Rte 691, Exit 7 at Lewis Ave, north to Westfield Shoppingtown on left, parking in front of Sears
Length: 39 miles
Lunch: There are quite a few restaurants, cafes, delis, and food markets along the route, especially at Kensington, Newington, and Wethersfield. A couple of cafes facing the Green in Wethersfield would make a pleasant stop, as there are no more after that, until Meriden.
Sights: Farms, forests, hilltop views, escarpments, historic churches and homes (especially the Buttolph-Williams House of 1710), Hubbard Park and Reservoir, and the vast Westfield Shoppingtown of Meriden.
Challenge: easy to moderate; rolling hills with many long, level stretches and paved roads with light traffic, except heavier in towns.

Three hundred years of housing in Connecticut would be an appropriate title for this ride, as it passes numerous new subdivisions as well as streets of Victorian houses in Meriden, Kensington, and Newington, and dozens of colonial houses—one dating back to 1710—in the charming center of Wethersfield. That's the prize at the northern end of the tour.

We begin our ride in Meriden in the huge parking lot of "Westfield Shoppingtown" and make our way south and west on Lewis Avenue, W. Main St., and Reservoir Avenue until we reach Hubbard Park, which is a vast wooded area with hiking paths and pedestrian roads. After passing around the gate, we head north on the park road past the long Reservoir, which is a beautiful sight with a high rocky escarpment on its west bank. Left on Edgewood takes us past a second reservoir and at the end Route 364 follows the edge of the Timberlin Golf Course to the end. Chamberlain Highway and Norton Road take us to Kensington Road north along the railroad all the way through the town of Kensington to New Britain. Here South Street and then East Street, Route 174, and Route 176 take us to Newington. All these towns have interesting examples of nineteenth-century architecture as well as shops. Route 175 heads east towards Wethersfield.

Wethersfield is worth the entire ride. Here is house after house built in the eighteenth century. With time, it would be a good idea to visit the Webb-Deane-Stevens Museum on Main Street—a line of three houses built from 1770 to 1789. Operated by The National Society of the Colonial Dames of America in the State of Connecticut, there are half-hour tours for a fee until 3:30 P.M. every day except Tuesday, May to October, and only weekends in April and November. The 1752 Joseph Webb House, with its great gambrel roof, served as George Washington's headquarters in 1781, where he plotted the surrender of Cornwallis at Yorktown. Down at the Green is the severely stately First Church of Christ (Congregational), built in 1757 in brick with a soaring tower and steeple, a good example of colonial Puritan architecture, on the model of many other wooden structures around the state. Around the bend on Broad Street is the Buttolph-Williams House of 1710-20, completely restored to its original medieval English style, and a visit is well worthwhile to see the house and gardens and the authentic period furnishings, including the woodenware in the kitchen. Broad Street is divided by a beautiful park which we pass on our way out to catch Route 3 South by way of Middleton Avenue.

The rest of the ride back to Meriden passes one colonial house after another, often marking the date of erection. These are long, uninterrupted stretches of Route 3, 160, a cut across Bacon to Wethersfield, then Beckley which becomes Savage Hill which becomes Atkins Street until it reaches Highland. Country Club, Westfield, and Britannia take us back to Meriden through neighborhoods of lovely, if neglected, Victorian homes, and Columbia Street follows aside Route 691 back to our starting point. Here, the many national department stores beckon us for some evening shopping.

First Church of Christ (Congregational), Wethersfield, 1757-1761

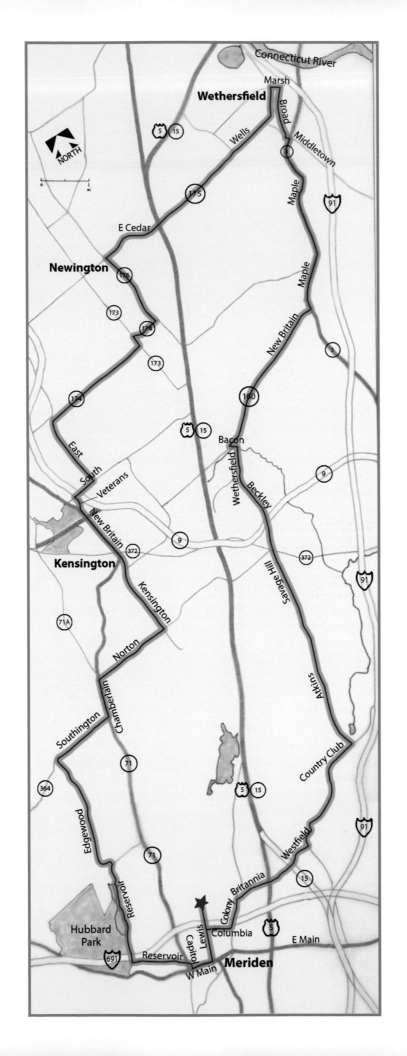

6. Meriden – Wethersfield
Meet: Meriden, Rte 691, Exit 7 at Lewis Ave, N.
to shopping center on L., in front of Sears

00.00	R	Lewis
00.88	R	W. Main
01.30	R	Capitol (just before gas station) to 1st X.
01.42	F	Reservoir to Rte 691 and down past gate into Hubbard Park to 1st R.
02.32	R	Reservoir (past another gate and under Rte 691)
03.90	L	Edgewood to end
05.70	R	Southington (Rte 364) to end
07.23	L	Chamberlain to 1st R.
07.85	R	Norton to 2nd L.
09.16	L	Kensington → New Britain over Rte 9 exit extension (signs to Rte 84)
11.65	BR	Veterans Dr to end at Rte 9
11.88	R	South St. under Rte 9 to 3rd L.
12.26	L	East St
13.52	R	Rte 174 to end at 173
15.35	L	Rte 173 to 1st R.
15.50	R	continue Rte 174
15.90	L	Main (Rte 176) to center of Newington
17.25	R	Rte 175 (E. Cedar → Wells) past Rte 99 & into Wethersfield
21.50	R	Marsh to 1st R.
21.63	R	Broad to end
22.52	L	Middletown to immediate R.
22.55	R	Rte 3 (Maple)
25.70	R	Rte 160 (New Britain)
28.28	L	Bacon 1 bl to end
28.38	R	Wethersfield across bridge up a steep hill to the 1st Y.
28.70	BL	Beckley → Savage Hill → Atkins to end
34.00	R	Country Club Rd
36.00		Westfield → Britannia over RR to 1st L.
37.54	L	Colony under Rte 691 to 1st R.
37.98	R	Columbia to end
38.38	R	Lewis
38.75	L	into parking lot and back to start

Hubbard Park Reservoir, Meriden

[7] Portland – Rocky Hill Ferry (seasonal)

Meeting Place: *Brownstone Intermediate School, Rte 17A (Main) & Middlesex, next to Post Office*
Length: *27 miles, with an optional 12 more*
Lunch: *There are no eating places from Portland to the Rocky Hill Ferry, except for a fruit stand where you could get something to take and munch by the ferry crossing. An optional ride before crossing the ferry, along the east side of the Connecticut River brings you to Glastonbury, where there are many restaurants and markets. Across the river into Rocky Hill there are many along Route 3, including a nice homemade ice cream shop.*
Sights: *Farms, tobacco barns, forests, hilltop views, state parks, historic churches and homes (especially the deacon Samuel Hall House of c. 1708 and the Thomas Hale House of 1714), the broad Connecticut River, and the Rocky Hill Ferry*
(since 1655).
Challenge: *moderate; rolling hills the first half, some steep but short, then long, level stretches on the return, paved roads with light traffic the first half, then heavier in towns on Route 3. Note: this bike route is not for those afraid of bridges and heights, as the last leg is on the very narrow sidewalk of the high bridge over the Connecticut River.*

The ferry does not have a permanent schedule, and will not open in the spring until the Connecticut River floods subside. So this is a summer ride, only from mid-May into early fall.

After leaving Portland on William Street, the roller coaster ride becomes increasingly vertical over Aims Hollow, Jobs Pond, Maple, and Penfield Hill roads. But the hills are not long, so the struggle to get to the top each time is brief. You've just begun, so you have your energy up to this task. Later on, when you've expended your energy, mercifully the route becomes relatively flat. But all the way, along South, Old Marlborough, Thompson, and Isinglass Hill roads, the climbs continue, with some downhill breaks. All along this way are wonderful early-eighteenth-century homes beginning on Main Street just before William Street in Portland, and wide open spaces of farmland, barns, and the ubiquitous, colonial low stone wall. From Route 17, the ride along Old Maids Lane (with its tobacco drying barns), Tryon Street, and Ferry Lane is fairly easy, especially the long stretch along the banks of the Connecticut River.

Taking an optional six-mile sidetrip back up Ferry Lane and north on Route 17 brings you to Main Street, Glastonbury, which is full of history; early-eighteenth-century homes; a magnificent, classical Congregational Church; greens and parks; shops; and restaurants. This would be a good place to have lunch before returning back to the ferry.

Waiting for the ferry is a good time to relax in the small park with picnic benches and walking trails along the river. The ferry has been in service since 1655, connecting the towns of Glastonbury on the east with Rocky Hill on the west. Once you embark, the ride is only four minutes to the other side. Here is a nice piece of history to ride on.

On the other side, there is another riverside park with picnic tables as another option for a lunch stop. Here, what has been Route 160, continues through Rocky Hill and the Dinosaur State Park to Route 3. A left on this route is the break you've been waiting for, almost completely flat, and even a little downhill, but there is nothing scenic about it, the shoulder is narrow, and the traffic is rather heavy. A good ice cream shop, however, breaks the monotony. And it's a direct route that gets you back to Middletown and to the end of the ride. Just after crossing the old Providence & Worcester Railroad, before reaching Route 66 in Middletown, a zigzag through some old neighborhoods on Liberty, Prospect, Spring, Rome, and Stack streets takes you to North Main and onto the rather dizzying Route 66 bridge (on the sidewalk) back across the Connecticut River, with spectacular views if you can stand the height, and down Main Street, Portland, to where you began.

Ames Hollow Road at Route 17, Portland

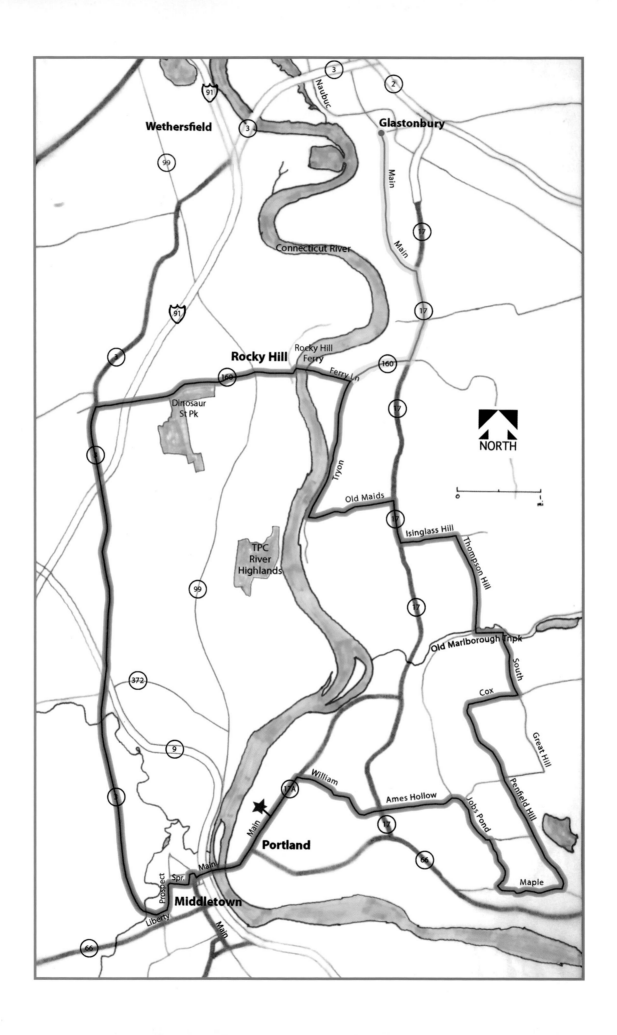

7. Portland – Rocky Hill Ferry
Meet: Brownstone Intermediate School,
Rte 17A (Main) & Middlesex, next to Post Office

00.00	L	Main
00.76	R	William to cross Rte 17
02.00	F	Ames Hollow
03.00	BR	Jobs Pond
03.78	BL	Maple to end
04.40	L	Penfield Hill
05.60	BL	Penfield Hill to end
06.30	R	Cox
07.02	L	South to end at bottom of hill
07.90	L	Old Marlborough Tpke
08.25	R	Thompson Hill to end at bottom of hill
09.64	L	Isinglass Hill to end
10.38	R	Rte 17 past fruit stand
10.90	L	Old Maids Ln to end
12.05	R	Tryon along CT River
14.00	L	Ferry Ln (Rte 160)
14.60	F	onto Rocky Hill Ferry across CT River

Optional:
Return on Ferry Ln

15.30	*L*	*Rte 160*
16.00	*L*	*Rte 17*

17.20	*L*	*Main into Glastonbury*

Return to Rocky Hill Ferry across CT River
(add 2.60 miles to each of the following)

Continuing main route from Ferry:

14.65	L	Rte 160 to end
17.30	L	Rte 3 to Middletown just over railroad
24.40	L	Liberty 2 bl
24.52	BL	Prospect to end
24.88	R	Spring
25.15	L	Rome 1 bl to end
25.28	R	Stack 1 bl to end
25.32	R	North Main 1 bl under bridge to Main
25.46	R	onto sidewalk, over bridge, onto Main
26.75	L	Middlesex into parking lot at school

Rocky Hill Ferry

[8] Air Line State Park Trail (South): East Hampton – Lebanon

Meeting place: *Trail parking lot, East Hampton*
(91 to Meriden, 66 east past Middletown to East Hampton, R on 196 1 bl, L on Flanders Rd. to 1st R, R on Smith St. to 1st L into Trail parking lot)
Length: *41 miles (31-44 optional)*
Lunch: *There are cafes, convenience stores, and gas stations in Willimantic.*
Sights: *Woods, forests, more woods, more forests, Salmon River, streams, big turtles, farmland, Windham Textile and History Museum, Windham Historical Society, Thread City Crossing and the four giant bronze frogs, and Old Comstock Covered Bridge (optional)*
Challenge: *easy on the crushed gravel trail, generally flat with some inclines; moderate on the paved streets and roads with very light traffic and a few steep hills (Riders can opt for just the trail ride, at 31 miles total). A hybrid bike is required, and a mountain bike always works.*

Getting away from civilization into the wilds is what this ride is about. Unlike some of the other rails-to-trails paths, this one is very sparsely used, especially at the northern end. There are walkers, other bike riders, and the occasional equestrian, but no skaters on this largely stone dust trail. The entire Air Line State Park Trail (originally named for the railroad that followed a straight line—as the crow flies—between New Haven and Boston) extends for 44 miles one-way, but this ride goes only 15 miles on the path, to the unfinished section at Cook Hill Road, and then deviates for about 10 miles around the country roads to the town of Willimantic. On the more remote sections you're likely to see the big turtles sunning themselves on the path. There is a good website to check for news and maps of the trail: http://pages.cthome.net/mbartel/ARR. A wonderful link to nature photography along the trail can be found at www.performance-vision.com/airline/index.htm.

The ride begins at the trail head in East Hampton by the small Cranberry Meadow Lake and soon heads down a long incline across the dramatic Lyman and Rapallo Viaducts, originally iron trestle bridges of 1873 now covered over with an immense earthwork 150 feet high, built in 1912-13, over the Flat Brook Valley and Dickinson Creek. You are riding over the only surviving nineteenth-century wrought iron viaduct construction, listed on the National Registry of Historic Places, even though it's hidden under tons of sand. Next we're plunged into the Salmon River State Forest, alongside the beautiful Salmon River, and then over the Blackledge River where it's possible to hike down the high embankment to the pebble beach and wade in the water. But along the way, a charming optional detour at Bull Hill Road takes you down to the Old Comstock Covered Bridge,

preserved as a landmark. Then back up to the trail, following the Salmon River and then its tributary, the Jeremy River, on our right side.

Next we cross the Bay Meadow Brook where it meets the Jeremy, and soon the gravel trail ends at a big parking lot, where it follows Westchester Road (Route 149) over Highway Route 2, and immediately right, down the embankment where the gravel trail continues. Just beyond, Judd Brook, under a high wooden bridge, is worth a rest stop. Continuing past Route 207 (there is no sign, but you can recognize it by a marked road crossing where the trail doglegs to the right and left, with a large sandy shoulder on both sides at the trailheads), you will pass the huge Williams Pond, with lots of birds among the swamp bushes, and then the big turtles (they won't move for bikes).

At the time of this writing, the path is improved to Cook Hill Road, although it's a little rough, composed of crushed stone, gravel, and ballast. From here, circling around on the country roads of Columbia and Lebanon there are nothing but houses and farms, with some very steep hills. A left on Cook Hill leads to Village Hill, Cards Mill for one block, then Baker Hill to Pleasant, into Willimantic, and Jackson across the bridge to Main Street and the giant bronze frogs. Here is the beginning of the northern section of Air Line State Park Trail, finished for only a few miles.

But we turn left on Main (Route 66), and left again across the next bridge to Mountain Street, Burnham, Trumbull, and finally Cook Hill Road again to bottom of the hill. Here we meet the Air Line State Park Trail again where we left it. Fifteen miles take us back the same way, this time with a long downhill to the Salmon River and then ending with a slight uphill to the trailhead where we began at East Hampton.

Judd Brook under the Air Line State Park Trail

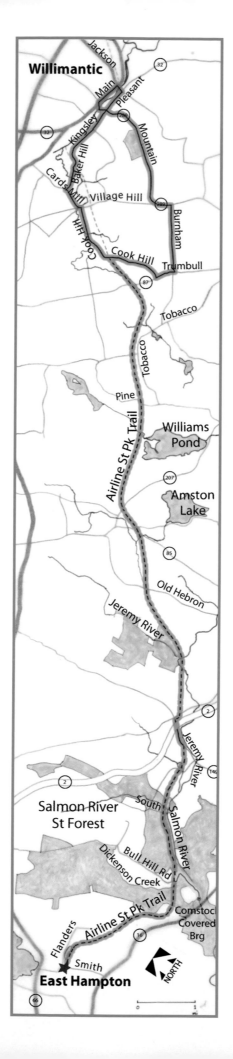

8. Air Line State Park Trail (South): East Hampton – Lebanon

Meet: I-91 to Meriden, 66 E. past Middletown to Lake Pocotopaug, R on 196 1 bl, L on Flanders to 1st R, R on Smith to 1st L into Trail parking lot

00.00	F	trailhead (with one detour on road at parking lot, over Rte 2) to end

Optional sidetrip: At 3rd Intersection c. 3 mi:
R   Bull Hill Rd. to end (steep hill down)
R   Comstock Bridge Rd. to covered bridge
Return to Trail—add c. 3 mi

15.50	L	Cook Hill Rd. to end
16.60	L	Village Hill Rd. 1/2 bl to end
16.66	R	Cards Mill Rd. 1 bl to end
17.00	R	Baker Hill Rd. → Kingsley → Pleasant
19.20	L	Jackson across bridge to Main (this is the beginning of the Air Line State Park Trail North, finished for only a few miles)
19.30	L	Main (Rte 66)
19.80	L	Bridge St. across bridge to 1st L.
19.90	L	Mountain St. (Rte 32) 1 bl
20.05	F	Mountain St. (Rte 289)
22.55	R	Burnham to 1st R.
23.80	R	Trumbull 1 bl to 1st R.
24.10	R	Cook Hill Rd. to bottom of hill
25.20	L	onto trailhead back to beginning
40.70	F	into parking lot

A large tortoise on the trail near Williams Pond

[9] Durham – Middletown

Meeting Place: Durham Town Hall, Rte 17 at Green, or across the street opposite Post Office
Length: 36 miles
Lunch: There are many cafes and restaurants in Middletown, as well as food markets here and there.
Or bring lunch to enjoy by Seven Falls or on the Wesleyan University campus or at Millers Pond.
Sights: Historic homes, churches and public buildings, state parks, lots of state forests, farms and horses,
lots of green, lakes, and Wesleyan University.
Challenge: moderate; paved roads with light to moderate traffic, 1 mile of dirt road, and continuous long hills

This is a very rural route with little traffic except at the larger towns. Just off the road to Haddam is, almost ubiquitously, the far-flung Cockaponset State Forest in different sections for those who would like a hiking detour.

We begin at the small town of Durham at the town Green with its early nineteenth-century Town Hall, and several eighteenth-century buildings such as the old schoolhouse; the former, very simple Congregational Church (now abandoned); and a number of stately homes. We head south on Route 17, to 79, and to 148, which takes us 9 miles almost continually uphill through beautiful farmland and forest, with very little traffic, and lots of ups and downs. At Route 81, which is surprisingly quiet, we head north past ponds and lakes and horse farms for eight more miles until we reach the town of Higganum with its reservoir on the left and the Higganum Reservoir State Park. This little town is worth a close look with its gorgeous early-nineteenth-century mansions and the stark white and simply magnificent Colonel Daniel Brainerd House from 1780. There are some eateries here. A quick detour straight ahead on Depot Road leads to the Connecticut River.

But our route north on Route 154 brings us soon to Seven Falls, a charming little local park with a stream that bubbles down seven layers, hence its name. As we continue north, paralleling the major highway, Route 9, the traffic gets a little heavier, and the road a little grittier, until we reach Middletown through its industrial backdoor. Here we go past City Hall and the center of town. A detour one block east would bring us again to the Connecticut River. But our route meets Route 66 and follows it north along Main Street with its many outdoor cafes, then continues west on Grand Street to south on High Street and right through the Wesleyan University and its leafy campus and its row of elegant nineteenth-century mansions in Classical and Gothic styles, now departments within the University. This is worth some detours and would be a good stop for a lunch on the grass along College Row by the brooding Memorial Chapel on the hill.

Continuing south to Loveland Street, Mill Street, Main, and East Main, we head out to open countryside again on Millbrook, Foot Hills, and Wiese Albert Roads, past Miller's Pond State Park (a popular picnic spots in the woods), through Cockaponset State Forest, on a steady and long incline for 6 miles. Suddenly straight ahead is a brief dirt road, Blue Hills, which is a pleasurable and well-deserved ride downhill all the way through the filtered sunlight of the dense forest. Turning at the next right on Higganum Road, we climb a little more, through Cockaponset State Forest again, until the road takes a sharp left, and then it's a glorious downhill all the way to the end. A right on Route 17 takes us quickly back to the Town Hall at Durham.

Seven Falls, Route 154, south of Middletown

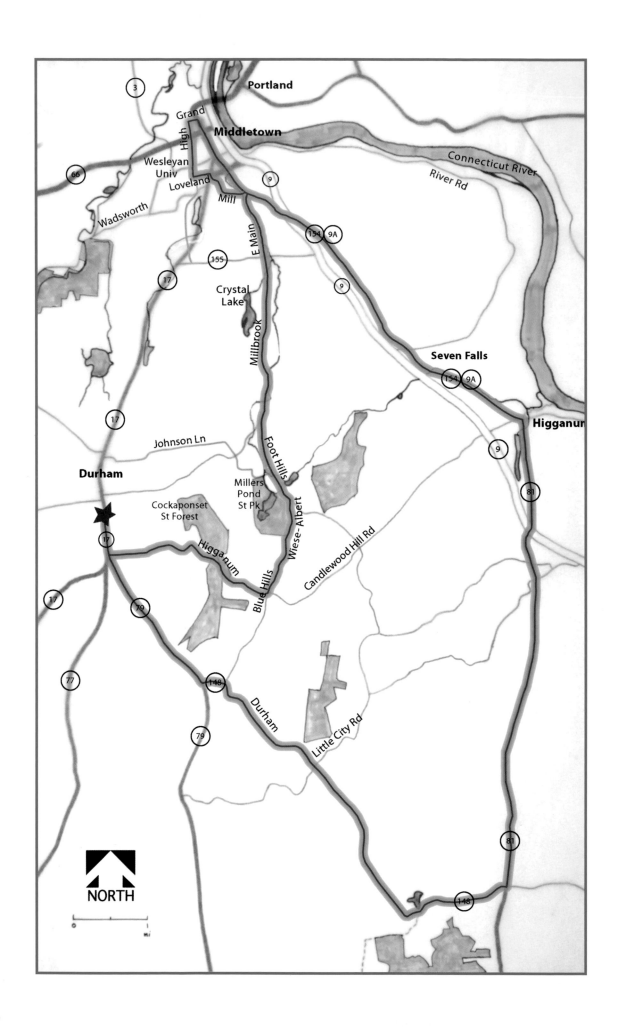

9. Durham – Middletown
Meet: Durham Town Hall, Rte 17 at Green

00.00	R	Rte 17
00.42	BL	Rte 79
02.95	L	Durham (Rte 148)
09.85	L	Rte 81 to end
17.33	L	Rte 154 (under Rte 9) into Middletown
24.43	L	Grand
24.70	L	High (past Wesleyan University)
25.55	L	Loveland (across S. Main to 1st R.)
25.85	R	Mill to end
26.40	R	Main (Rte 154) to immediate R

26.44	R	E. Main
27.15	BR	Millbrook
30.12	BL	Foot Hills to Y
31.50	BR	Wiese-Albert
32.50	F	Blue Hills (dirt, then macadam) to 1st X.
33.10	R	Higganum
34.60	L	Higganum continues, to end
35.88	R	Rte 17
36.30	L	into Town Hall parking

Colonel Samuel Camp House, 1790, in the new Federal style

[10] New Haven to Stony Creek

Meeting Place: New Haven Green at Chapel & College Streets
Length: 35 miles
Lunch: There are several small cafes. Or bring lunch to enjoy at Stony Creek wharf.
Sights: Long Island Sound, harbors, Lighthouse Point, beaches and beach houses, gorgeous eighteenth and nineteenth-century houses, beautiful Branford Green, and historic churches.
Challenge: easy; generally flat, some light hills, and paved streets with some traffic.

Beginning in New Haven at the historic Green, we hug the coastline all the way to Stony Creek. On the way we hit some of the most beautiful sights along the Long Island Sound. Chapel Street, then Olive, and Water streets lead us across the bridge over the New Haven Harbor, with ships anchored on the eastern side. A ride through the gritty area of docks and warehouses and the trucks that serve them, down Waterfront, Alabama, and Fulton, is interesting in itself, leading to a road through the East Shore Park, where a wooden fisherman's wharf protrudes out into the water giving a spectacular view of downtown New Haven. Out of the Park, Woodward Avenue takes us through Fort Hale Park, named for the patriot, Nathan Hale, onto Townsend Street (Route 337), which follows a beautiful promenade along the water. All this is called "The Annex." Lighthouse Road takes us out to Lighthouse Point, Lighthouse Point Park, and the octagonal Lighthouse itself, a charming nineteenth-century structure, with its lightkeeper's house. A nice family beach, with a historic 1920s carousel, swings, a "Splashpad," a long stone jetty, and other delights for children, stretches to Morgan Point. On the way back on Lighthouse Road, make a stop to explore the huge colonial Pardee-Morris House, rebuilt in 1780 after it was burned by the British.

Heading east on Routes 337 and 142, we pass the cove at Stanley Point, with its wonderful waterside homes and sandy beach. Cutting through the south side of Branford on Maple and Indian Neck, with their elegant neo-Gothic homes, we follow Route 146 through Pine Orchard with its charming, wooden, Union Chapel built in 1897. After much meandering on 146, with numerous local name

changes, we head south on Thimble Island Road to the end at Stony Creek, with the harbor at the picturesque Flying Point. From the wooden wharf, we get a grand view of the little Thimble Islands everywhere—with names like Potato, Rogers, Bear, Thimble, Money, Pot, Horse, Cut-in-Two, and the Outer Islands—a single house perched on each of the littlest. Some of the larger islands comprise little villages, and the largest, Horse, is a Yale University marine biology study site. These islands have been a destination for boaters since Captain Kidd in the seventeenth century. There are several restaurants and cafes here at Stony Creek overlooking the harbor and boat docks.

We return the same route except for a more direct ride from Route 146 on Damascus Road and Pine Orchard, taking Montowese into the heart of Branford. Here on the beautiful Green are found The Academy of 1820, the large brick First Congregational Church, and the modest early nineteenth-century First Baptist Church. Main Street west, and then Alps Road south takes us back to Route 142, where we retrace our path through The Annex, past Gothic mansions, and then the old factory district of Forbes Avenue and East Street. Chapel Street brings us back to the start, past Wooster Square, surrounded by classical-revival, early-nineteenth-century homes, and then the New Haven Green and the dark stone 1816 Trinity Episcopal Church. With time to spare, here you are in the middle of history, with the three churches on the Green, the High Victorian-style City Hall, built in 1861 by Henry Austin, to the East, and the neo-Gothic campus of Yale to the West.

Lighthouse Point, the New Haven Annex, with downtown New Haven in the distance

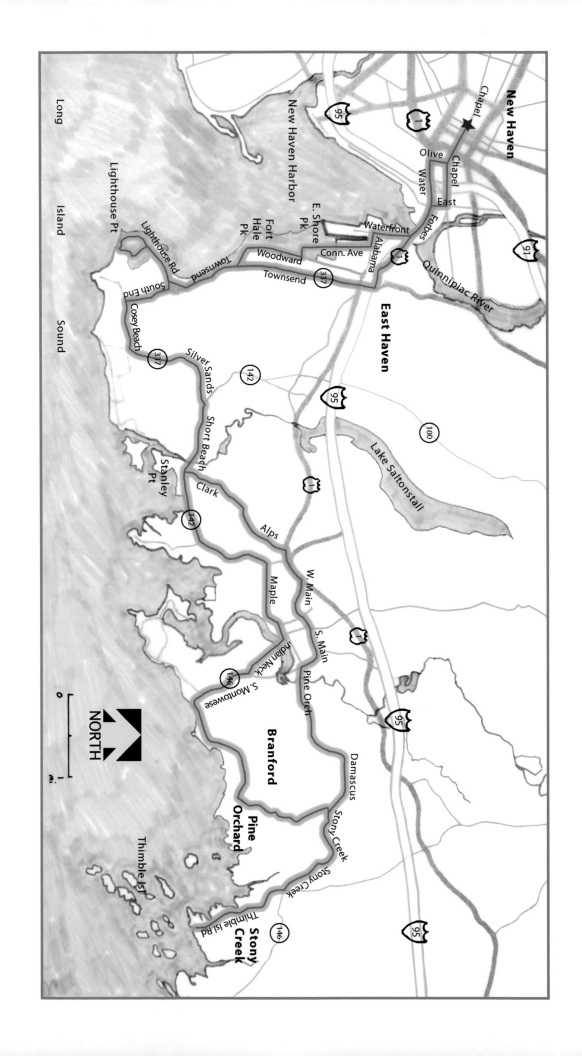

New Haven

Long
Island
Sound

New Haven Harbor

Lighthouse Pt

Lighthouse Rd

E. Shore
Pk

Fort
Hale
Pk

Townsend

Woodward

Conn. Ave

Waterfront

Alabama

Olive
Water
Chapel
East
Forbes

Chapel

Quinnipiac River

95

1

91

1

337

Townsend

South End

Cosey Beach

Silver Sands

337

East Haven

142

95

100

Lake Saltonstall

Short Beach

Stanley
Pt

Clark

142

Alps

1

W. Main

Maple

S. Main

Indian Neck

146

S. Montowese

Pine Orch

95

Branford

Pine
Orchard

Damascus

Stony Creek

Stony Creek

95

Thimble Isl

Thimble Isl Rd

146

Stony
Creek

NORTH

0   ½   1
mi.

10. New Haven to Stony Creek
Meet: New Haven Green at Chapel & College

00.00	L	Chapel
00.70	R	East
00.82	L	Water (cross drawbridge)
01.86	BR	Waterfront (just after bridge, before 95)
02.19	L	Alabama
02.25	R	Fulton → Connecticut
02.82	F	through East Shore Park (keep left, on road)
03.11	R	Woodward → Fort Hale Park Rd. [Fort Hale Park]
03.97	R	Townsend (Rte 337)
04.71	BR	Lighthouse Rd
05.20	F	around gate thru Lighthouse Point Park (on old road—circle around Park to beach and exit at east end)
06.20	R	Lighthouse Rd
06.64	R	Douglass 1 bl to 1st R.
06.68	R	Townsend → South End (Rte 337)
07.25	L	Cosey Beach (Rte 337)
07.84	L	Silver Sands (Rte 337 to Coe) to end
09.08	R	Short Beach (Rte 142)
11.54	R	Maple
12.30	R	Indian Neck
12.55	F	South Montowese (Rte 146)
16.10	F	Rte 146
16.72	R	Stony Creek Rd. (Rte 146)
17.99	R	Thimble Island Rd. to end
18.84		[Stony Creek] Return on Thimble Isl Rd
19.70	L	Stony Creek Rd. (Rte 146)
21.06	F	Damascus
22.60	F	(not L) Pine Orchard to end
22.91	R	Montowese to Branford Green
23.05	L	S. Main
23.45	F	W. Main (pass Rte 142)
23.90	L	Alps → Clark
25.13	R	Short Beach (Rte 142)
25.60	L	Silver Sands → Rte 337
27.60	R	Cosey Beach (Rte 337)
28.86	R	South End (Rte 337)
29.20	F	Townsend (Rte 337)
32.39	L	Forbes (Rte 1) → Water
34.13	R	Olive
34.40	L	Chapel
34.64		New Haven Green

The colonial Pardee-Morris House, rebuilt in 1780 after a fire, Lighthouse Point, The New Haven Annex

[11] Guilford – Hammonasset State Park

Meeting place: Park & Ride, Exit 58, Route 95, Guilford
Length: 38 miles.
Lunch: There are several cafes, restaurants, and convenience stores in Guilford and Madison but I recommend bringing your own for lunch out on the beach.
Sights: Long Island Sound, harbor, seventeenth and eighteenth-century houses, oldest stone house in New England, a spaceship condo, beautiful Greens at Guilford and Madison, historic churches, a monastery, and the glorious long beach and nature preserve at Hammonasset. Bring your swimwear and a towel just in case you get the urge to sunbathe or take a dip.
Challenge: easy to moderate; generally flat paved roads, a few hills on the northern stretch, some traffic, and a gravel path.

Along this route we find the oldest stone house in Connecticut as well as possibly the most futuristic house in Connecticut, if not in the world. The route is modified from Ride 33 in Mullen & Griffith, *Short Bike Rides.* We begin at the superlatively charming town of Guilford. Beginning at the Park & Ride on the north side of the exit at Route 95, passing under 95 and heading south, in a few minutes we arrive at the beautiful Green of Guilford, with its white-spired Congregational Church and historic houses all around. Continuing south past the Green, the Henry Whitfield House, the oldest existing stone house in New England, and Connecticut's oldest house, built in 1639, is on the left. This is open to the public, and it's worth a visit to see the interior and the period furniture, including the first tower clock made in the American colonies in 1726. Continuing down Whitfield Street, a surprise in this quaint little town awaits you on the left—an ultra-modern condominium that looks like a spaceship taking off, designed by a Guilford architect, Will Armster. A couple more blocks and we're at the wharf with a glorious view of the Long Island Sound. Now we return to the Green and turn right on Boston Street.

One the way of out town, we pass a row of wonderful wooden seventeenth- and eighteenth-century houses, of which the Highland House (1660) and the Griswold House (1735) are most notable. At the end we follow Route 1 and detour north a bit on Wildwood, Green Hill, and Horse Pond over hills and through woods, leading to the broad Hammonasset Connector over Route 1 again and into the Hammonasset State Park, the most popular State Park in Connecticut, acquired for public access 1913-1925. Here is a couple miles of sandy beach which we first encounter at West Beach with its boardwalk and dressing rooms with showers at the end of a huge parking lot. From here a gravel path leads along the coastline to the end at Meigs Point, where there is a rocky outcropping with a hiking path about a half

mile to the Point, which is definitely worth it for the views and the driftwood sculptures that beachcombers erect every summer. There is a nature center here alongside the nature preserve. And the water of the Long Island Sound is clean and worth a swim.

We return on Route 1, taking Liberty, Waterbury, and Seaview along the coast, arriving at the beautiful Green in Madison with its majestic, neo-classical First Congregational Church at the top of the triangle. Along Route 1 is one charming eighteenth or nineteenth-century home after another. We continue back on Route 1 to its meeting with I-95 just west of Guilford. Here we turn north on Goose Lane, passing under Route 95 again and traveling for several miles while the road changes names a couple of times. Along the way are dozens of eighteenth-century houses, all occupied by owners. After passing a series of lakes, and a short climb on Route 80, we arrive on Hoop Pole Road at Our Lady of Grace Monastery for Dominican nuns built in the twentieth century, with a wooded retreat by a bubbling brook. Turning west here on Race Hill Road, we meet Route 77 and ride south to the first right, Hemlock Avenue. This takes us up a hill to meet Great Hill Road which becomes Long Hill Road, but don't let the names scare you, because after a few short climbs, it's all downhill. Stop to see the beautiful early-nineteenth-century North Guilford Congregational Church with its open cupola instead of a spire. After about five miles we meet a circle and go left on Flat Meadow Road, then immediately right on Saw Mill Road, which takes us right back to the parking lot on Route 77.

For those who would like to explore a bit of history at the end of the ride, the town of Guilford has more than 100 eighteenth-century homes and a beautiful central Green surrounded by historic churches, interesting shops, and numerous cafes to sit down and relax.

Hammonasset State Park, the view west from Meigs Point

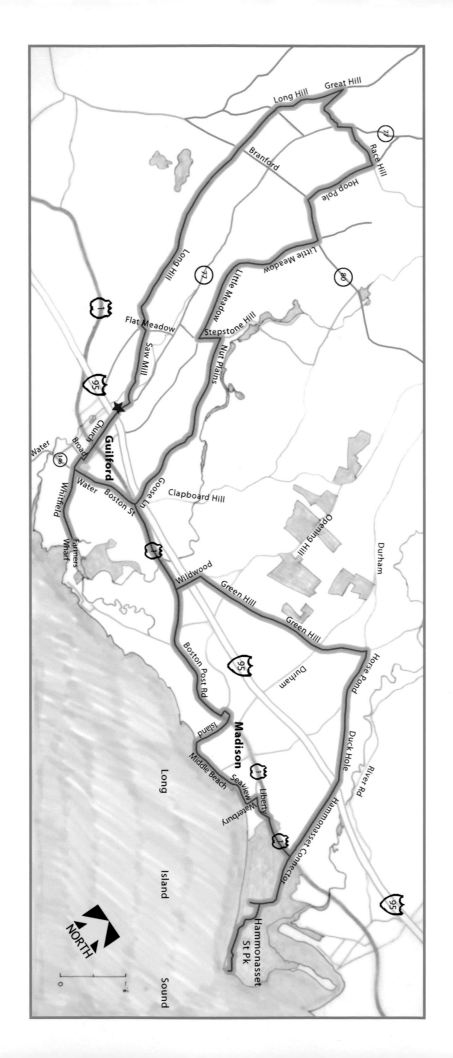

11. Guilford – Hammonasset
Meet: Park & Ride, Exit 58, Rte 95, Guilford

00.00	R	Rte 77 (Church) S under Rte 95 to end at Green	17.65	L	Waterbury to end
			17.91	R	Seaview → Middle Beach to end
00.82	R	Broad 1/2 bl	19.00	R	Island to Rte 1
00.85	L	Whitfield → New Whitfield past Green to end at Farmers Wharf	19.58	F	around Green in a circle to Rte 1
			19.88	R	Rte 1
			23.10	R	Goose Lane (at Rte 95) → Nut Plains
02.30		Return to Green			
03.41	R	Water → Boston (Rte 146) to end	25.96	L	Stepstone Hill to 1st intersection
04.64	R	Rte 1	26.31	R	Little Meadow
05.71	L	Wildwood	28.92	L	Rte 80 (Killingworth) to 2nd R
06.10	BR	Green Hill to 2nd light	29.55	R	Hoop Pole to monastery
08.73	R	Horse Pond → Duck Hole → Hammonasset Connector to Hammonasset State Park to W. Beach	30.61	L	Race Hill to end
			31.33	L	Rte 77 1 bl
			31.50	R	Hemlock
			32.06	L	Great Hill → Long Hill to circle
13.18	L	(gravel path to end at Meigs Pt.)	36.96	L	Flat Meadow 1 bl
14.60		Return on road to exit	37.13	R	Saw Mill to end
16.70	L	Rte 1	38.29	R	Rte 77
17.26	L	Liberty	38.33	R	into parking

The Henry Whitfield House, 1639, Guilford

[12] Clinton – Old Saybrook – Essex

Meeting Place: Rte 95, Exit 62 South, left on Rte 1 to parking at Parkview on left, 1291 Boston Post Rd
Length: 41 miles.
Lunch: There are many cafes, restaurants, and convenience stores all along the route from Clinton to
Old Saybrook and Essex—some really cute eateries by the seaside that cater to fishermen, and then great ice cream
in Essex. Alternative is to bring your own for lunch by the beach or the river or by an old church or historic estate.
Sights: Long Island Sound, the Connecticut River, boat docks, hawks nests, historic churches and homes,
eighteenth-century cemeteries, and the Connecticut River Museum.
Challenge: easy; generally flat paved roads, a few short hills on the northern stretch, and little traffic except along Route 1.

This is certainly one of the most bucolic routes in all of Connecticut, from the lovely beach coves and marinas along the Long Island Sound to the Connecticut River and the charming little villages just inland.

We start and end just near the entrance to Hammonasset State Park, which is included on the previous ride. But this ride follows Route 1 eastward across the Hammonasset River with its boat docks, then down to the coast of Long Island Sound on Grove, to the point with its great view of the Clinton Harbor. A couple of folksy eateries here on the water give some local flavor. Back up Commerce Street we continue eastward on Route 1, through Clinton, passing the magnificent early-nineteenth-century First Congregational Church, the monument to the first Yale College of 1701, The Academy of 1801, and numerous eighteenth-century homes, most notably the Adam Stanton House of 1789, which is now a museum. At Beach Park Road we head down to Clinton Beach, which is private, along Shore Road to Old Mail Trail, where it ends in a wonderful view of the harbor at Hawks Nest. The ancient-sounding Menunketesuck Road and Indian Trail takes us back to Route 1 and east again, with a little detour on South Main in Westbrook to see the 1678 David Bushnell House, and the charmingly understated Gothic St. Paul's Episcopalian Church and cemetery. At the grand First Congregational, the gravestones from the 1750s make a fascinating stop.

The next hike down to the waterside is Old Salt Works Road and around Sagamore and Old Kelsey Point, with more private beachfront with shingled houses, and then eastward on Route 1 again. Here, a grander Bushnell House of 1678 stands on a large estate that has been made public. Down the road a piece, Route 154 begins, and takes us around the coast to Knollwood and across the South Cove causeway to Old Saybrook, with its bright colonial red Old Buckingham House of 1671 (a private home), the clapboard and shingled 1679 William Parker House, which is now a museum, and the stately, classical 1840, First Church of Christ (Congregational), among block after block of historic sites.

After 10 miles on Route 154 we reach the exquisitely charming harbor village of Essex on the Connecticut River. This is good for some serious exploration—the First Congregational of 1852 high on a bluff, the expansive Captain Henry Lay Champlin House of 1818, and the harbor itself with its Connecticut River Museum giving a good historical view of the shipping and ship building, as well as the events of the Revolutionary war. The ice cream shop along Main Street, with its garden courtyard, is a must. It would be tempting to spend the whole day in Essex, but our route takes us out of town to the quaint little villages of Centerbrook, with its Robert Pratt House, (a 1714 saltbox and enlargement about 1760), then the old Congregational Meetinghouse, originally built in 1792 with a later belfry tower, and then the village of Ivoryton, where we find the most intriguingly dark, medieval-looking, totally shingled All Saints Episcopal Church hovering on top of a knoll. Then we're out Pond Meadow, Denison, Cross, Chittenden Hill, Kelseytown, and Hurd Bridge Roads, winding through woods and hill and dale, passing colonial saltboxes, the venerable old "Piano Factory" (where ivory keys were made—thus the name Ivoryton) and the tiny Mill District School. This takes us over Route 95, where we take North High and finally Route 1 back to our starting point. If there's still sunshine, it would be worth a visit to Hammonasset Beach and the rocky promontory at the eastern end.

The Bushnell House, 1678, Route 1, Saybrook Manor

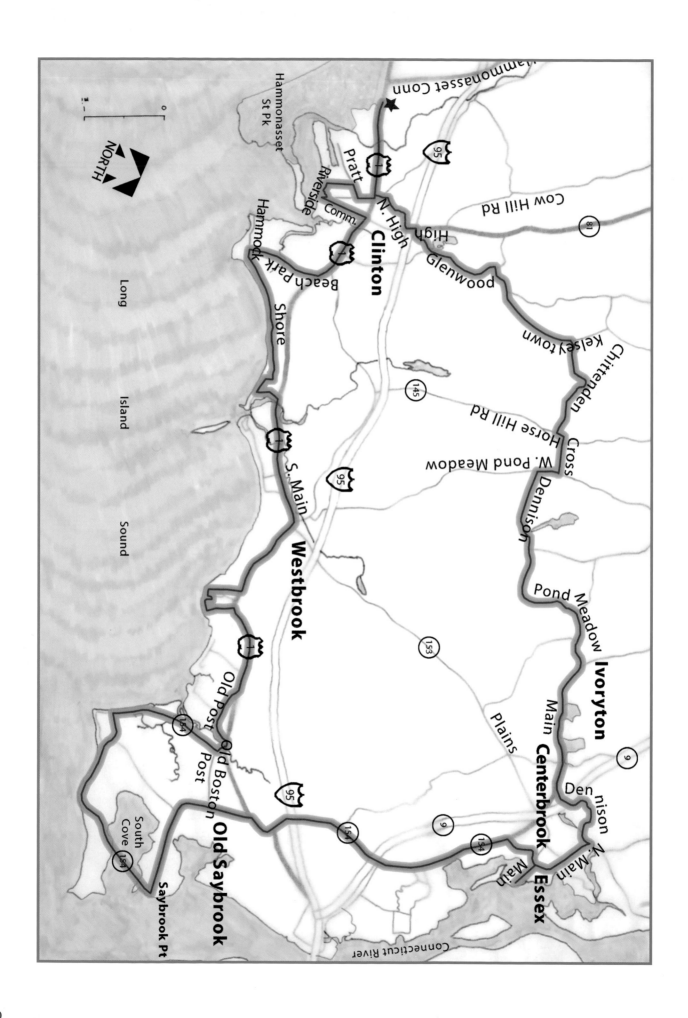

NORTH

Long Island Sound

Hammonasset St Pk

Wm Comm.

Riverside

Pratt

Hammonasset Conn

95

1

N. High

Clinton

High

Glenwood

Cow Hill Rd

81

Beach Park

Hammock

Shore

Kelsey town

Chittenden

Horse Hill Rd

W. Pond Meadow

Cross

145

1

S. Main

95

Dennison

Westbrook

Pond Meadow

Ivoryton

153

Main

Centerbrook

9

Old Post

1

Plains

Den nison

Old Boston Post

154

N. Main

Main

Essex

95

South Cove

154

9

154

154

Old Saybrook

Saybrook Pt

Connecticut River

12. Clinton – Old Saybrook – Essex
Meet: Rte 95, Exit 62 S, L on Rte 1 to parking at Parkview on left, 1291 Boston Post Rd

00.00	L	Rte 1
01.31	R	Grove to 1st X.
01.55	R	Pratt to 2nd L.
01.75	L	Harbor Pkwy to end
02.08	L	Riverside to end
02.34	R	Grove 1/2 bl to end
02.40	SL	Commerce to end
03.08	R	Rte 1
04.08	R	Beach Park to end
05.15	L	Hammock → Shore Rd
06.23	BR	Groveway → Grove Beach to end
06.94	R	Elm 1 bl to end
07.00	L	Beach Way → Old Mail Trl
07.27	L	Menunketesuck
07.45	BR	Indian Trl to end
07.60	R	Rte 1
09.00	BR	S. Main to end
09.30	R	Rte 1
10.53	R	Old Salt Works Rd. to end
11.00	L	Sagamore Ter S. to end
11.88	L	Sagamore Ter E. to 1st R.
11.14	R	Sagamore Ter Dr around curve R to end
11.24	L	Old Kelsey Pt Rd. around curve to end
11.80	R	Rte 1
13.12	R	Old Post Rd. to end
13.80	R	Rte 1 across bridge
13.90	R	Old Boston Post Rd. to
		Rte 154 at 1st R.
14.00	R	Rte 154 (many turns, many names) through Old Saybrook to Essex
24.75	R	S. Main
25.35	R	Main to end at harbor
25.74		return on Main
25.68	R	Ferry 1 bl to end
25.94	L	Pratt to end
26.20	R	N. Main
27.05	L	Dennison Rd. (many curves) to end
28.25	R	Rte 154 (Main) to Centerbrook
28.50	F	Main to Ivoryton
29.92	F	Main (not N. Main) → Pond Meadow → Dennison to end
33.33	R	W. Pond Meadow → Winthrop to 1st L.
33.62	L	Cross Rd.
34.05	F	Old Horse Hill Rd. to 1st R.
34.23	R	Chittenden Hill to end
35.73	L	Kelseytown → Glenwood
37.33	L	Hurd Bridge Rd. → Glenwood to end
38.76	L	High over Rte 95 to 1st R.
38.85	R	N. High to end
39.60	R	Rte 1
40.90	R	Parkview parking lot

Port Clinton Marina, Commerce Street, Clinton

GOODSPEED OPERA HOUSE

★ EAST HADDAM ★

[13] Old Saybrook – East Haddam

Meeting Place: Park & Ride, Exit 70 on I-95 at Rte 156 in Old Lyme
Length: 43 miles
Lunch: There are many cafes and restaurants, as well as food markets, at Old Saybrook, Chester, and East Haddam. Or bring lunch to enjoy at the Goodspeed Opera House or at Gillette Castle.
Sights: Connecticut River, lakes, state forests, farms and horses, Chester artists' studios, historic homes, churches, public buildings, cemeteries, Goodspeed Opera House, Gillette Castle, and Florence Griswold Museum.
Challenge: moderate; paved roads with light to moderate traffic, 1 mile of dirt road, and continuous long hills.

Beginning at the majestic mouth of the Connecticut River at Old Saybrook, the route follows its shores north to East Haddam where it crosses the river again and heads southward through rolling countryside back to the beginning at Old Lyme. With an initial ride on the bike trail along Route 95 over Baldwin Bridge, we get a fantastic view of the wide river and the boat docks along its shores. Heading south through the charming town of Old Saybrook, we pass wonderful eighteenth and nineteenth-century homes on Main Street (Route 154), including the General Hart House and the Town Hall before turning west on Old Boston Post Road to Route 1. Route 166 and then 153 to 154 passes through Centerbrook, with its 1792 Meetinghouse, then Deep River, passing the First Congregational Church, built in 1835, a simple but charming example of the classical style situated on the small Green. At Chester, a quaint nineteenth-century village is full of shops, cafes, and artsy residents, with a food festival every Sunday in the summer.

Along the route towards Tylerville we get a glimpse of the lacy iron "swing bridge" of 1913 that crosses the Connecticut River on Route 82, and the magnificent, shimmering white Goodspeed Opera House with its mansard roof. Built in 1876 by William Goodspeed to combine his shipping and banking business with a venue for theatre, the mansard-style Opera House stands six stories high above the river, with a portico as well as picnic grounds along the shore. East Haddam is full of neo-Gothic houses with mixed mansard and colonial styles with a grand restaurant overlooking the river.

Outside of the town, Route 82 takes us south to River Road, which leads to the "Gillette Castle" on a bluff overlooking the Connecticut River (open to the public). This was built in 1919 as the home of director, actor, and playwright, William Gillette (the original Sherlock Holmes), with walls of sinister jagged stone meant to re-create the Normandy castle of William the Conqueror's father, Robert Le Diable ("The Devil"), but its plan and its interior are in the modern American prairie style, with built-in furniture, a mix of stone and wood inside, and window walls that blend the inside and outside. This would be a place to have lunch overlooking the Connecticut River far below. Heading south again we come to the historic Chester Ferry which has been operating since 1769 (albeit not with the same boat). A little picnic ground affords a place to relax and view the river again.

The ride south from here on Route 148 and Joshuatown Road is extremely hilly but picturesque as can be, through woods and farms and over streams until it comes to the upper reaches of the Hamburg Cove. Here, along the Old Hamburg Road, are some of the loveliest eighteenth and nineteenth-century homes of the whole ride. Crisscrossing Route 156 on Cove, Elys Ferry, Bill Hill, and Saunders Hollow Roads takes us through rolling farmland with eighteenth and seventeenth-century houses back to Old Lyme. Here is a wonderful, historic town, with its delightfully bipolar Florence Griswold classical-revival house of 1817 and ultra-modern museum of Impressionism. At the wedding-cake white, classical tower of the First Congregational Church (1817, rebuilt 1910), we take Ferry Road and Route 156 back to where we started.

Goodspeed Opera House, 1876, East Haddam

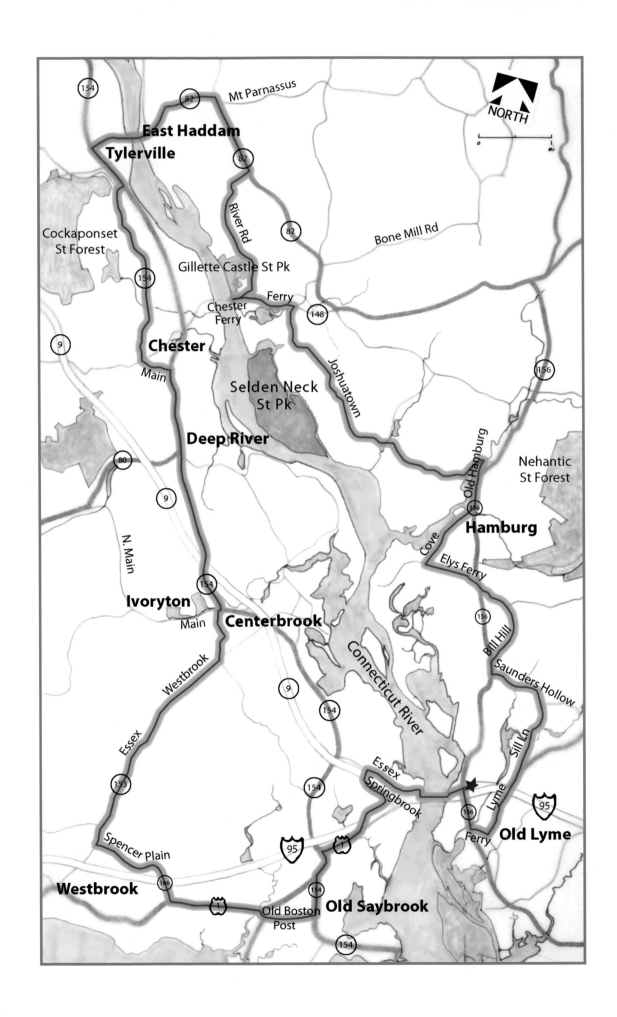

13. Old Saybrook – E. Haddam
Meet: Park & Ride, Exit 70 on I-95 at Rte 156 in Old Lyme

00.00	F	on pedestrian/bicycle path (to the R. of the entrance ramp) across Baldwin Bridge (I-95) over CT River into park
01.00	L	Essex
01.32	L	Floral Park Rd. to Rte 1 through underpass
01.44	L	Springbrook (to Rte 1)
02.33	BR	Rte 1
03.00	L	Rte 154 (Main)
03.44	BL	Rte 154
04.00	R	Old Boston Post Rd
04.85	L	Rte 1
06.22	R	Rte 166 (Spencer Plain Rd) to end
07.90	R	Rte 153 (Essex Rd)
11.42	L	Westbrook Rd. to Centerbrook, Main St
12.25	R/L	dogleg onto Rte 154 N., then under Rte 9 past Deep River
16.25	L	Main St. into Chester
16.75	F	N. Main to 1st Y.
16.95	BR	Goose Hill Rd. to end at Parkers Pt
18.87	L	Rte 154 to Tylerville
20.78	R	Rte 82 across bridge thru E. Haddam past Petticoat Ln to sign for Gillette Castle

24.35	R	River Rd. to 1st R.
25.98	R	into Gillette Castle St. Pk to end at Castle
26.60		circle & return to River Rd.
27.32	R	continue on River Rd. to end
28.12	BR	Rte 148 (Ferry Rd) to Chester Ferry
28.27		return on Rte 148 to 1st R.
29.25	R	Joshuatown Rd. (very hilly) to Hamburg Cove & across bridge
34.06	R	Old Hamburg Rd
34.40	F	Rte 156 to 1st R.
34.77	BR	Cove Rd. to end
36.02	L	Elys Ferry Rd. to Rte 156
36.85	R	Rte 156 to immediate L.
36.94	L	Bill Hill Rd. to end
38.53	BL	Rte 156 to 1st L.
38.72	L	Saunders Hollow Rd
39.75	F	Sill Ln
40.75	F	Lyme St. through Old Lyme to end
41.95	R	Ferry Rd. to end
42.24	R	Shore Rd. (Rte 156) under I-95
42.80	R	into Park & Ride

An artist's studio, Chester

[14] Colchester – Bashan Lake – Salem

Meeting Place: *Route 16, shopping center (Stop & Shop) immediately east of Route 2*
Length: *40 miles*
Lunch: *There are no eating places outside of Colchester, so buy at the starting point and take to eat by a lake.*
Sights: *Historic churches and houses, horse farms, Devils Hopyard State Park, Chapman Falls, Lake Hayward, Bashan Lake, and lots of smaller lakes and ponds.*
Challenge: *moderate; hilly, paved roads mostly with light traffic, continuous traffic on Route 82, and one short dirt road.*

This is a figure 8, so it's possible to cut it shorter, although we don't begin at the center, but, rather, at the northernmost point at the town of Colchester. This is the only reasonably populated place we'll see, with many shopping centers and eateries where lunch could be taken out at the beginning or reserved for the end.

Heading straight south from Route 16 on Cabin Road, we continue straight on with various name changes past Lake Hayward, a community of modest waterfront homes where motorboats are banned (except for quiet electric motors), and a small beach at the lower end is a private club. The road continues through the tiny village of Millington, with its eighteenth-century homes, graveyard, and small green, through even tinier Mount Parnassus, to its end at Town Street (Route 82 to 151), where we turn north through the appropriately named Little Haddam, with its grand Congregational Church built in 1794. Soon, East Haddad-Colchester Pike takes us northeastward right over the center of the huge, meandering Bashan Lake, with its private homes, canoe paddlers, vast stretches of water lilies, and a private community beach. The road continues southward, becoming Wickham, where it is a state-designated scenic dirt road for a half mile, through sun-filtered forests and past isolated historic homes.

Back on Millington Road we retrace our path briefly to head south on Hopyard Road through the Devils Hopyard State Park with its vast forests, hiking paths, Eight Mile River, and Chapman Falls cascading sixty feet to the rocky pool at the bottom, currently under consideration for national designation as a "Wild and Scenic River." The road follows the river (more of a brook) out of the park and down to Route 82 East.

The best thing about Route 82 (which has continuous traffic and not much of a shoulder) is a great homemade ice cream shop with picnic tables right before the Route 11 overpass (to escape Route 82, an alternative would be a right on 82; a quick left on Hamburg Road; left on Salem Road, which becomes Essex Turnpike; and Darling Road, back to 82 just beyond the ice cream shop). Then it's just a little further before we head north on Route 85. The village of Salem has more public buildings than it has homes—the classical Congregational Church built in 1838, the little Gothic-style Center School with its belfry built around 1885, and the inexplicably eclectic classical/Gothic Episcopal Church (now the Historical Society) built in Norwich in 1749 and moved to Salem in 1831. For the next seven miles, it is simply open country until we reach Colchester, a mix of shopping malls and nineteenth-century churches and homes on the center Green, and our starting point on Route 16.

A swamp along Hopyard Road, Millington

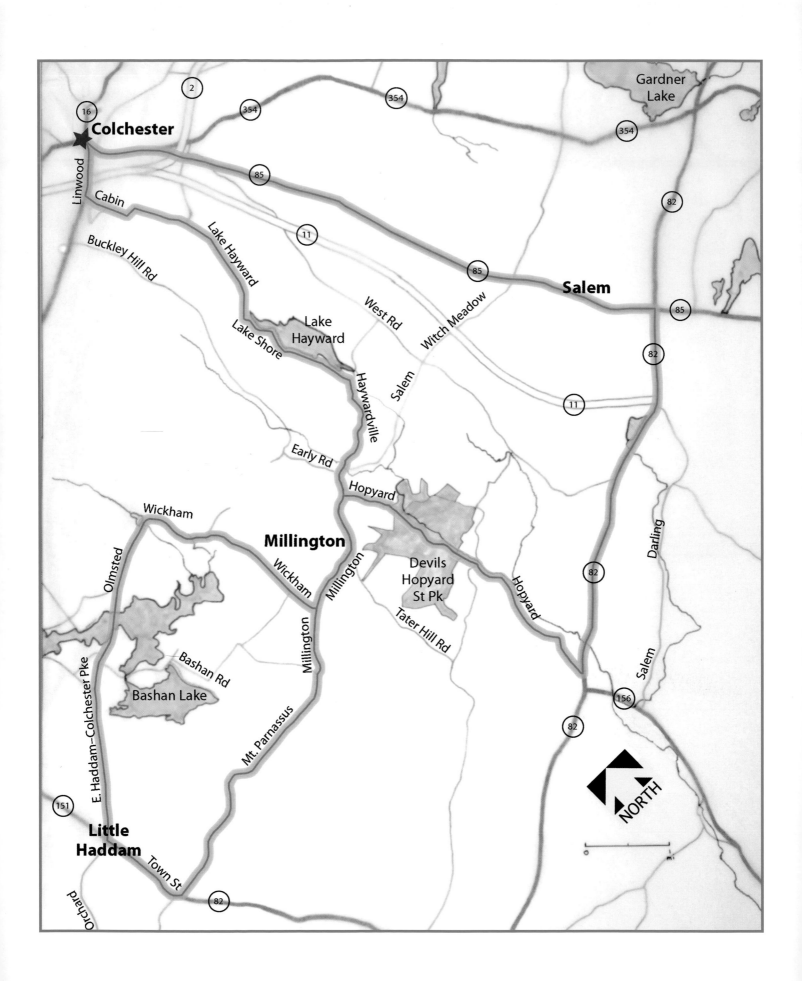

14. Colchester – Bashan Lake – Salem
Meet: Rte 16, shopping center (Stop & Shop)
E. of Rte 2

00.00	L	Rte 16 (Linwood)			Olmsted → Wickham
00.40	L	Cabin			(dirt road from 18.94 to 19.44)
01.83	BR	Lake Hayward Rd. → Lake			to end
		Shore Dr → Haywardville Rd	20.72	L	Millington
07.45	BR	Millington Rd. → Mt. Parnassus	22.35	R	Hopyard to end
		Rd. to end	26.55	L	Rte 82
12.58	R	Rte 82 → 151 (Town St)	31.40	L	Rte 85
13.85	R	E. Haddam-	39.15	L	Rte 16 (Linwood)
		Colchester Pke →	39.38	L	into parking lot

A horse farm on Route 82, Salem

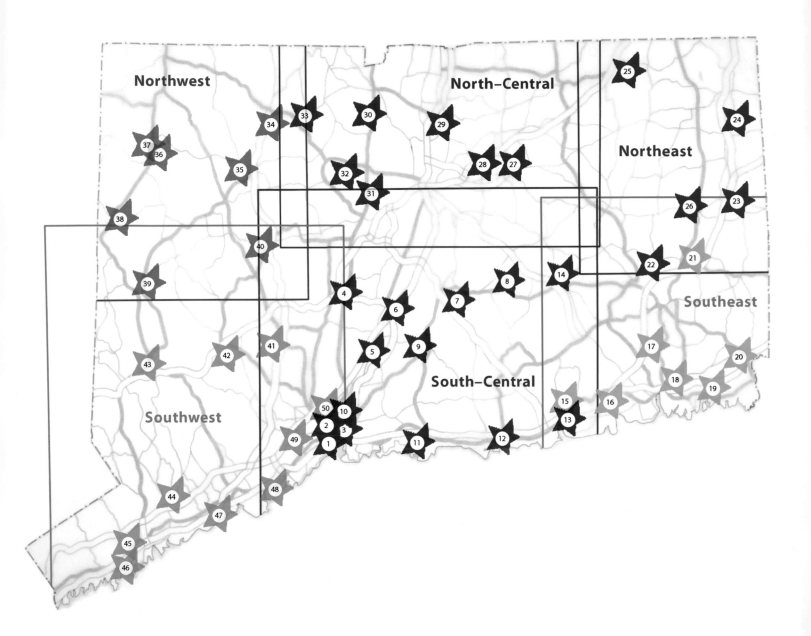

Southeast

The Lymes – The Seacoast – The Thames River – Mystic River – Windham and Colchester

Rocky Neck State Park Beach, South Lyme

[15] The Lymes (Old, South, & North)

Meeting Place: Old Lyme, Rte 95, Exit 70, at Rte 156, Park & Ride
Length: 30 miles
Lunch: There are several cafes, restaurants, and convenience stores in Old Lyme and along Rte 156 to South Lyme,
 but then no more once you leave the coast. Best to bring your own for lunch out on the beach or by a lake
or an old church.
Sights: Long Island Sound, sandy beaches, lakes, rivers, hawks nests, historic churches, eighteenth-century cemeteries,
farms and cows, and the Nehantic State Forest.
Challenge: easy to moderate; generally flat paved roads, a few hills on the northern stretch, and some traffic
on northern part of Route 156.

This route goes from the bustling summer home communities along the Long Island Sound to the extremely rural areas of Lyme. Beware of road closings, as many leading to the coastline are marked "private." The route is modified from the Connecticut Bicycle Map. It begins on the quiet southern stretch of Route 156 that heads down to the small beach communities of White Sands, Hawks Nest, Old Lyme Shores, and Point O'Woods. The lovely, spired St. Anne's Episcopal Church along the first stretch is a peaceful sight, followed by the great stretch of the Black Hall River with expanses of marshland and two white lighthouses in the distance. Here we branch off onto Old Shore Road passing Griswold Point and White Sands Beach, both unfortunately private and off limits to us. After we're back on Route 156, the next right onto Center Beach Avenue takes us to Hawks Nest Beach, although signs here also say private, but the monitor at the entrance allowed me to pass. West End Drive has no outlet, but it's an interesting diversion, with its rows of simple, gray shingled beach houses. Returning along the coast and then up Columbus and Flagler, we continue down Route 156, past the Old Colony Beach Association (where, again, we are not invited). The next road down to the coast is Sea Spray Road, and marked as private, again, but the monitor allowed me to pass, and the beautiful, small beach at the end of Sea Lane is public, and worth a stop to explore the water and the rocky coves to the east before heading around and out Billow Road and east again on Route 156.

Before we reach the sharp left bend in the road, we take one more jaunt to the waterside, down Connecticut Road (unmarked, with signs warning "No Trespassing," but, again, I was allowed to pass) to the charming little harbor full of sailboats and out to the end of Champion Road. Returning back around the peninsula to the end of Hillcrest Road, we get a magnificent view from the high promontory across the estuary of the Four Mile River to Rocky Neck State Park and Watts Island.

Circling back the coastline on Seaview, Walnut, Oak, and Hillcrest, we return back to Route 156 North through South Lyme and up Four Mile River Road and then what must be the loneliest stretch of Route 1 in all of Connecticut. North on Grassy Hill Road takes us through some of the most charming countryside—first the beautiful Rogers Lake (all private waterfront, unfortunately, except for one small boat ramp on a branch at the northern end), then the forests of Stone Ranch Military Reservation, the tiny, colonial, Grassy Hill Congregational Church originally of 1746, and the Grassy Hill Preserve with its old cemetery amid farmland and colonial era homes. Left on Beaver Brook Road, we pass through North Lyme, with its old Town Hall residing in a former eighteenth-century Congregational Church, crossing Route 156 and down Macintosh and Mount Archer Roads, twice across the Eight Mile River past magnificently landscaped estates at the edge of the dam. Finally we head back down Route 156 again, worth a few rest stops at a pre-Revolutionary War cemetery, the colonial First Congregational Church of Lyme (remodeled in the early nineteenth century), and expansive fields of comfortably lounging cattle. Just before we reach the starting point, Pilgrims Landing gives us a great view across the Connecticut River to Calves Island, Goose Island, and down to the Route 95 bridge.

Rocky Neck State Park Beach, South Lyme

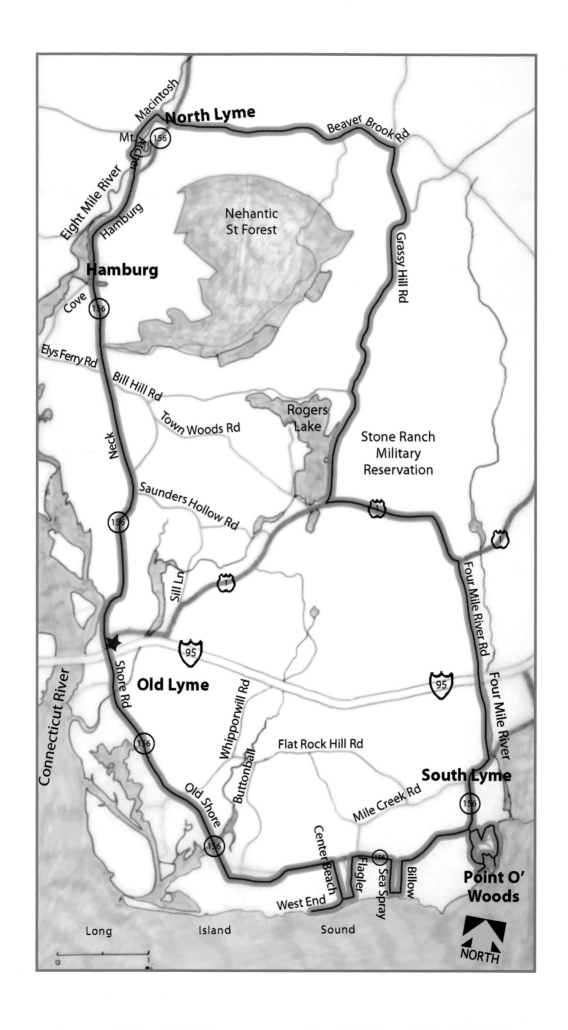

15. The Lymes (Old, South, & North)
Meet: Rte 95, Exit 70, at Rte 156, Park & Ride
(Beware of road closings, as many leading
to the coastline are marked "private.")

00.00	L	Rte 156 (Shore Rd)
02.90	R	Old Shore to end
03.93	R	Rte 156 (Shore Rd)
04.45	R	Center Beach to end
04.92	R	West End to end
05.34	(return on West End) →	
	Avenue A to end	
05.88	L	Columbus to 1st X.
06.02	BR	Flagler to end
06.35	R	Rte 156 (Shore Rd)
06.80	R	Sea Spray to end at water
07.17	L	Sea Ln to end
07.28	L	Billow to 1st R.
07.60	R	Rte 156 (Shore Rd) to just before a sharp bend left
08.55	R	Connecticut (unmarked) under RR bridge, BR, to end
09.08	R	Ridgewood 1 bl to end
09.10	R	Champion to end
09.24	(return on Champion to end)	
09.36	L	Ridgewood
09.53	R	Hough 1 bl, BL to end
09.62	R	Sargent 1 bl, BL to end
09.70	R	Hillcrest to end
09.82	(return on Hillcrest to 1st Y.)	
09.97	BR	Seaview to bend left → Walnut to end
10.55	R	Oak 1/2 bl to end
10.56	R	Hillcrest to end
10.79	R	Connecticut 1 bl to end
10.83	R	Rte 156 (Shore Rd) to 1st Y.
11.74	BL	Four Mile River Rd. to end
14.17	L	Rte 1
16.08	R	Grassy Hill Rd
20.80	L	Beaver Brook Rd. across Rte 156
23.57	F	Macintosh to end
24.14	F	Mt. Archer to end
24.70	BR	Rte 156 (Hamburg → Neck) to Rte 95
30.80	L	into parking

The beach life at Old Lyme Shores

[16] South Lyme – New London

Meeting Place: Rte 95, Exit 72 S. to Rte 156 E., 1/2 mile to Samuel M. Peretz Park on left
Length: 44 miles
Lunch: There are charming cafes, restaurants, and convenience stores in Niantic, and again in New London, but most of the way is residential. Try lunch by the beach or in one of the great state and local parks, or by the lake at the Arboretum.
Sights: Long Island Sound, sandy beaches (private and public), boat docks, the Niantic River, hawks nests, Rocky Neck State Park, Harkness Memorial State Park, Ocean Beach Park, Fort Trumbull State Park, New London Harbor, Connecticut College Arboretum, seventeenth to nineteenth-century historic homes, schools, mills, cemeteries, and early government buildings.
Challenge: easy to moderate; generally flat paved roads with little traffic along the coast and a few long but gentle hills on the northern route back. Beware of road closings in the restricted communities.

Looping down and out of numerous peninsulas on the Long Island Sound, this route is longer than it appears on the map, with glorious views of the Sound, inlets, river deltas, grassy wetlands, beaches, and historic New London. Much of the trip follows Route 156 eastward, with many departures down to little communities on the coast, and the more rural return is a steady peddle over long, gentle hills back to our start. The route can easily be shortened by skipping any of the long stretches down to the seaside points, although these are the easy parts.

Heading west from the athletic fields of Peretz Park in South Lyme, we pass the dark, brooding Thomas Lee House on the left, open to the public during the summer, of which the core was built in 1660 and the rest by 1765, with the bright red Little Boston School of 1734 next door. Immediately after, we meet the entrance to Rocky Neck State Park. This is an enormous expanse of lawns, trees, picnic tables, and marshland culminating, through a passage west of the parking lot, under the railroad, in a long public beach packed with sun worshipers. The parking lot along the railroad leads to the eastern access, where a footpath winds out through the woods to Giants Neck Road. This takes us out to the point of Giants Neck, with its private beaches and marina, where a circle around the coast takes us back out Giants Neck Road to Route 156 again.

Now eastward, the next circle down to the coast, by way of Fairhaven, Black Point Road, and Attawan follows the eastern waterside down to Black Point. Here, we circle around back on Great Wight Way (certainly a euphemism for this restricted neighborhood) and out Old Black Point Road along the Pataguanset River, with gorgeous views of sailboats stretching out to the Sound. Terrace, Beach, Washington, Crescent, Atlantic, and Columbus Avenues take us past Crescent Beach, which is also private, and McCook Point Park, with a huge community beach.

Route 156, again, leads us into Niantic, a cute little town with lots of interesting cafes, before crossing over the Niantic River bridge with a spectacular view up and down the river, and the fishermen's docks full of lobster traps. Quickly we head down Gardiners Wood, Jordan Cove, Shore, and Great Neck Roads, crossing the inlet of Jordan Cove, to Harkness Memorial State Park. This is a huge 230-acre expanse of grass, trees, and sandy beach—a great place to spend all day for a picnic, a splash in the water, and a visit to the beautiful formal gardens beside the Harkness family's 1906 Eolia summer mansion (named for the island home of the Greek god of winds). Around the classical revival mansion is a carriage house, nursery, and other farm buildings. Lush gardens flank the mansion on both the east and west lawns, and an Alpine Rock Garden faces a grand seaside panorama.

Great Neck and Ridgewood Roads lead us out and down to another peninsula across the Alewife Cove. After passing the village of Ridgewood on Peninsular Avenue, Ocean Avenue takes us down to Ocean Beach Park, a huge public playground including a vast sandy beach, arcades, miniature golf, and fairground rides. Neptune and Pequot Avenues take us up the coast of the Thames River, with more private sandy beaches, gorgeous nineteenth-century homes on the bluff, the Eugene O'Neill Theater, O'Neill's Monte Christo Cottage dating to 1700, and a view of Groton and the submarine yards across the Thames River.

At the circle, we enter right into Fort Trumbull State Park (which used to be Fort Trumbull US Navy Reserve but is now public) down to the river and around the Park to the Riverwalk with great views across the harbor to New London. Turning back along the railroad and right on Walbach and then Howard Street, we enter the town on Bank Street, passing the US Customhouse designed by Robert Mills in 1833, to the square surrounded by the City Pier, Richardson's Union Railroad Station of 1888, the Schoolhouse of 1774, where Nathan Hale taught until his hanging by the British, and up State Street the 1784 Superior Courthouse, the oldest continuously used courthouse in the country. Northward on Huntington Avenue we pass a row of stately Greek revival

Crescent Beach, Niantic

houses built in 1832 by whale oil merchants and captains, then the Antientest Burial Ground with seventeenth and eighteenth-century gravestones. Williams Street heads north to a little detour down under the Route 95 overpass on State Pier Road to the little wooden Old Town Mill first built in 1650. Back up Williams we pass the Lyman Allyn Museum and the great lawns of Connecticut College, to its vast Arboretum of native plants, a great place to lounge for lunch by the lake, and through it on Gallows Lane, where we enter Waterford.

Zigzagging south on Bloomingdale, north on Pilgrim, and west on Chapman across the lake, there is an easy but long climb to the northwest on Vauxhall, Douglas, and then briefly on the busy Route 85. Now it's all downhill and leafy on Way Hill and Oil Mill Roads. On Route 1 we cross the upper end of the picturesque Niantic River basin through Flanders and finally head straight south—at the landmark Scott's Yankee Farmer Market—on North Bride Brook Road, again downhill, ending up at Route 156 and our parking at Peretz Park.

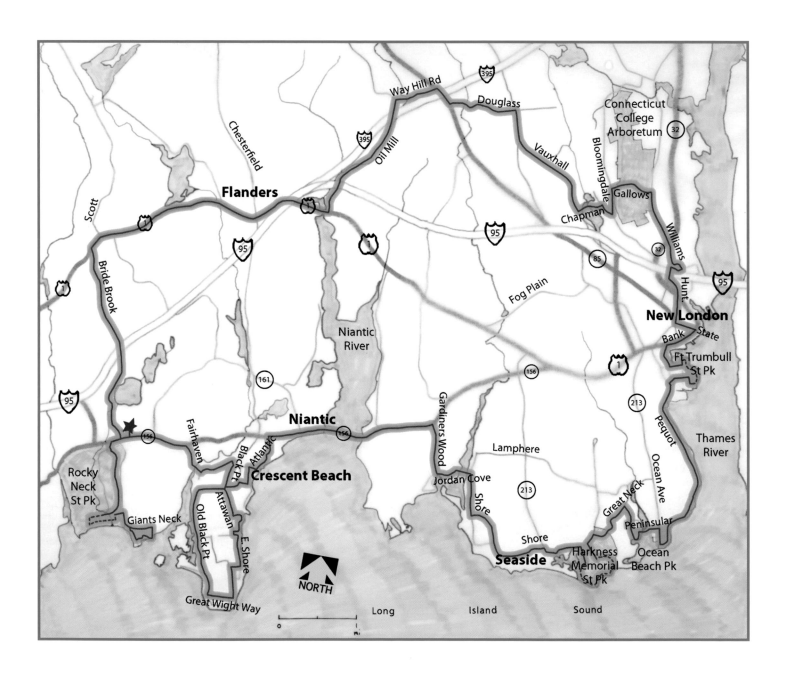

16. S. Lyme – New London
Meet: Rte 95, Exit 72 S. to Rte 156 E., 1/2 mi to Peretz Park on L.
(Beware of road closings in the restricted communities.)

00.00	R	Rte 156
00.28	L	into Rocky Neck State Park: to beach at end of parking lot
01.79		before the railroad tunnel leading to the beach, turn left on the path to the eastern entrance to the beach
02.28		L then R onto footpath through the woods just after the park sign
02.42	R	Giants Neck around shoreline (many turns) to marina
03.10	L	W. Pattagansett
03.28	L	Bride Brook to end
03.57	R	Giants Neck
04.87	R	Rte 156 to 1st full R.
05.69	BR	Fairhaven to end
06.25	L	Fairhaven ←Gada to 1st R.
06.70	R	Black Point
06.75	R	Black Point
07.13	L	Attawan Rd. to split
07.50	L	Attawan Ave along shoreline to end
07.84	R	Bidwell 1 bl to end
07.92	L	W. End to end
07.96	L	Billow 1 bl to end
08.03	R	E. Shore to end
08.68	R	Bond to end
08.77	L	West Ln (unmarked private) past barrier
09.07	R	West Ln → Great Wight Way to end
09.40	R	Old Black Point
11.32	L	Black Point to immediate R.
11.35	R	Terrace
11.50	F	Terrace
11.57	R	Beach to 2nd L.
11.69	L	S. Washington
11.93	R	Crescent
12.15	BR	Atlantic to end
12.31	R	Columbus to end
12.65	R	Rte 156 over Niantic River
14.85	R	Gardiners Wood to end
15.55	L	Jordan Cove to end
16.02	R	Shore Rd
16.70	L	Shore Rd
16.85	R	Shore Rd. to end
18.03	R	Great Neck (Rte 213)
18.59	R	into Harkness Memorial State Park—follow path R. around the shoreline and around to mansion; then out mansion drive
19.95	R	Great Neck (Rte 213)
20.85	R	Ridgewood around coast
21.50	R	Peninsular → bridge → Highland to end
21.77	R	Ocean
22.19	L	Neptune to end
22.30	R	Mott to end
22.48	R	Ocean
22.60	R	Neptune
22.70	L	Pequot to end at circle
25.15	R	into Ft Trumbull St. Park— past gate downhill to footpath around waterside, out gate on other side— R on Riverwalk to end
26.55	L	on Goshen following RR track
26.62	R	Walbach 1 bl under RR to end
26.67	R	Howard
27.15	R	Bank
27.59	R	State 1 bl to City Pier
27.72		return on State St
28.05	R	Huntington to end
28.75	R	Williams under I-95
28.95	R	State Pier Rd. to 2nd L.
29.05	L	Mill 1 bl to end
29.09	L	Cole to end
29.26	R	State Pier Rd. 1/2 bl to end
29.30	R	Williams
30.45	L	Gallows to end
31.07	L	Bloomingdale to 1st R.
31.45	R	Pilgrim to 2nd L.
31.65	L	Chapman to end
32.00	R	Vauxhall
33.72	L	Douglass to end
34.65	R	Hartford Tnpk (Rte 85) under 395 to 1st L.
34.93	L	Way Hill Rd. to end
35.47	L	Oil Mill to end
37.40	R	Rte 1
41.00	L	Bride Brook to end
43.84	L	Rte 156
43.95	L	into parking

Whale Oil Row, captains and merchants houses, 1832, New London

[17] Montville – Norwich

Meeting Place: Route 395, Exit 79, Uncasville, to Route 32 South to Montville Town Hall parking lot
Length: 37 miles
Lunch: There are lots of eating places from Uncasville through Norwich to Yantic. After that there are none.
Sights: Historic churches and houses, Mohegan Sun, the Thames River, Gardner Lake, Lake Konomoc, and lots of smaller lakes and ponds.
Challenge: easy to moderate; some hills, paved roads mostly with light traffic, and fast traffic on Routes 82 and 85.

Our starting point is named after the Mohegan chief Uncas who, in 1659, sold nine square miles to Major John Mason and the Reverend James Fitch to establish the settlement which eventually became Norwich. Up Route 32, you wouldn't recognize the Mohegan Indian Reservation at Trading Cove unless you knew in advance that that is the site of the giant glass Mohegan Sun casino resort, gleaming like an enormous crystal shooting up toward the sun. This is not your grandfather's Indian reservation.

Continuing along Route 32 we pass antique shops and the little Thamesville, reaching the Thames River (we pronounce it like "James" unlike the Londoners) at Norwich, with its boat slips on Holly Hock Island at the confluence of the Shetucket River. Crossing over the wharf and continuing left on Route 32 through the main part of town, we pass the large Green with its heavy stone, Gothic-style 1874 Park Congregational Church and the Slater Memorial Museum next to it. Forward on Washington and Town Streets, we pass the bright-red early-eighteenth-century Leffingwell Inn by the upper Thames, now a museum, which began life nearby in 1675 as the two-room house of Stephen Backus. Further on is the older Green and the late-eighteenth-century First Congregational Church, surrounded by eighteenth-century homes with the 1772 Joseph Carpenter Store. Following West Town Street we end up at Yantic, a quaint little nineteenth-century factory town overlooking the upper reaches of the Thames, a good place to have lunch. Now hemmed in by the New England Central Railroad, Route 32, and the Route 2 freeway, there's only one way out on an overgrown footpath around the old factory, following the Route 2 exit.

Across the bridge on Route 32, a right on Fitchville Road leads us south on Yantic Lane and then Browning Road. Wawecus Hill Road is one glorious, long, downhill ride all the way to where it bears a quick right at Goldmine Road, takes a quick hop up and then gently down all the way to its end. Route 82 West doesn't have steady traffic, but, because it is a long, relatively straight two-lane road, the traffic is fast, and there is no substantial shoulder to avoid it. It passes through woodlands for seven and a half miles, but otherwise, there are no remarkable landmarks. Just past Route 163, Gardner Lake spreads out to the north, but is visible only by a detour right on Eden Park Drive to the end at the waterside. Just past the entrance to the Route 11 freeway, we turn left on Darling Road, where a stop for delicious homemade ice cream is a must.

Fortified, we head east on Old New London Road. Route 85 South has horrendous traffic, but for most of the way it has a broad shoulder, which makes it bearable for the brief time we're on it, and the big dinosaur on the right adds a point of interest. Left on Turner Road takes us past the long sliver of Lake Konomoc, which is visible only at certain breaks in the heavily wooded shores. Left on Lake Road and right on Fire Street leads through woodlands to Unger Road, becoming Moxley Road and leading us back to Uncasville. A right on Jerome Road and a left on Jerome Avenue lands us back on Route 32 and our parking at the Montville Town Hall.

The Mohegan Indian Reservation at Trading Cove: Mohegan Sun

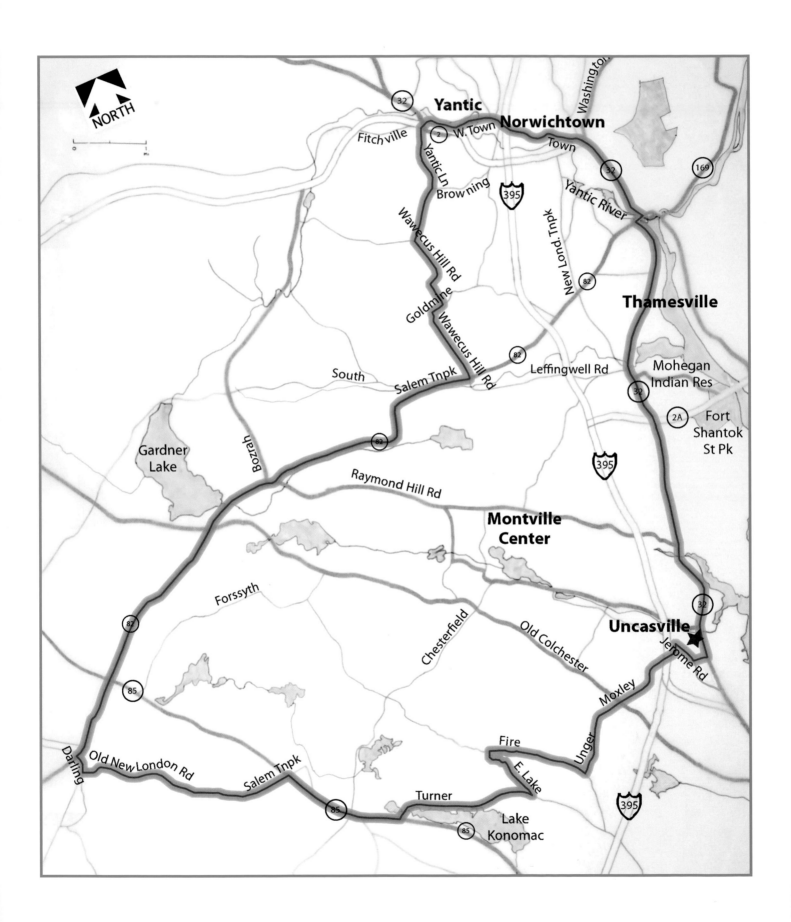

17. Montville – Norwich
Meet: Rte 395, Exit 79, Uncasville, to Rte 32 S. to Montville Town Hall parking lot

00.00	L	Rte 32
06.75	R	Rte 32 across bridge to 1st X.
06.90	L	Rte 32
08.37	F	Washington 1 bl to 1st Y.
08.45	BL	Town St. to end at Green
08.90	L	W. Town St. under Rte 395 to just before underpass Rte 2
10.45	R	Yantic Rd. (ignore "No Outlet" sign) to Y. at factory
10.80	BL	Chapel Hill Rd. 300 ft, past factory
10.90	BR	footpath alongside Rte 2 exit ramp
11.20	L	Rte 32 over bridge over Rte 2
11.30	R	Fitchville Rd. to 1st L.
11.36	L	Yantic Ln
12.36	BR	Browning
13.18	BL	Wawecus Hill Rd. to Goldmine Rd
14.35	BR	Wawecus Hill Rd. to Old Salem Rd
15.61	R	Wawecus Hill Rd
15.93	R	Rte 82 (Salem Tnpk) past Rte 11
24.28	L	Darling to 1st X.
24.57	L	Old New London Rd. → Salem Tnpk to end
29.00	R	Rte 85
29.62	L	Turner
31.73	L	E. Lake Rd. to end
32.64	R	Fire St. to 1st L.
34.13	L	Unger → Moxley to end
36.60	R	Jerome Rd. to 1st L.
36.97	L	Jerome Av 1 bl to end
37.18	L	Rte 32
37.38	L	parking at Montville Town Hall

Lake Konomoc, Turner Road, Chesterfield

[18] Groton – Mystic – Mashantucket

Meeting place: Groton, Wal-Mart parking lot facing Kings Hwy. Take 95 E., Exit 86, 1 bl on Route 184 to parking lot on left.
Length: 37 miles
Lunch: There are several small cafes and restaurants in Noank and Mystic. Or bring lunch to enjoy at the waterside.
Sights: Long Island Sound, harbors, forests and farmland, historic homes, magnificent views at the University of Connecticut SE Branch, a beautiful beach and woods at Bluff Point State Park, Haley State Park, the quaint villages of Noank and Mystic and Old Mystic, Thames River and Mystic River, Mystic Seaport, and Mashantucket Pequot Indian Reservation.
Challenge: easy to moderate; generally flat with some rolling hills, mostly paved streets and roads with some traffic, one dirt path through Bluff Point. A hybrid bike is best, but a road bike will do OK.

Even the names are intriguing—Mystic, Groton, Mashantucket. After heading south on Kings Highway and Bridge Street, we begin in historic Groton along the Thames River south of the US naval base, and travel down the narrow main street, the Thames, named after the river, with a view of ships sailing up the harbor. Following the river to the point at the Long Island Sound, past the US submarine building plant (no photographs) and giant Pfizer plant, we reach the glorious campus of the University of Connecticut at Avery Point with a magnificent view of the sea, lawns dotted with large outdoor contemporary sculpture, and the grand Branford summer house in all its Gothic splendor. Circling around the perimeter of the campus, past the Oceanological Research Center, we continue out of the campus and off the peninsula by way of Shennecossett and Thomas Roads and Tower Avenue until reaching Route 1.

Fortunately, we have only a few blocks to ride east on this very commercial strip until we reach Depot Street, which takes us straight down under an old railroad bridge, along a dirt road to the parking for Bluff Point State Park, where we continue straight ahead on the dirt path all the way to the end of the Park on the Long Island Sound again. Here is a beautiful shell and pebble beach, worth a stop to take a dip in the cool, clean water along this cove, and then to scramble to the top of the low bluff for a panoramic view of the sea and the coastline. The park is left in the pristine condition as it might have been seen by the first European visitors, and a walk through the woods would be pleasant. Now we can return the way we came (or, with a mountain bike, we can continue around the trail which circles through some very rough spots back to the beginning at the parking lot). Back at the trailhead before the parking lot, we turn right on the gravel trail heading toward Haley Farm State Park. For about a mile, we follow the railroad and then cross over the bridge to the other side, where quickly we find an entrance into the park on a path that takes us straight through to the main entrance on the east side. There we find the foundations of the old Haley farmhouse. Haley Farm Lane and Brook Street take us to Route 215, and a right down the hill towards the sea.

Rather than visiting Groton Long Point community, we make a sharp left turn to continue on 215 where it turns toward Noank. Turn right at the sign for Noank and tour around the perimeter of this extremely charming nineteenth-century fishing town at the mouth of the Mystic River by way of Mosher, Ward, Silvan, High, Spring, Pearl, and then Main down to the dock, and circling out by way of Front, Church, Main, Ward, and Mosher again, to turn right and continue north on Route 215. Finally we reach Route 1 again. If you look to the left you see the serene, classical, white, Union Baptist Church at the top of the hill. But turn right along the charming shops of Mystic for only one block to the drawbridge for a grand view of the Mystic River and replicas of nineteenth-century sailing ships that take visitors for a tour.

Returning from the bridge, we turn right immediately on Gravel Street, and follow the Mystic River north, zigzagging on Pearl, Star, and then River Road for more than two miles, with magnificent views of Mystic Seaport across the water with its tall sailing ships. This takes us through charming neighborhoods with eighteenth and nineteenth-century homes, until we reach Route 27 and turn right for one block for a view of eighteenth-century Old Mystic. Returning, we take Shewville Road north for several miles where it ends at the Mashantucket Pequot Indian Reservation (Foxwoods Resort, with its casino and museum, is just a couple miles to the right, for an interesting detour). We turn left on Route 214 for several miles through glorious farmland, and then, at a beautifully restored early-eighteenth-century farmhouse, we head south on Whalehead, Vinegar Hill (mostly uphill, and Long Cove (all downhill), passing the Ledyard Oak Open Space, with its Museum of Farm Implements, and then the Ledyard Reservoir. A brief right on Route 117 and right again on Route 184 for a couple of miles takes us back to our starting place.

Bushy Point Beach from Bluff Point, Groton

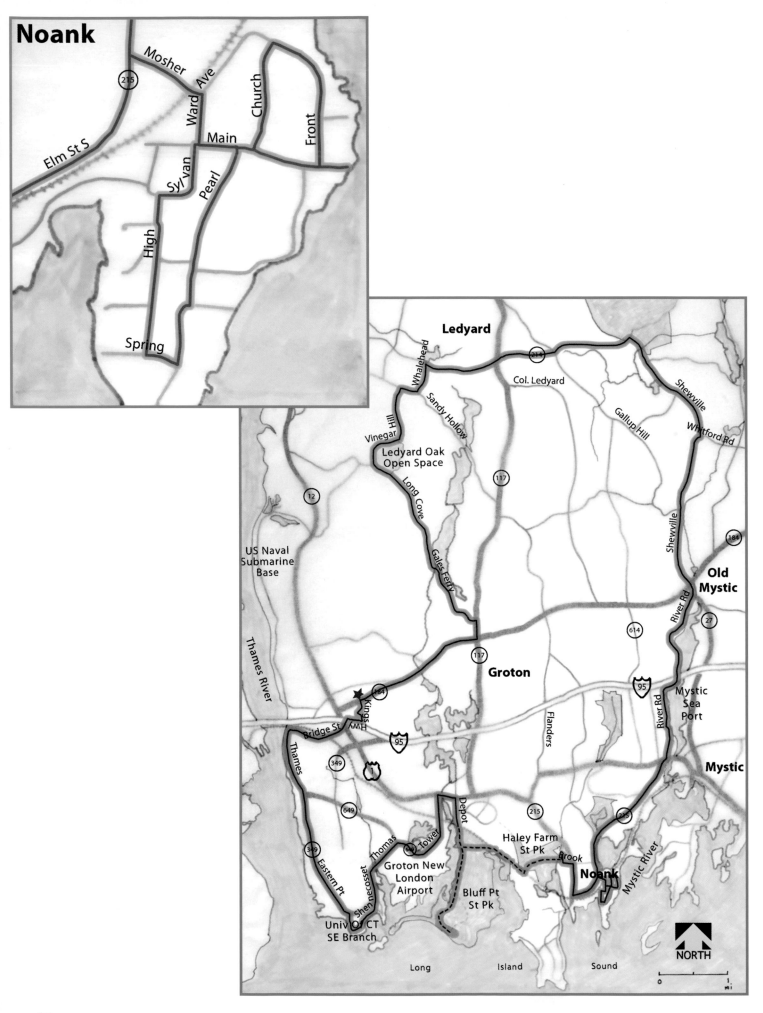

Noank

Mosher Ave

215

Elm St S

Ward Ave

Church

Front

Main

Sylvan

Pearl

High

Spring

Ledyard

214

Whalehead

Col. Ledyard

Shewville

Sandy Hollow

Gallup Hill

Whitford Rd

Vinegar Hill

Ledyard Oak
Open Space

117

12

Long Cove

Shewville

184

US Naval
Submarine
Base

Gales Ferry

Old
Mystic

River Rd

27

614

Thames River

117

Groton

95

Mystic
Sea
Port

184

Kings Hwy

River Rd

Bridge St

95

Mystic

Thames

349

1

Flanders

649

Depot

215

215

349

Eastern Pt

Thomas

Tower

649

Haley Farm
St Pk

Brook

Mystic River

Shennecosset

Groton New
London
Airport

Noank

Univ Of CT
SE Branch

Bluff Pt
St Pk

Long   Island   Sound

NORTH

0   1
mi

18. Groton – Mystic – Mashantucket

Meet: Wal-Mart parking lot facing Kings Hwy.
Take 95 E., Exit 86, on to Rte 184, 1 bl to parking lot on L.

00.00	F	Kings Hwy (several curves, under 95)
00.70	BR	Bridge St. to end
01.50	BL	Thames to end
02.58	BR	Eastern Point → Rte 349 to end
04.67	R	into U. Conn—R around circle, keep following the waterside to the Marine Center (either on road or brick path) (If by road circle right around Marine Center to the end. If by path, at the end ride down over the embankment to the road by the waterside)
05.46		(Head out and keep to R around waterside to exit university)
05.60	R	Shennecosset to stop sign
06.03	L	continue on Shennecosset to 1st R.
06.45	R	Kamaha/Thomas to end
07.08	R	Tower (Rte 649) to end
08.65	R	Rte 1 to 1st R.
09.93	R	Depot St. under bridge thru Bluff Point State Park to beach & up to bluff
11.17		Return on same path trailhead parking lot (with a mountain bike it's possible to continue on the same path, which circles around the park back to the entrance)
12.68	R	on trail leading to Haley State Park
12.83	BR	continue on trail
13.80	SL	across bridge over railroad to the 2nd trail R. (the 1st follows the railroad)
13.93	R	through gate and onto trail
14.50	F	Haley Farm Lane to end
14.60	R	Brook St
14.88	R	Rte 215 (makes a sharp left at the bottom)
15.38	SL	Rte 215 to Noank
15.94	R	Mosher 1 bl to end
16.05	R	Ward 1 bl to end
16.13	F	Sylvan to 1st L.
16.25	L	High to end
16.50	L	Spring 1 bl to end
16.55	L	Pearl to end
16.90	R	Main to end at dock
17.02	L	Front
17.25	L	Church to end
17.42	R	Main to 1st R.
17.50	R	Ward 1 bl
17.58	L	Mosher to end
17.70	R	Rte 215 to end
20.07	R	Rte 1 → drawbridge
20.15		Return to 1st R.
20.19	R	Gravel St. to end
20.45	L	Eldridge to end
20.53	R	Pearl
20.78	R	River Rd. to Rte 27
23.10	R	Rte 27 1 bl into Old Mystic
23.20		Return 1 bl on Rte 27
23.30	BR	Shewville across Rte 184 to bridge over brook at white farmhouse on Whitford Rd
24.85	L	Shewville to end
27.70	L	Rte 214 (Indiantown → Iron → Stoddards Wharf)
31.28	L	Whalehead
31.97	L	Vinegar Hill to end
33.46	L	Long Cove → Gales Ferry to end
36.64	R	Rte 117 (North Rd) to 1st X.
36.88	R	Rte 184 to Groton
39.10	R	into parking lot

Mystic Seaport

[19] Old Mystic – Stonington

Meeting Place: *I-95, Exit 90, Olde Mystic Village parking at Aquarium*
Length: *34 miles*
Lunch: *There are several cafes and restaurants at Olde Mystic Village and Stonington. Or bring lunch to enjoy at Stonington Point or by a farm on an old stone wall.*
Sights: *Long Island Sound, harbors, historic homes and farms, B. F. Clyde's Cider Mill, the quaint villages of Mystic, Old Mystic and Stonington, Olde Mystic Village shopping, and Old Mystic Aquarium, Mystic Seaport.*
Challenge: *easy to moderate; generally flat with some rolling hills, mostly paved streets and country roads with little traffic.*

This is a route that takes us through some of the most charming old coastal villages in Connecticut. We begin, however, at the convenient parking at the very commercial Olde Mystic Village, a modern reinterpretation of an old village with shops and restaurants and the more interesting Mystic Aquarium. From here we head out to Jerry Brown Road, where we first head north to Route 27 and the Pequot Trail into Old Mystic (the real one), full of charming little eighteenth and nineteenth-century houses, a grand plantation-style classical mansion, and the classical Methodist Church. But the real treat is just up North Stonington Road, where we find B. F. Clyde's Cider Mill, which has been going since 1881 (open only in apple season—the fall). This is worth a stop not only to taste the cider but also to gather around the old press and watch the production of cider from the dumping of the apple mush onto the trays to the slow cranking of the press to the disposal of the enormous cloth wraps.

From here we continue north, then head south on Al Harvey Road back to the Pequot Trail and then south on Flanders, passing the huge Greco-Italianate 1852 mansion of Captain Nathaniel B. Palmer, a national historic landmark. A zigzag over the railroad viaduct brings us into Stonington, an eighteenth-century fishing village that became the center of the Portuguese fishing industry in the nineteenth century, and still retains its Old World charm. Check out the luxurious nineteenth-century homes around Wadawanuck Square surrounding the library, some cute little cafes, and then head down High Street past the Captain Jessie Beebe House of 1765 down to the Town Dock, and Connecticut's only existing fishing fleet. Back on Water Street, we pass the James Merrill House, Wayland's Wharf off Union Street, the

Arcade Building of 1836, and Cannon Square. At The Point, we find the Old Lighthouse Museum and a grand view of the water and the long sandbar of Sandy Point to the north. Returning back on Main Street, we pass the Customs House of 1823, the Amos Palmer House of 1809 (once occupied by James MacNeill Whistler), the Portuguese Holy Ghost Society in the Courtlandt Palmer House of 1836, Dr. Lords Hall (before 1784), and the St. Mary Church, before heading out of town on Elm Street.

Off Route 1, South and North Anguilla Roads take us past swamps with giant white egrets and farms to Route 184, where we then head west to our next descent south on Wheeler Road back to the Pequot trail and then south again on Dean's Mill, Mistuxet, and Cove Roads, passing early-eighteenth-century farm houses and picturesque barns, and then the beautiful Quiambog Cove, until we finally spill out on the heavily traveled Route 1 and back to Mystic.

Here, Route 27 leads north to many wonders to the left and to the right. Mistuxet Avenue leads west to the Denison Pequotsepos Nature Center featuring native plant and animal life, with indoor exhibits and outdoor trails. Further on Route 27, to the left, is Mystic Seaport on the Mystic River, a vast open-air museum celebrating Mystic's position as America's preeminent shipbuilding port in the eighteenth century, with authentic historic buildings brought to the site from around the area. If you still have an hour or two before closing time, this is definitely worth the education and pleasure of going back in time. Much better than browsing the "shoppes" at Olde Mystic Village, back at our starting point, although a visit to the Aquarium would be worthwhile. Too many options, too little time. Come back!

Captain Nathaniel B. Palmer House, 1852, Stonington

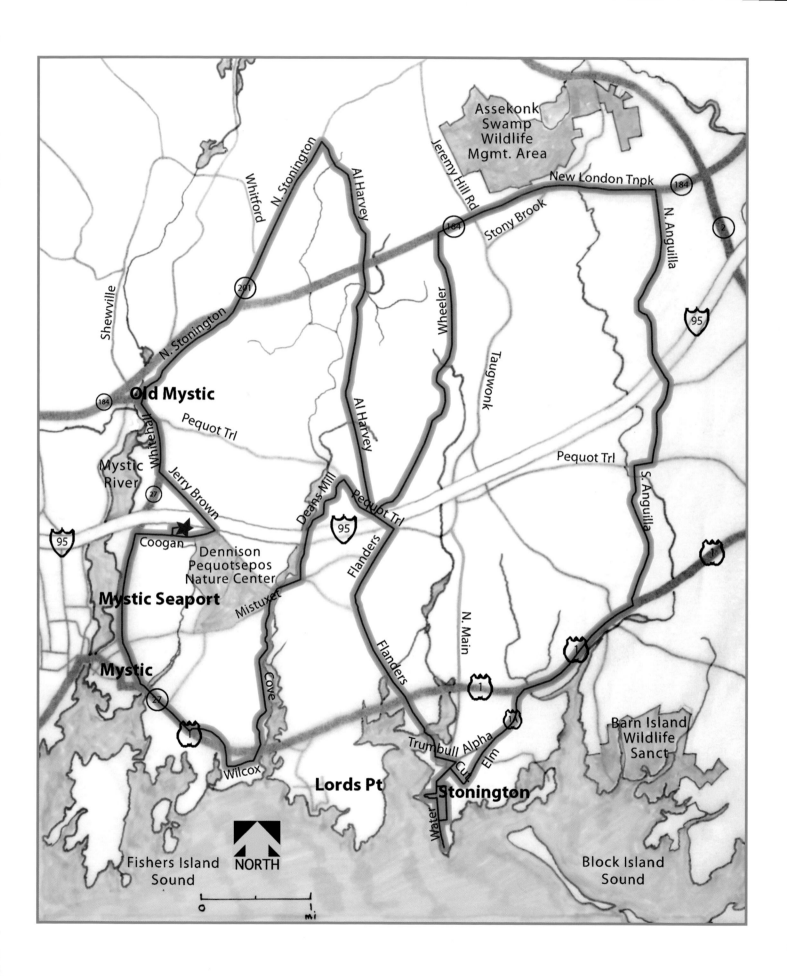

Assekonk
Swamp
Wildlife
Mgmt. Area

New London Tnpk

N. Stonington

Whitford

Al Harvey

Jeremy Hill Rd

Stony Brook

184

N. Anguilla

184

2

95

Shewville

201

Wheeler

Taugwonk

Old Mystic

184

Pequot Trl

Al Harvey

Pequot Trl

S. Anguilla

Whitehall

Mystic
River

Jerry Brown

27

Deans Mill

Pequot Trl

95

1

Coogan

Dennison
Pequotsepos
Nature Center

Flanders

Mystic Seaport

Mistuxet

Flanders

N. Main

1

Mystic

27

Cove

1

Barn Island
Wildlife
Sanct

1

1

Trumbull Alpha

Cutler

Elm

Wilcox

Lords Pt

Water

Stonington

Fishers Island
Sound

NORTH

0   1
mi

Block Island
Sound

19. Old Mystic – Stonington
Meet: I-95, Exit 90, Olde Mystic Village
parking at Aquarium

00.00	R	Clara Dr (at Aquarium)
00.05	L	Coogan Blvd. to end
00.46	L	Jerry Brown to end
01.14	R	Whitehall → Pequot Trail (Rte 27)
01.95	BR	Main (Rte 184)
02.52	R	N. Stonington (Rte 201) across Rte 184
05.20	R	Al Harvey to end
09.15	L	Pequot Trail over I-95 to 1st R.
09.38	R	Flanders
12.00	L	Trumbull (Rte 1A) to 2nd R.
12.20	R	Alpha (Rte 1A) over RR to end
12.42	L	Water St
12.55	R	High to Town Dock parking lot to end
12.82		(Return from parking lot by Pearl St)
13.04	R	Water St. to end at The Point
13.58		(return on Water St)
13.86	R	at Cannon Square to end
13.88	L	Main to end
14.26	L	Broad
14.32	R	Water St
14.36	R	The Viaduct (Alpha, Rte 1A) to 1st R.

14.60	R	Trumbull to end
14.67	L	Cutter St. to end
14.82	L	Elm to end
15.30	F	Elm (Rte 1A)
16.05	BR	Rte 1 (Stonington Rd)
17.33	L	S. Anguilla to end
18.78	R	Pequot Trail to 1st L.
18.97	L	N. Anguilla to end
21.88	L	New London Tnpk (Rte 184)
24.08	L	Wheeler to end at I-95
27.25	R	Pequot Trail to 1st L.
27.70	L	Deans Mill under I-95
28.85	R	Mistuxet past Jerry Brown
29.30	L	Cove → Wilcox to end
31.35	F	Old Stonington Rd
31.65	F	Rte 1 (Stonington Rd) across river
32.40	R	Rte 27 to just before I-95
33.98	R	Coogan Blvd.
34.28	L	Clara
34.38	L	into Mystic Aquarium parking

B.F. Clyde's Cider Mill, 1881, Old Mystic

[20] Old Mystic – Glasgo

Meeting Place: Park & Ride, I-95, Exit 91, left on Taugwonk
Length: 39 miles
Lunch: There are no restaurants, cafes, or food markets along the entire route, but there is a great ice cream farm halfway, and a famous cider and baked goods stop toward the end. Better to bring lunch to enjoy beside a pond, in a state forest, or in a small village.
Sights: Farms, historic homes and churches, quaint villages, Assekonk Swamp Wildlife Management Area, Pachaug State Forest, Pachaug Pond, Glasgo Pond, and Pequot Indian Reservation and Foxwoods Resort.
Challenge: easy; many long, level stretches with just a couple of short steep hills, paved roads with light traffic, except for Route 164 with moderate traffic and Route 2, which has broad shoulders but heavy, high-speed traffic.

This is a quite bucolic tour even though the roads are mostly major routes, but they go through large forests and open countryside with farms the entire way. The small villages are pleasant and tidy but not upscale. While there are no major landmarks on the route itself, a couple of detours can be made for more excitement. This is a quiet, placid tour.

We begin heading north from I-95 in Stonington on Taugwonk Road, which becomes Jeremy Hill Road in North Stonington, passing the Assekonk Swamp Wildlife Management Area on the right. Route 201 takes us on a winding road, briefly merging and turning with Route 2, passing some enchanting cemeteries, expansive farm scapes, hills, and forests. Where Route 2 splits again from Route 201, Route 2 goes left to Foxwoods Resort, with its museum of Native American art, which would make a nice detour, perhaps even for the night, for those who have time. But our tour turns right to continue on Route 201 to Glasgo. Glasgo Pond and its adjoining Doaneville Pond are one of the last bucolic havens for the working class in Connecticut, where trailer parks, festooned with laundry on the clothes lines, sit at the water's edge. Turning right on Route 165, we come shortly to one of the best farm-made ice cream places in Connecticut, Buttonwood Farm, a great place to relax on the stone benches for a delicious cone.

Six miles later, through more farmland and cows and horses, we arrive at the optimistically named Preston City, which is little more than a crossroads with few houses in sight. Nevertheless, there are two major churches, the lovely combination Gothic-Romanesque Congregational Church built in the 1860s, and down Route 164 a few hundred yards, the Preston City Bible Church, rather dilapidated but in a stately Federal style, built in 1812 by the Baptists (the foyer and belltower added in 1835 after lifting and turning the entire building 120 degrees). After a brief ride along the heavily trafficked Route 2, we turn left at Shewville Road where a rotting one-room shack that served as a filling station stands as a reminder of the simplicity of yesteryear. Along Shewville are more picturesque farms and eighteenth-century homes.

After a brief cut across Whitford Road, which becomes Wolf Neck Road, past a pond and thick woods, we head south on Route 201. At 33.83 miles we come to an institution in this neck of the woods—B. F. Clyde's Cider Mill built in 1881—a must-stop to sample some of the delicious ciders, including hard cider of various flavors, and maybe to accompany it with lunch before completing the last five miles of the ride. Down the road is the extremely quaint Old Mystic on Whitford Brook, which leads to the Mystic River. Down Main Street we pass some of the most charming eighteenth and nineteenth-century homes. Finally, out Route 27 and 234 along the Pequot Trail, we cross over I-95 and pass through a scenic route of historic homes and a quite austere, Federal-style church, The Road Church Congregational, before heading back to Taugwonk Road back under I-95 to the Park & Ride.

Eggleston Cemetery, Route 201

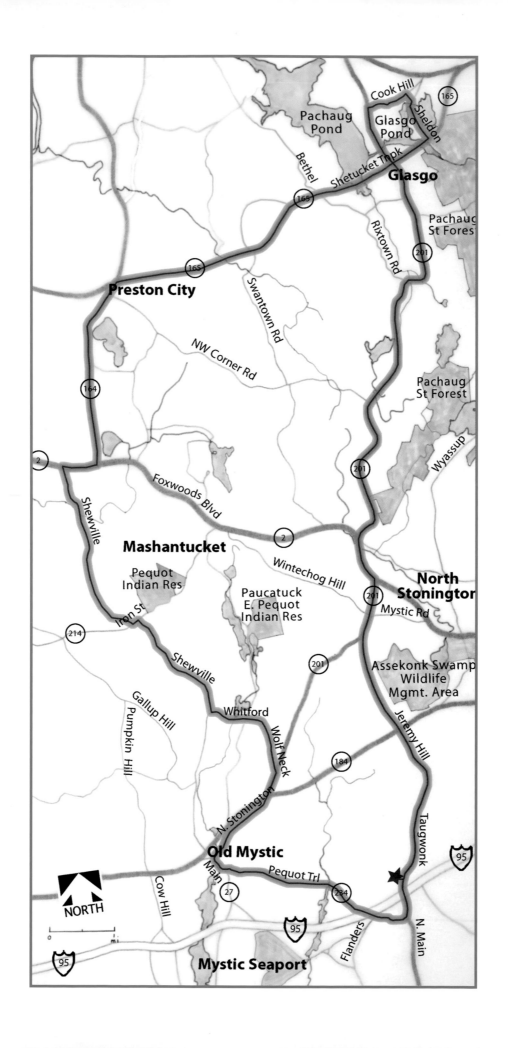

20. Old Mystic – Glasgo
Meet: Park & Ride, I-95, Exit 91, L on Taugwonk

00.00	L	Taugwonk → Jeremy Hill to end
04.56	R	Rte 201 to Mystic Rd
04.90	BL	continue Rte 201 to Rte 2
05.55	L	continue Rte 201/Rte 2 to split with Rte 2
06.32	R	continue Rte 201 to Rte 165
13.55	F	continue Rte 201 past Glasgo Pond dam
14.70	R	Cook Hill
15.38	R	Cross 1 bl to end
15.53	R	Sheldon to end
16.20	R	Rte 165 (Shetucket Tnpk) to Preston City
21.95	L	Rte 164 to end
25.16	R	Rte 2 to 1st L.
25.65	L	Shewville
28.80	L	Rte 214 (Iron St) to immediate R.
28.87	R	Shewville to T
30.90	L	Whitford → Wolf Neck to end
33.80	R	Rte 201 to 1st X (Rte 184)
34.00	F	N. Stonington Rd
34.56	BL	Main → Rte 27
34.75	BL	Rte 234 (Pequot Trail) to end
38.35	F	Taugwonk under I-95
38.55	L	into parking lot

Farm display, Shewville & Whitford Roads, Ledyard

[21] Griswold – Voluntown – Sterling – Plainfield

Meeting Place: Route 138 S. at Route 12 in Jewett City (north of Route 395, Exit 85)
Length: 36 miles
Lunch: There are several eateries in Jewett City, Moosup, and Plainfield, and a wonderful farm market with ice cream, pies, and sandwiches on Route 49 just south of Route 14A. Or bring lunch to enjoy beside a pond, in a state forest, or in a small village.
Sights: Farms, historic homes and churches, quaint villages, Hopeville Pond State Park, Pachaug State Forest, bubbling brooks, and the Moosup State Park Trail.
Challenge: easy; many long, level stretches with some short steep hills, paved roads with very little traffic, except for Route 12, which has broad shoulders.

Lots of farmland whizzes by us here, with cattle herds and horses and barns all along the way; interrupted, for the most part, only by forests and lakes. Not hard to take. This is a fairly breathless ride, with no long, grueling hills, but a few short steep ones that take just brief bursts of energy. There are some charming tiny hamlets along the way north, and then some larger villages on the way back south. These villages are what one fellow rider called "the next big real estate opportunity," that is, they've seen some hard times with the closing of mills, but there is some charming, if neglected, architecture.

One of these towns a little worse for the wear is Jewett City (optimistically named), where we begin the ride. Although the main strip where we park is particularly unattractive, a little detour down to the lower town by the Quinebaug River reveals a more pleasant past of wooden Victorian homes. Heading out of town on Route 201, we pass the Ashland Pond on the right, which connects to the Hopeville Pond in the State Park of the same name, where there is a pleasant picnic ground and cozy little beach for swimming. Route 138 takes us through the hamlet of Voluntown (named for the land given to volunteers in the Revolutionary War), where we catch Route 49 North. A worthwhile stop is the Pachaug State Forest, with its large bog full of a variety of large and small birds, and the occasional canoe gliding through the vegetation, all of which can be viewed from a wooden platform over the water. Trails through the woods lead to several ponds. Further north have a nice stop for a picnic lunch at a farm selling delicious baked goods, organic sandwiches, and ice cream.

Sterling Hill is just an intersection with a few houses, but all are historic and beautifully maintained, and the little hill is crowned by a serene and simple First Baptist Church (a rarity in this Congregational state). North on Sterling Hill Road and then Goshen Road, through pastoral scenery, we head back east and south on Route 14, which becomes Main Street through the town of Moosup. The road follows the Moosup River. Along the river is the Moosup State Park Trail, as of this writing suitable only for mountain bikes, which starts at the town of Moosup and follows Route 14 and the river all the way to the Rhode Island border. Eventually it will be connected to the Air Line Trail as a part of the East Coast Greenway.

South on Grove and Starkweather Roads and more bucolic scenery, we head west on Route 14A through the village of Plainfield, where someone in the nineteenth century took a strong liking to mansard roofs, placing them atop even little square houses, with stately decorative trim. The town is a curiosity and won't remain shabby for long. Continuing south on Weston and Lillibridge Roads, we turn right on Route 12, through Dairy Queens, trailer parks, and a scene right out of the 1950s straight back to our starting point at Jewett City.

Sheep farm at Sterling Hill

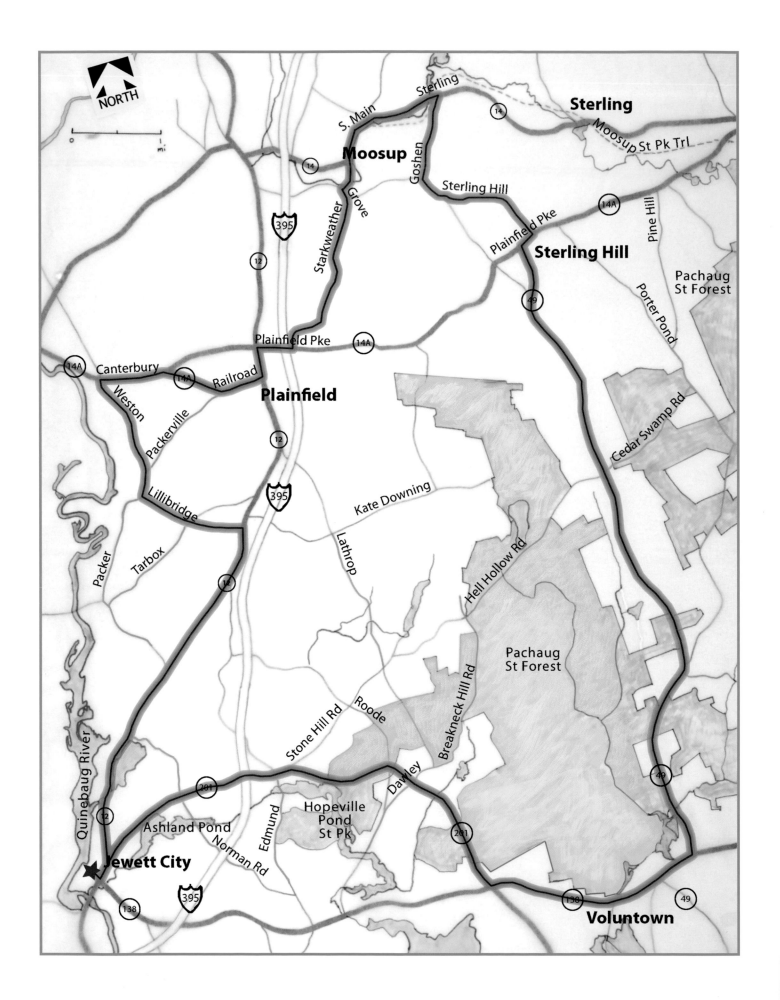

21. Griswold – Voluntown – Sterling – Plainfield
Meet: Rte 138 S. at Rte 12 in Jewett City
(north of Rte 395, Exit 85)

00.00	R	N. on Rte 12 to Y.
00.20	F	Rte 201
02.74	BR	continue Rte 201
06.00	L	Rte 138
08.69	L	Rte 49 N to end
16.95	R	Rte 14A (Plainfield Pke) to 1st L.
17.00	L	Sterling Hill to 1st R.
18.70	R	Goshen to end
19.85	L	Rte 14 (Sterling)
21.34	F	S. Main to right curve across little stream
21.75	L	Grove to 1st Y.
21.94	BR	Starkweather to end
24.09	R	Rte 14A (Plainfield Pke) under Rte 395 through Plainfield
24.48	L	Rte 14A (Rte 12) to 2nd R.
24.89	R	Rte 14A (Railroad)
25.39	BR	Rte 14A (Canterbury)
26.91	L	Weston to end
28.24	F	Packerville to 1st L.
28.52	L	Lillibridge to end
30.00	R	Rte 12 to Jewett City
35.50	L	into parking lot at Rte 138

Pachung State Forest, Voluntown

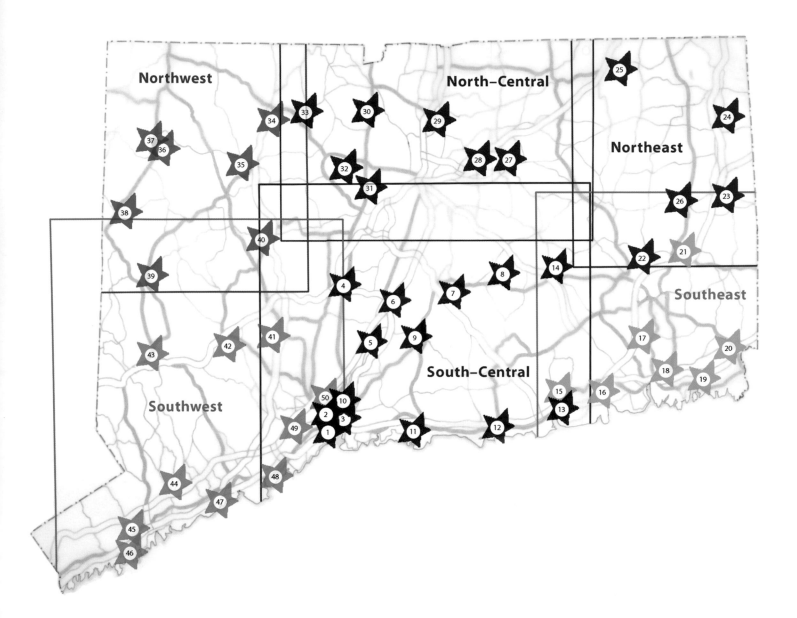

Northeast

The Quiet Corner: Franklin & Griswold to the Massachusetts Border

A stone wall on Cook Hill Road, Killingly

[22] Occum – Windham – Westminster

Meeting place: Park & Ride, Route 97, off I-395, Exit 83 at Occum.
Length: 39 miles
Lunch: There are no cafes once we get past Occum and Baltic, although there are service stations with food. Bring lunch to enjoy on the Green at Windham or at Bibbons Pond at the Beaver Brook State Park.
Sights: Historic homes and churches, quaint villages, state parks, lakes, horses, and farms.
Challenge: moderate; flat and rolling hills, all paved roads with little traffic.

Here is rural Connecticut with quaint villages unspoiled by modern commercialism, so don't expect any fast food places, but do expect roads with little traffic and people who greet you with a smile. The route is modified from Cue #3 on the Connecticut Bicycle Map. We begin at the junction of Route 395 and 97, where the view is of a typical Thruway stop with gas stations and parking lots, but this is the last you'll see of that. Riding north on 97, we zigzag through the small village of Occum, with a big playing field and a country store. You can tell it was a company town by the lineup of nearly identical, multi-family houses, right out of the industrial early twentieth century.

Further north, as we turn left on Route 207, is the charming village of Baltic, with the rather startling, high, gold-domed cupola of St. Mary's church on the grounds of the Academy of the Holy Family. The village is a hodgepodge of nineteenth-century churches, commercial brick buildings from the turn of the twentieth century with bay windows, and double-terraced residential buildings with decorative balustrades featuring shops below. For a village in the middle of nowhere, there is the incongruous assembly of small, urban, brick apartment houses, including a miniature, brick version of New York's Flatiron Building, possibly the skinniest building in Connecticut, wedged in between West Main and Upper High Streets. Out 207 a bit is a magnificent Victorian home with turret, wrap-around porch, and too many gables to count. This road takes us past Gagers Pond to Route 32, past horse farms and eighteenth-century homes. After a short detour on Williams Crossing Road and Babcock

Hill Road, we arrive at the beautiful little village of South Windham, with its magnificent mid- to late-nineteenth-century mansions in classical and shingle style. Turning on Machine Shop Hill Road (Main Street), we continue on Route 203 to 14 and the beautiful Green and village of Windham Center. Before reaching the village, make a stop at the Windham graveyard and take time to look at the headstones, many from the early eighteenth century, with wonderful inscriptions and delightfully curious images of angels' heads with wings and other fanciful designs. Then, surrounding the Green in Windham are some stately Gothic and classical homes and the white, Gothic, Congregational Church. Around the Green are the tiny 1790 office of Sheriff Shuebel Abbe, the colonial 1750 Fuller house next to the bright pink Italianate 1850 Huntington house, and the austere eighteenth-century Windham Inn, said to be haunted by the ghost of Elisabeth Shaw, hung in 1744.

Leaving Route 14 on Back Road we pass Bibbons Pond at the Beaver Brook State Park, which is worth a visit for lunch by the waterfall. The rest of the trip takes us north on Parrish Hill Road, south on Brook, and east on Kemp which becomes Windham and Raymond Schoolhouse as we cross town lines. Finally, we turn south on Brooklyn, zigzagging through Westminster, with its beautiful, classical, Congregational Meeting-House, and from there for a ten mile ride through farmland and forests south on Water, which becomes Westminster, Potash Hill, Inland, Versailles, and Main, through woods and farms, mostly downhill, past Versailles Pond, before bringing us back to 97 at Occum.

Cemetery, Windham Center

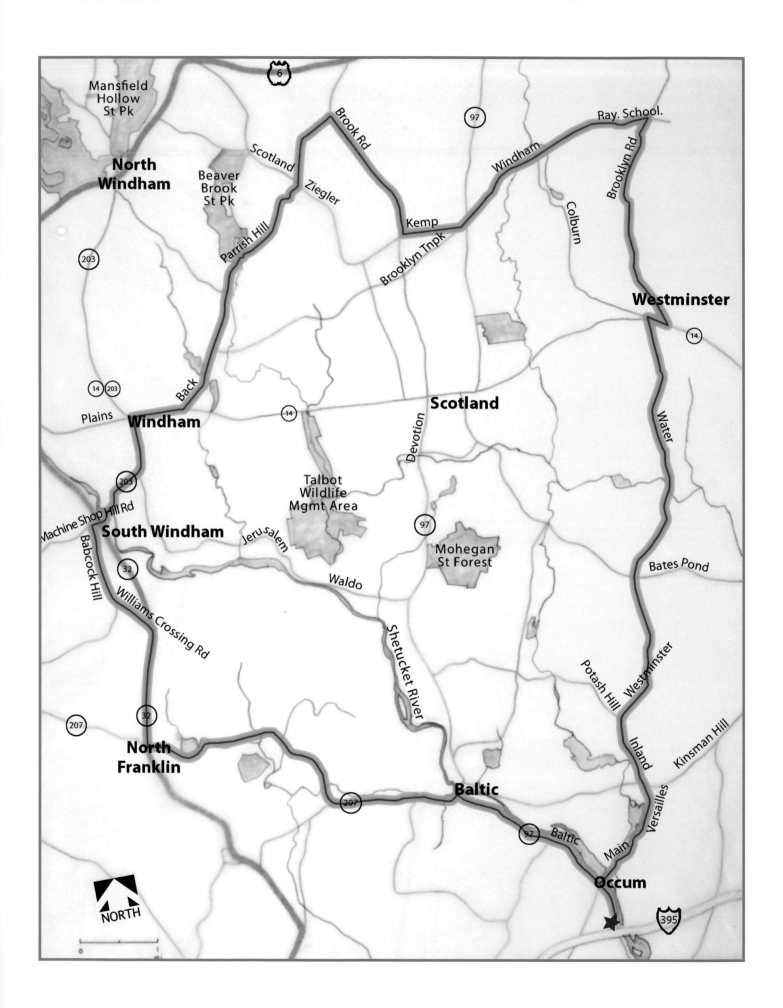

22. Occum – Windham – Westminster
Meet: Park & Ride, Rte 97, off I-395, Exit 83 at Occum.

00.00	R	North on Rte 97
00.78	L	Bridge St
00.84	R	Rte 97 (Baltic)
03.35	L	Rte 207
08.40	R	Rte 32
10.10	BL	Williams Crossing Rd. to end
11.00	R	Babcock Hill Rd
11.90	R	Machine Shop Hill Rd. → Main (in South Windham)
12.02	F	Cross Rte 32 onto Rte 203
13.75	R	Rte 14 (at Windham Center)
14.48	L	Back Rd. to Bibbons Pond
16.90	BR	Parrish Hill Rd
19.42	R	Brook Rd. to T
21.50	L	Kemp Rd. to end
22.24	BL	Brooklyn Tpke → Windham Rd. (Cross Rte 97)
22.91	BR	Windham Rd. (in Hampton) → Raymond Schoolhouse Rd
25.45	R	Brooklyn Rd. to end
28.68	R	Rte 14 (Westminster Rd) 1 bl
28.87	L	Water St. → Westminster Rd. to end
35.14	F	Potash Hill → Inland Rd
36.17	F	Versailles → Main → Bridge St
37.82	L	Rte 97
38.63	L	into Park & Ride

Early–nineteenth-century home, South Windham

[23] Moosup – Putnam – Quaddick

Meeting Place: *Moosup, off Route 395, Exit 89, Route 14 to Main Street and across to parking at the trailhead bridge of Moosup State Park Trail (parking to the left of bridge, behind the bank)*
Length: *46 miles*
Lunch: *There are several small delis and restaurants in Putnam, so buy here and take to eat by a lake.*
Sights: *Historic towns, state parks, farms, abandoned mills, sand quarries, the Putnam River Trail, the Quinebaug River, the French River, the Quaddick Reservoir, and lots of lakes and ponds.*
Challenge: *easy to moderate; mostly flat and gently rolling hills, a few short steep hills toward the end, paved roads with light traffic, a couple of short bike paths, and one short dirt road.*

This is the very rural, once-industrial northeast, with some hardscrabble little towns. The first 30 miles of this route are fairly easy, on mostly flat roads with just a few small hills. We start at the town of Moosup, which lies on the little Moosup River. Here is found the Moosup State Park Trail, beginning at a trestle bridge across the river and going a few miles, where it ends up as a dirt trail and becomes impassable to road bikes (at this time of this writing), although when it's developed it will stretch all the way to Providence, Rhode Island.

At the elegant, but abandoned, United Methodist Church, facing a hub of gas stations and convenience stores, we leave behind some of the crusty old idlers hanging out together at the corner and head north on Main Street and then Lake and Mortimer to begin our circle with a left on Moosup Pond Road past the pond of the same name down the hill to our right. Along the way are some rustic looking farms and farmhouses until we reach Route 12. Making a right, we ride for four miles to the town of Danielson, branching onto the Route 6 highway to meet the bridge over the Quinebaug River. Just before crossing the river, there is a bike path following the river south for a bit, which would be a nice little diversion. The small town of Danielson, to the right, is worth a little side trip down Main Street to see the magnificent Westfield Congregational Church sitting in a little park down from the library and the town hall.

But our route takes us right on Maple Street (with name changes to Tracy, Park, and Kennedy Drive) for an eight-mile ride until we reach the town of Putnam. Just before entering the town, at 16.30 miles, opposite Arch Street, a diversion across a 200-foot pedestrian trestle bridge to the left takes you across the Quinebaug River to the paved Putnam River Trail heading south, good for those who would like to explore this picturesque waterway a little bit. But our main route

straight ahead branches left shortly into a little park and on to the Putnam River Trail (following the Quinebaug River) heading north for two miles. Exhibits along the route tell of Putnam's railroad history and textile mills, one of which stands prominently across the river, and the great flood of 1955, which brought everything crashing down, including the Boston, Hartford & Erie Railroad service. The Pomfret Cotton Mill was built to produce textiles in 1807, and it is the oldest existing cotton mill in the United States today, consisting of a four-story stone mill, a hip-roofed office building (c. 1823), a three-story stone mill added in the mid-1840s, another three-story brick mill (1856), and a final three-story mansard-roofed brick mill (1869).

At the end of the trail we turn right on Providence Street and then head north on Route 12 to where the railroad crosses the pond on the French River, bordered by a little picnic area. Right on Route 193 takes us to the charming little village Green of Thompson, with its tall white spire of the Congregational Church soaring above the trees. Continuing on, we turn right on Brandy Hill Road, crossing the Quaddick Reservoir surrounded by lakefront homes, and then south on Quaddick Town Farm Road. Munyan Road takes us past the arid mountains of sand at the Rawson Materials Company, and then we're on to Tucker Road and Five Mile River Road to Cady Brook Pond. From here, it's fifteen winding miles south over a few more challenging hills on East Putnam, Cutler, Yosemite Valley, Chestnut Hill, Valley, Burlingame, and Cook Hill Roads to South Killingly, a tiny little crossroads of a village with a charming little Federal-style Congregational Church. Another 6 miles straight south seems endless, but wooded and picturesque, until it drops us back at Moosup on Lake Street to Main Street and the parking at the trestle bridge trailhead.

The Pomfret Cotton Mill, 1807, on the Quinebaug River, Putnam

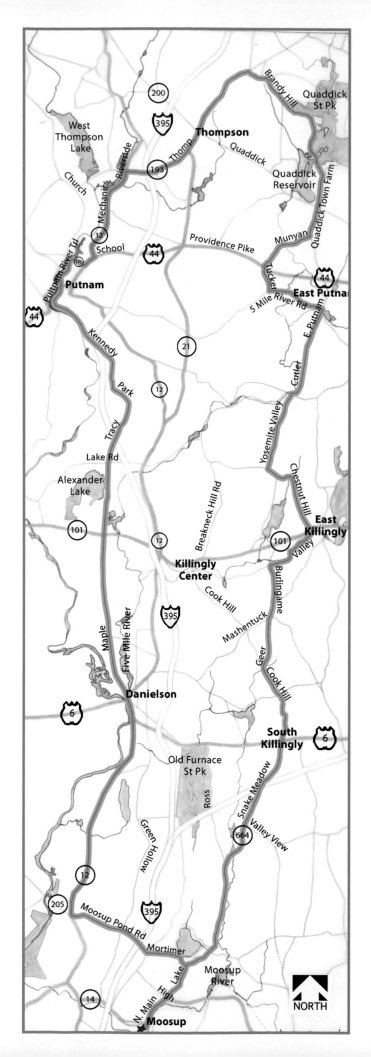

23. Moosup – Putnam – Quaddick
Meet: Moosup, Rte 14 to Main and across to parking at trailhead bridge of Moosup State Park Trail

00.00	N	N. Main
00.56	L	Lake
01.35	L	Mortimer
01.60	L	Moosup Pond Rd
03.80	R	Rte 12 (Putnam) to Danielson
07.85	L	Rte 6 across river
08.25	R	Maple to end at Lake Rd
12.90	R-L	(dog leg) Tracy → Park (bikepath part way at 13.90-14.50) → Kennedy
16.40	L	into park and onto Putnam River Trail (continuing on sidewalk after Woodstock Ave) to end
17.62	R	Rte 171 (Providence) to end
17.88	L	Rte 12 (School St) 1 bl to 1st L.
18.10	L	Rte 12 (Mechanics → Riverside)
20.05	R	Rte 193 (Thompson Rd) through Thompson
23.30	R	Brandy Hill across reservoir to end
26.05	R	Quaddick Town Farm
27.27	R	Munyan to end
28.50	L	Rte 44 (Providence Pke) 1/2 bl to 1st R.
28.54	R	Tucker to end
28.90	L	Five Mile River Rd. to 1st X.
29.97	R	E. Putnam Rd. → Cutler to end at Y. (do not cross bridge)
31.80	L	Yosemite Valley (becomes dirt road at 32.17) to end
32.28	L	Chestnut Hill (unmarked)
34.87	L	Rte 101 (Hartford Pke) 1 bl to 1st R.
34.94	SR	Valley
36.10	L	Burlingame → Geer
38.07	L	Cook Hill (BR at 39.30) across Rte 6
39.60	F	Snake Meadow
44.23	BL	Lake to end
42.28	R	N. Main
45.88	L	into parking at the Moosup State Park Trailhead

Late–nineteenth-century home on the Green, Thompson

[24] Thompson – Woodstock

Meeting place: Park & Ride at Dayville in Killingly. Take I-95 to 395 N—Exit 93 (Dayville/Killingly Center)—left under 395 to Park & Ride on left
Length: 35 miles
Lunch: There are several small delis and restaurants, one big one with outdoor seating at Rte 169 and Rte 44 E. Or bring lunch to enjoy at Roseland Cottage.
Sights: Historic homes and towns, state parks, abandoned mills, and farms.
Challenge: moderate; mostly rolling hills, a couple of short steep hills, and paved roads with light traffic.

This ride takes us to the hilly northeast corner of Connecticut, through small towns and villages in an area that was once thriving with large mills. The mills are silent now, some of the mill towns are suffering, some new commerce has come in, and here and there are large productive farms with beautiful old farmhouses and barns.

We start the ride at Dayville in Killingly, and head north on Route 12. (To experience the small town of Putnam with its charming antique shops and cafes, continue on Route 12.) For a more rural and smaller road with less traffic, bear right on Route 21. This takes us to the village of Thompson, with its charming village Green opposite the stately white Congregational Church, and surrounded with Victorian and colonial homes. Turn left here on Route 200, which takes us back to Route 12 and the mill towns of Grosvenorsdale and North Grosvenorsdale, quintessential company towns dominated by the huge brick mill with its ornamental towers perched by the old railroad. Here there are a few delis, where lunch could be taken to the small Green overlooking the mill.

We continue on Route 131 which runs along an abandoned railroad (which would make a great rails-to-trails bike path) stopping short of the village of Quinebaug to turn left at the light on the smaller Fabyan Road. This takes us past beautiful farmland on a very hilly road.

(An alternative route would be to continue on 131 into Quinebaug and then left on 197, and left at 169 at North Woodstock, for more main roads with lower hills.)

Continuing forward for several miles, with many road name changes, we arrive at the charming village of Woodstock, with its expansive Green, surrounded by the sprawling Woodstock Academy, a classical Congregational Church, and the amazing, pink, Gothic-style Roseland Cottage built in 1846, with its beautiful formal garden, as a summer home for Henry Chandler Bowen, a Woodstock native who made his fortune in New York and became an active abolitionist. The cottage is open on weekends from June 1 to October 15. Here, and on the Green, would be a good place to have lunch on the grass. Otherwise, further down 169, at 44, is a big outdoor restaurant and beer garden, where you're likely to see dozens of motorcyclists hanging out. Routes 44 and 169 continue together here, passing the magnificent Pomfret school with its stone, Gothic chapel across the street from the white Congregational Church.

Where Routes 44 and 169 split again, we turn left on Route 101 to arrive back at our starting place at Dayville, another old mill town. For a slight diversion, turn right on 101 instead and then a quick left on Wolf Den Drive into the Mashamoquet Brook State Park, and then return to Dayville.

Congregational Church and the Academy, on the Green, Thompson

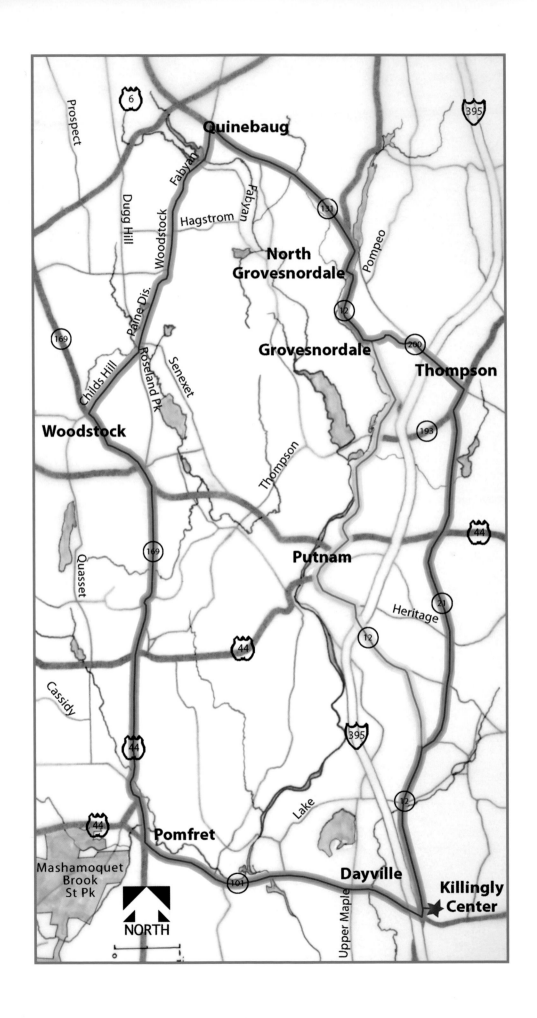

24. Thompson – Woodstock
Meet: 95 to 395 N—Exit 93 (Dayville/
Killingly Center)—L under 395 to Park & Ride on L

00.00	N	Rte 12		13.00	BL	Rte 131 to 1st light
02.70	BR	Rte 21 to end *(alt. continue on Rte 12 thru Putnam for c. same mileage to 13.00 at Rte 131)*		15.94	L	Fabyan past bridge & dam
				16.62	F	Fabyan → Woodstock—BL at next Y (no sign) → Paine District → Roseland Park
08.00	BR	Rte 193 to 1st X at Thompson Green		20.00	BR	Childs Hill
08.93	L	Rte 200 to end		21.40	L	Rte 169 to light at Rte 44 W
10.87	BR	Rte 12		28.80	L	Rte 101 to Dayville
				33.50	R	into Park & Ride

Roseland Cottage, 1846, Woodstock

[25] Union – Chaplin

Meeting Place: *Union Green, Congregational Church: I-84, Exit 73, Route 190 East*
Length: *45 miles*
Lunch: *There is not a single cafe or restaurant or even a gas station. Bring lunch to eat along a lake or stream.*
Sights: *Bigelow Hollow State Park, state forests, lakes and ponds, farms, cows and horses, and historic homes and churches.*
Challenge: *moderate; paved roads with very light traffic, short hills up and long hills down.*

This route takes us through some of the most idyllic farmland in all Connecticut on little country roads with only a rare car sighting; there are no towns but only small clusters of houses barely meriting the term "villages," and no commerce. The route is modified from Cue #4 on the Connecticut Bicycle Map. The entire route is hilly, although most are fairly low-grade, with only a few long inclines, but some may find the relentless ups and downs a bit difficult. We begin at a three-way stop that forms the Green of what is registered on the map as the town of Union, although all we see is the simple Congregational Church, an old schoolhouse, and a couple of scattered houses. By 1633 it was the source of graphite purchased from the Indians, but the first settler came from Massachusetts in 1727.

We follow Route 190 east from the Green. East again on Route 171 takes us flying downhill and then up past Bigelow Hollow State Park, where it would be a good idea to turn off the odometer and follow the Park Road one-quarter mile to the canoe launch at the southern point of the Mashapaug Pond, and further on to the beautiful picnic grounds at the edge of the lake. Out of the park and continuing up a steep hill on 171, and then 197, we take Center, then Bradford Corner to West Woodstock, again, nothing more than a three-way stop, but it is home to the charming little 1894 neo-Gothic Church of the Good Shepherd Congregational with its pointed belltower, a grand but decrepit nineteenth-century colonnaded front to an eighteenth-century colonial, and several other colonial homes. And a little further on Perrin Road is the colonial Elias Child house built in 1714. This becomes Old Colony Road, taking us to 198 South past the huge Natchaug State Forest.

Chaplin Street, at a little country store (abandoned, as of this writing), takes us to Tower Hill Road and fields of grazing cattle. Turning right on Wormwood Hill Road, past a little triangular park across from the Hiram Parker House of 1750 (painted a deep colonial red), we continue north on Knowlton Hill Road, left on Route 44 briefly, and then right on rural roads called Marsh, Daleville School, Cowles, Parker, and Moose Meadow across streams and past red-painted barns with square cupolas. At the end, the cemetery on the hill is a good place to collapse for a deserved rest for the weary. Turnpike Road takes us east to Route 89 North (where just beyond is a lovely old abandoned barn complex with a wooden silo) past Lake Chaffee, then east on Hillside and north on Lead Mine Road to Barrows and finally east on Route 190 at the turnpike exit back to our start at the Green at the hamlet of Union.

For a charming end to the day, if one has just a little more energy to ride on a mile and a half, a downhill ride to the Bigelow Hollow State Park on Route 171 to relax at the lakeside would be a great idea.

Church of the Good Shepherd Congregational, West Woodstock, 1894

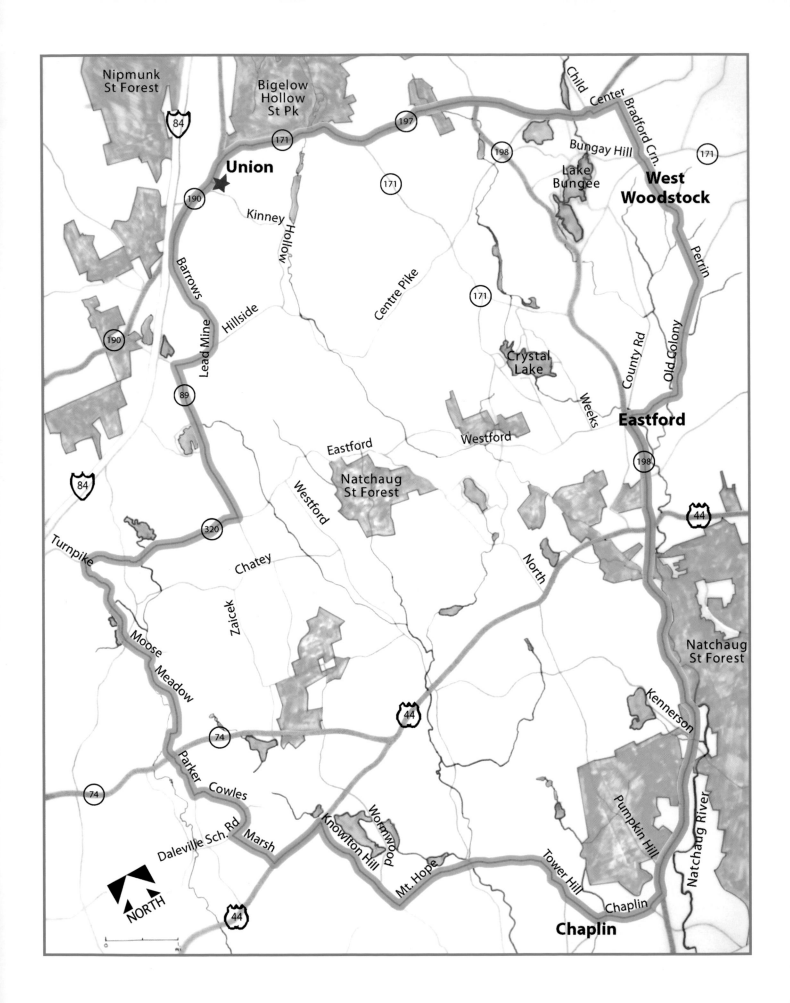

25. Union – Chaplin
Meet: Union Green, Congregational Church:
I-84, Exit 73, Rte 190 East

00.00	F	Rte 190 to 1st R.
00.33	R	Rte 171 (01.70, L. into Bigelow Hollow State Park: 1/4 mile to Mashapaug Pond) (steep hill on 171 after Park)
02.67	BL	Rte 197
06.36	R	Center (across from Child) to 1st R.
06.82	R	Bradford Corner across Rte 171
07.86	F	Perrin → Old Colony
12.83	L	Rte 198 (cross Rte 44 at 14.36)
20.88	R	Chaplin (at little country store) to 1st R.
21.16	R	Tower Hill → Mount Hope across Rte 89 to end
25.75	R	Wormwood Hill, BR at triangle, then to next Y.
26.23	F	Knowlton Hill to end
27.67	L	Rte 44 to 1st R.
28.59	R	Marsh to end
29.40	R	Daleville School Rd. → Cowles to end
30.79	R	Parker (across from Mason) → Moose Meadow (after Rte 74) to end at cemetery
35.41	R	Turnpike
37.97	L	Rte 89 N (direction: Union)
41.35	R	Hillside to 1st L.
40.40	L	Lead Mine → Barrows
42.03	L	continue on Barrows to end
42.97	R	Rte 190 to Union
44.50		to start at Union Green

A farm on Turnpike Road (Route 89), Westford

[26] Canterbury – Brooklyn – Hampton

Meeting place: Canterbury, 395, Exit 88, left on Route 14A to 14 to Park & Ride at baseball field just before Route 169
Length: *37 miles*
Lunch: *There are a couple of cafes. Bring lunch to enjoy at Mashamoquet Brook State Park, or on the Green at Brooklyn, Abington, Hampton, or Scotland.*
Sights: *Mashamoquet Brook State Park, historic homes, three of the earliest churches in Connecticut, quaint villages, lakes, horses, farms, and forests.*
Challenge: *moderate; rolling hills, all paved roads with little traffic.*

This picturesque route on good roads less traveled by is selected for the charming little villages that it connects: Canterbury, Brooklyn, Abington, Hampton, and Scotland. The ride is relatively easy for 14 miles north to Abington, and then returning south it hits some hills, increasing on the ride eastward from Scotland over some very rural roads where there may not be a single car.

Canterbury is worth a stop either at the beginning or the end to see various sites. Just south of the starting point at Route 169 and 14 is the First Congregational Church, a huge, white, early-nineteenth-century edifice in the customary classical style. Just adjacent is the Green Schoolhouse, built in 1850, that was in use until 1947. It's completely furnished inside, and open to the public. Across the street is the Prudence Crandall House, built in 1792 by Elisha Paine, made famous for the school the very brave Prudence opened for Black girls in 1833, an offense by Connecticut law for which she was convicted in court in the Windham County Courthouse in Brooklyn. This home is open to the public.

Along Route 169 are bucolic farms. Reaching the village of Brooklyn, we find one of the most charming old churches in Connecticut built by the First Ecclesiastical Society in 1771, which became Connecticut's first Unitarian Universalist Society in 1816 in a split from the original Puritan church. Across Route 6 is the Town Hall, built as the Windham County Courthouse in 1820. Continuing on Route 169 we pass old abandoned family gas stations and more farmland, with horses and cows, and then we turn left on Route 101 and then 44.

Mashamoquet Brook State Park on the left is a large rambling forest along a bubbling brook, with the bright red Brayton Grist Mill, which is now a museum, overlooking the brook from which the park takes its name. Take a stumble down the short hill to revel on the rocks crossing the clear water below the three-story mill. Further on we cross the undeveloped Air Line State Park Trail (difficult to notice here), and find a great seafood rest stop. Shortly we reach the village of Abington, which boasts the oldest Congregational Meetinghouse in continuous use, built in 1751, although the front facade is surely an early-nineteenth-century extension. South of Abington on Route 97, just after Brooklyn Road on the left, we soon cross again the unfinished Air Line State Park Trail (more noticeable) which should eventually connect with the trail at Willimantic, but unfortunately for bicyclists seems destined to double as a bridle path if it ever is finished. Further along Route 97, Hampton, at the top of a long hill, has a lovely and large Congregational Church, built in 1754 but, unfortunately given a classical facade in 1838. There is also the charming General Store that is good for a bite on the front porch.

Reaching Scotland, we find a little Green surrounded by eighteenth and nineteenth-century homes and the Congregational Church built in 1842. South of this there are many old seventeenth and eighteenth-century cemeteries, as we travel east over constantly rolling hills, past farmland, on the aptly named Cemetery Road, then Hanover, then Cemetery again, and Water, Kinne, and Lisbon Roads, and finally Route 14 back to Canterbury.

Unitarian Universalist Society, 1771, Brooklyn

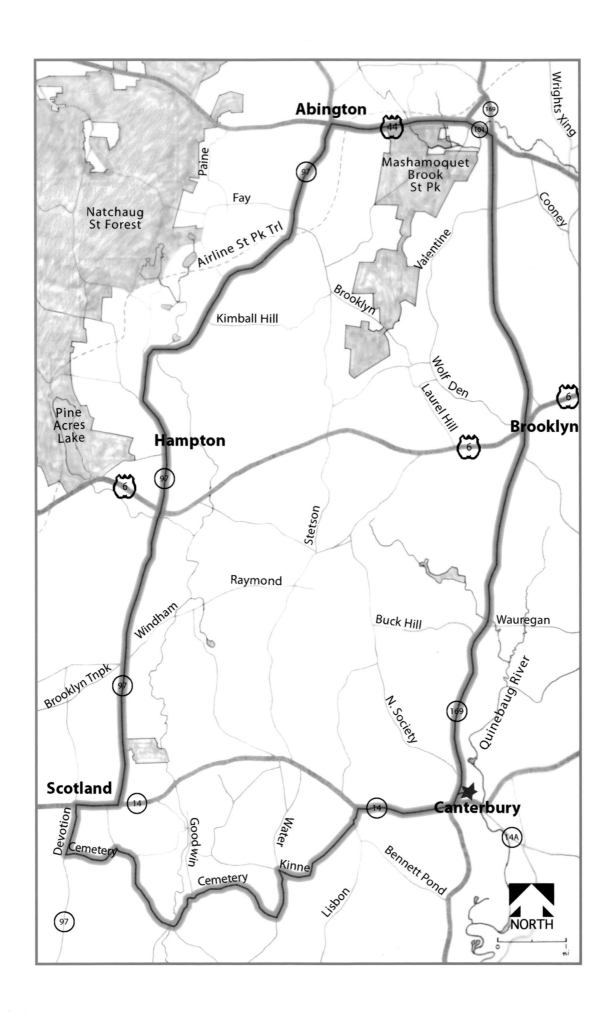

26. Canterbury – Brooklyn – Hampton
**Meet: Canterbury, 395, Exit 88, L on Rte 14A to
14 to Park & Ride at baseball field just
before Rte 169**

00.00	R	Rte 169
11.50	L	Rte 101
11.90	F	Rte 44
14.08	L	Rte 97
26.50	R	Rte 14
27.12	L	Rte 97
27.95	L	Cemetery Rd. to end
28.85	R	Hanover → Woodchuck Hill over creek
30.55	L	Cemetery to end
32.00	L	Water
32.78	R	Kinne to end
35.10	L	Lisbon to end
35.35	R	Rte 14 to Canterbury
36.80	F	Rte 14 & L into parking

Brayton Grist Mill, Mashamoquet Brook State Park

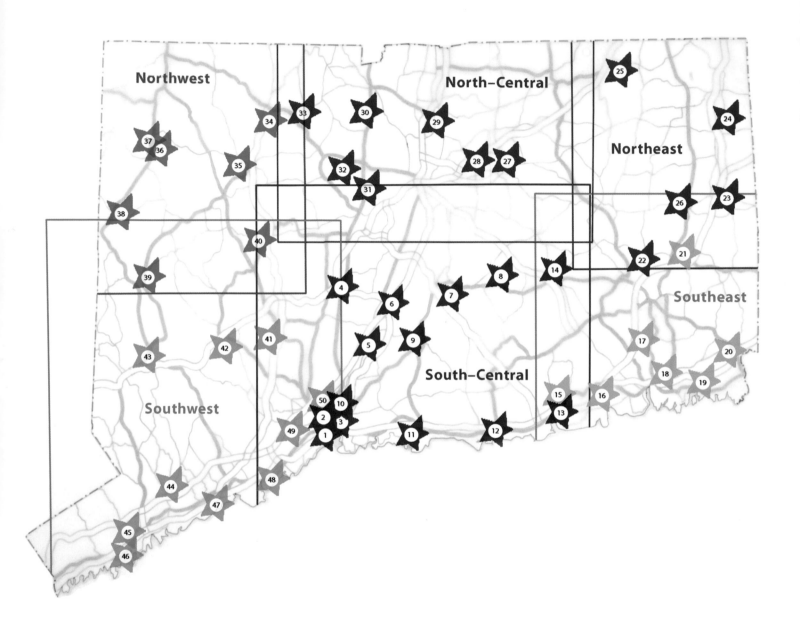

North-Central

The Farmington and Connecticut River Valleys

Hop River State Park Trail in Valley Falls Park, Vernon

[27] Bolton – Storrs – Hebron

Meeting Place: Bolton, end of Freeway 384 on Route 44, parking lot on right
Length: 43 miles
Lunch: There are restaurants and food markets in Storrs, around the University of Connecticut, and also one of the best ice cream spots at the UConn Dairy Bar. Otherwise bring lunch to enjoy beside a pond, in a state forest, or in a small village, especially along the stream at Merrow Meadows.
Sights: Farms, historic homes and churches, quaint villages, forests, lots of lakes, the University of Connecticut (main campus), and Nathan Hale home and monument.
Challenge: moderate; many long, level stretches with some long, gradual hills, paved roads with light traffic, and two stretches of dirt road.

There are probably more small lakes on this route than any other, including a beach or two for a sunbathing and swimming break. We begin at a convenient parking lot at the end of Freeway 384, where it becomes the two-lane Route 44. Bolton Lake immediately grabs our attention on the left with its boat ramp on our side and a small beach across the water. At Route 31 North, curiously called Bread and Milk Street, we head north briefly and then east on North School Road, which becomes Broadway and then Merrow. North School Road is a dirt road with bumpy stones until 4.5 miles at Dunn Road, but the rest of the way to the village of Merrow is paved. At the Willimantic River, a charming walking path through the Merrow Meadow has been created, worth a little detour either riding or walking. Pebble beaches along the river make a nice place to relax under the trees or spread out for a sun bath.

South on Route 32 and then west on 44 takes us past a large correctional institution, with an expansive exercise ground to the left behind a fence and a row of trees through which hundreds of inmates can be seen jogging. Do not even think of stopping here to take a look. The guards are extremely edgy, and in seconds you'll be surrounded by some rather severe officers who will question your intentions. Just keep moving and turn as quickly as possible on Bone Mill Road, which soon turns to dirt for a mile. North Eagleville Road east takes us past some eateries through the campus of the University of Connecticut, Storrs, leading to the end at Route 195. Before turning right to continue our route, it is highly recommended that you dogleg left and right down to the UConn Dairy Bar, where the delicious ice cream is so famous that there are lines out the door. The shaded picnic area makes a nice stop for lunch. Route 195 follows the edge of the campus along a beautiful pond with weeping willows before we head west on 275.

Heading toward Coventry, we pass the Pine Lake Reservoir and then Wangumbaug Lake, with a nice sandy beach at Patriot's Park, and, further on, the Nathan Hale grave and monument. At the dead end, we take South Street left and immediately right on Bunker Hill. But a detour right for a couple of miles on South Street would be interesting to visit the Nathan Hale Homestead (the present house built just before his death), which commemorates one of America's greatest heroes, a Yale graduate, executed by the British (but not before his famous declaration, "I only regret that I have but one life to lose for my country").

Out Bunker Hill Road, we head south to Hop River Road, a winding, partly dirt road through thick forest, passing the Hop River State Park Trail (unimproved in this area at the time of writing) and then the Hop River until we reach Route 6. We bypass the heavy traffic here on Oakwood Lane, which takes us back to Route 6 briefly before we turn south on Whitney Road. This takes us to Route 87 past Columbia Lake, ringed with vacation homes, and then we head south on Lake and Hennequin Roads, and west on Route 66 to Hebron. This little town is not much more than a crossroads, but with a lovely Gothic Congregational Church, where we catch Route 85 for a winding and turning twelve miles through lovely farmland and forests, past numerous small lakes and the Gay City State Park, which is worth a rest stop. At the T, where 87 turns left, we turn right on Bolton Center Road and then an immediate left on Notch Road back to Route 44. Use extreme caution turning right and crossing the exit for Route 6 onto the lane for 44, which are both exit ramps of Freeway 384 (with speeding traffic ignoring the limit signs) to the little shopping strip and parking lot where we began.

Monument to Nathan Hale, Lake Street, Coventry

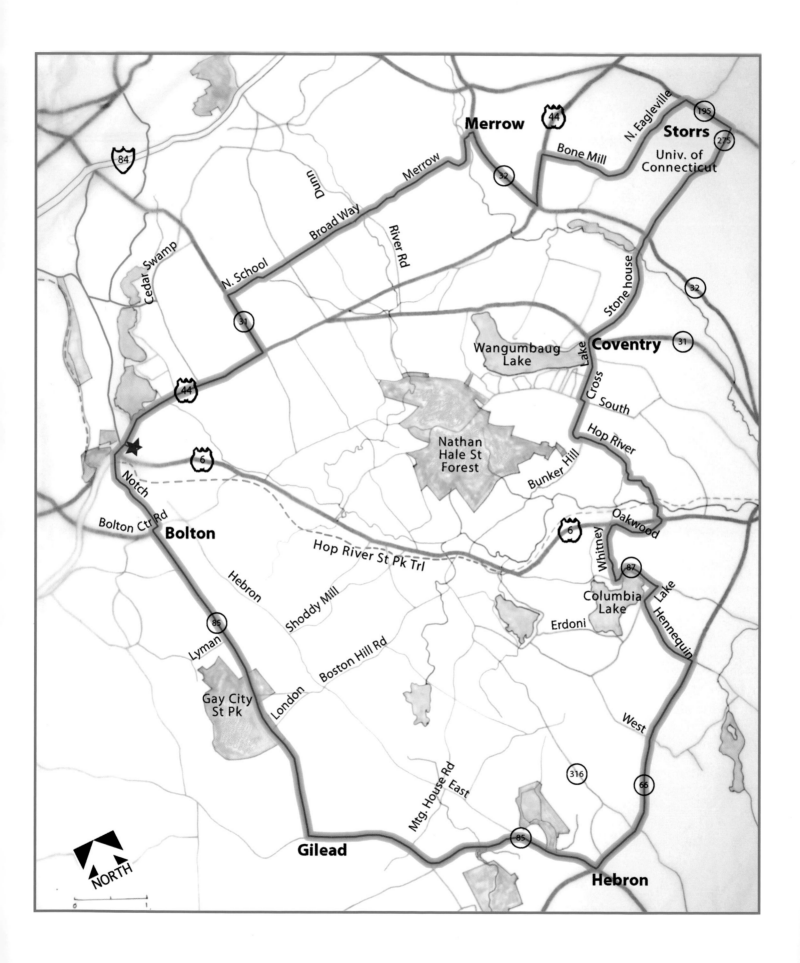

27. Bolton – Storrs – Hebron
Meet: Bolton, end of Freeway 384 on Rte 44, parking lot on right

00.00	R	Rte 44 E
02.60	L	Rte 31
03.60	R	N. School (dirt road) → Broad Way → Merrow to end
08.58	R	Rte 32
10.08	L	Rte 44
10.85	R	Bone Mill
11.24	BR	continue Bone Mill (dirt road)
12.17	L	N. Eagleville thru UConn to end
13.82	R	Rte 195 to light at end of campus
14.67	R	Rte 275 (S. Eagleville→ Stonehouse) to Rte 31
18.91	F	Lake→Cross to end
19.98	L	Dogleg on South to immediate R.
20.05	R	Bunker Hill
20.58	L	continue on Bunker Hill
20.70	BL	Hop River (becomes dirt road) to Rte 6
22.88	F	Oakwood to end at parking and path to Rte 6
23.70	L	Rte 6
23.90	L	Whitney to end
24.85	L	Rte 87 around lake
25.65	R	Lake Rd. to 2nd L.
25.98	L	Hennequin to end
27.30	R	Rte 66 to Hebron
31.00	R	Rte 85 (Gilead)
35.93	R	continue on Rte 85 to T
41.60	R	Bolton Center Rd. to 1st L.
41.70	L	Notch to end
43.10	R	Rte 44 (cross Rte 66—caution!)
43.32	R	into parking lot

University of Connecticut, Storrs

[28] Hop River State Park Trail

Meeting Place: Trailhead on Colonial Rd at Parker St, Manchester (Rte 84, Exit 63, east on Route 30, right on Parker to Colonial)
Length: 42 miles
Lunch: There are no eating places by the Trail, but many in Willimantic. Buy a lunch there to enjoy on the way back by one of the bubbling brooks or at the lake.
Sights: Forests, Hop River, Bolton Lake, and Historic Andover and Willimantic.
Challenge: Moderate; trail ranging from smooth dirt and gravel to stony dirt. Hybrid or mountain bike is best, but a road bike is OK for 12 miles only.

Woods, woods, and more woods, and a gravel trail from beginning to end is what this ride is all about. There are no villages to speak of. This is a "rails to trails" park, built on the route of the Hartford, Providence, and Fishkill Railroad that opened in 1863 and closed in 1929, although some rail use continued until 1970. The western end is an easy ride on relatively level ground, but the eastern end, as of this writing, is stony and rough riding. The Trail sometimes rises high above its surroundings, rounds the bends of mountainsides, cuts through rocky cliff sides, and goes over high bridges. A detailed map of this section of the East Coast Greenway may be found at the website: http://greenway.org/maps/ECG-CT.kml.

The first six miles are a steady, slight incline, almost imperceptible to the sight, but it soon dawns on you that you are pushing your gears to a higher notch. After four miles, through the deep forest and far below in the deep valley, is the bucolic Bolton Lake with a sandy beach at one end at Indian Notch Park and good fishing spots around the other sides. Hiking trails wind down from the bike trail all the way to the lake. This would be a good spot to put on a swimsuit and take a break by the waterside.

At around six miles we see a restoration site of the Railroad Brook, long-ago destroyed for the building of the railroad, where a new streambed has been created, and fish such as the brook trout have been reintroduced. Another nice stop would be at around ten-and-a-half miles, where a bubbling stream to the right below the trail pours over short rocky falls into a shallow pool; a cool dip would be really refreshing. At around twelve miles, the trail ends at Route 316, just past the tranquil, white, First Congregational Church of Andover on Route 6. A quick detour (stop your odometers) on Route 316 over the little bridge brings us to the old village of Andover at Cider Mill Road and the most charming eighteenth-century cemetery with wonderful old stones bearing primitive angels' heads and wings. This is worth a stop to wonder over the lives of such people as "Mrs. Louisa Loomis, Comfort of Mr. Levi Loomis (daughter of Rev Elijah & Mrs. Silence Lothrop) who departed this life January 9, 1792...." Otherwise, we continue across the road to retake the Trail again.

From here it deteriorates into a rather stony double-tire track. Although the going is a bit bumpy, the view of the Hop River below is delightful, and we're out in the middle of nowhere. After eighteen miles, the trail is interrupted again because of a broken bridge that needs to be restored. So we are detoured on the dead-end King Road that leads to Flanders River Road, where we turn right, over a little brook, and then find the trail again to our left, now greatly disintegrated into an overgrown footpath. It's rough going for one third of a mile, but who cares as long as we're out in the wilds. At nineteen miles the Trail is undiscernible (remains of the railroad cross the ruins of a bridge ahead, and then disappear) and we are unceremoniously dumped out into a vast area of car dealerships.

The town of Willamantic is straight ahead on Route 66, where there is the imposing nineteenth-century red brick courthouse; a Railroad Museum; Eastern Connecticut State University; the Windham Textile and History Museum; the Windham Historical Society in the elegant, stone Jillson House facing the river; and many restaurants for lunch. This intriguing eighteenth-century town is worth a day in itself. We cross the Thread City Crossing Bridge, which is guarded by four mammoth bronze frogs, officially named Willie, Manny, Windy, and Swifty, perched upon giant concrete spools. These bizarre and wonderful sculptures are meant to commemorate the town's historic thread mills and, at the same time, the mind-freaking night in 1754 when the villagers huddled in their homes thinking they heard the local Native Americans at battle, only to learn the next morning that it was the bull frogs fighting over water in a dried up pond. Circling back again on Route 32, we head back Route 66, where we meet the trail again and retrace our route.

To avoid going back over the same bumpy trail, an alternative would be to return on Route 66 and then Route 6 (both of which have heavy traffic but also broad shoulders good for riding) back to the First Congregational Church at Andover. From here you can pick up the trail again, and it's smooth sailing back to the starting point, with a glorious six-mile coast downhill all the way to the end.

Hop River State Park Trail under Notch Road and Route 44, Bolton

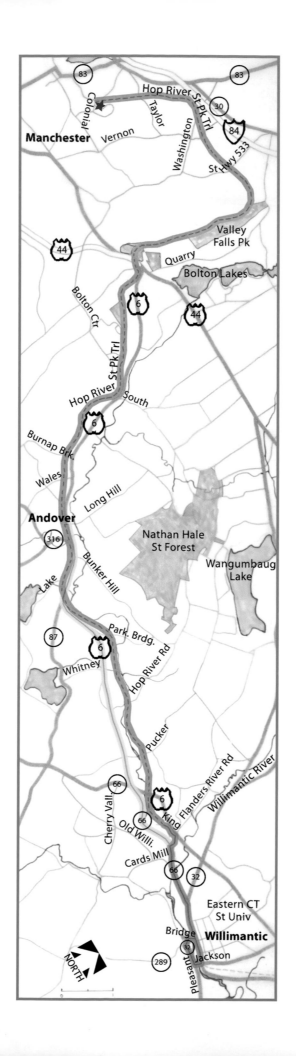

28. Hop River State Park Trail
Meet: Trailhead on Colonial Rd. at Parker St, Manchester (Rte 84, Exit 63, east on Rte 30, R on Parker to Colonial)

00.00	F	Trailhead from Colonial Rd
02.34	F	continue on Trailhead to Vernon
12.15		(Trail interrupted at Rte 316)— descend embankment and continue forward on Monument Lake to trail (stony surface here) to end at impassable bridge
18.04	L	King (unmarked dead-end road)
18.30	R	Flanders River Rd. over a creek
18.44	L	Trail (entrance is paved but soon becomes an overgrown footpath)
18.80		(end of Trail) F on Rte 66 into Willimantic
20.83	R	Jackson, across bridge to 1st X.
20.93	R	Rte 32 (Pleasant)
21.36	BR	Rte 32 (Mountain)
21.48	R	Rte 32 (Bridge) across bridge to 1st L.
21.63	L	Rte 32/66
22.40	BL	Rte 66
23.17	R	onto Trail

(To avoid the stony eastern section of the path: Continue on Rte 66:

26.00	*BR*	*Rte 6 to Andover to the First Congregational Church*
30.00	*L-R*	*shift onto Trail and continue to end)*
23.50	R	Flanders River Rd. to 1st L.
23.66	L	King to end
23.95	R	Trail to end
42.00		end at starting point, Colonial Rd

Fungi along the Hop River State Park Trail near Bolton Lake

[29] East Windsor – Crystal Lake – Windsor Locks Canal

Meeting place: *I-91, Exit 44, south on Route 5, left on Thompson Rd into parking at East Windsor Industrial Park*
Length: *40 miles*
Lunch: *There is one restaurant at Ellerton and a couple of delis just before Crystal Lake. Better to bring your own lunch. The trailhead at the Windsor Locks Canal along the Connecticut River has picnic tables on a grassy overlook.*
Sights: *Historic churches, homes, and towns; state parks and forests; tobacco country; horses; farms; abandoned mills; the Connecticut River; and Windsor Locks Canal Trail.*
Challenge: *moderate; mostly rolling hills, a couple of long steep hills, paved roads with light traffic, and one mile of dirt road, five miles of paved bike path.*

This is really rural Connecticut with rolling farmland, tobacco fields, and horses. We begin in the town of East Windsor at Route 5, taking Wagner Lane past tobacco farms to the River and then left on South Water Street and down Route 5 again to a left at Tromley Road. Along this road we encounter the charmingly simple First Congregational Church of East Windsor and the historic Scantic Cemetery, with its old brown stones. At the end, where we turn left on Omelia Road, we cross the Scantic River and then on to the eerie, green-covered Windsorville Pond, with its lovely weeping willows.

From here we follow Thrall Road, then Frogs Hollow Road to the village of Ellington, with its enchanting Victorian houses and the 1730 John McKinstry house painted a deep red. Taking Route 140, we pass the secluded Lake Bonair and at Route 30 we head north past the large Crystal Lake. On this Route is a small cafe where bikers hang out.

Past the Lake, we head west and uphill Handel Road, which is partly dirt, then Gulf, where we fly down a long wooded section through the dense Shenipsit State Forest. Now we turn left on Mountain View, which is a hard climb to the top but then a breezy sliding board at the halfway point down again. Now south on 83, and west again on Billings Road and Pinney, past expansive fields of horses and white fences, to the small village of Somersville. Here there is a charm in the abandoned mills that once operated off the Pond, the dam used for boating, a small historic Congregational Church in brown stone, the newer Gothic-style Congregational Church, and the nineteenth-century houses.

Returning on Maple Street southwest, turning into Fletcher Road, we pass more tobacco fields and one tobacco barn after another. These are emblematic of the preeminence of Connecticut tobacco as cigar wrappers, with the barns used just for a few weeks in late July and early August to dry the leaves. We reach the Grassmere Country Club and Town Farm Road, which turns into Post Office Road and takes us to the town of Enfield. Here it's worth another short side trip south on Route 5 as far as the colonial Martha Parsons house and gardens, which is open as a museum from May through November 1 on Sunday afternoons. But our route turns north past the magnificently classical Congregational Church and rows of stately nineteenth-century homes. After crossing the Route 190 overpass, we turn west on Franklin Street, which takes us to the new bike path at the side of the Route 190 bridge across the Connecticut River. Just on the other side, the path takes a sharp right and down under the bridge onto the beautiful Windsor Locks Canal State Park Trail (www.traillink.com) for nearly five miles. A grassy spot with benches and picnic tables overlooks the Connecticut River where the trail begins, and walking paths go through the woods. The trail is paved, but narrow, hugging the top of the old towpath between the canal and the river, with some root bumps and a few pedestrians, so we cruise this trail at a relaxing speed. The view on both sides is peaceful and gorgeous. Almost five miles later, at Windsor Locks, the trail ends at a private industrial drive, where we cross the Route 140 bridge, and a right on South Water Street takes us back to Wagner Lane and the starting point.

Ellington Congregational Church, rebuilt 1915

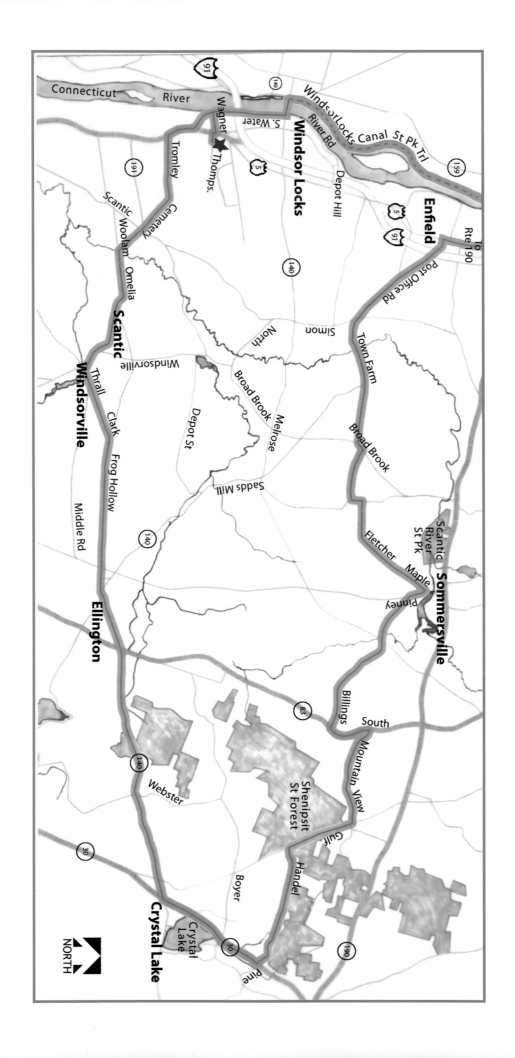

NORTH

29. East Windsor to Crystal Lake
Meet: I-91, Exit 44, S. on Rte 5, L on Thompson Rd. into parking at E. Windsor Industrial Pk

00.00	RL	dogleg onto Wagner Lane (across Rte 5 from Thompson) to end	24.84	BR	Pinney 1 bl to end
			25.12	BR	Maple 1 bl to triangle
00.42	L	South Water to end	25.27		Return around triangle and back Maple → Fletcher
00.90	R	Rte 5 to 2nd L.			
01.37	L	Tromley → Cemetery to end	27.40	L	continue on Fletcher
03.65	L	Woolam → Omelia → Apothecaries Hill	28.42	L	Broad Brook 1/2 bl
			28.47	R	Town Farm → Post Office to end
05.43	F	Windsorville Rd. to end	32.54	R	Rte 5 (Main) thru Enfield across Rte 190 to 1st L.
05.85	L	Thrall			
06.37	F	Clark to end	33.89	L	Franklin
07.02	BR	Frog Hollow	34.11	F	onto bike path across the bridge
09.50	LR	dogleg onto Rte 140	34.61	R	Windsor Locks Canal Trail under Rte 190 bridge to end at Bridge St. (Rte 140) Depot Hill (Rte 510)—cross over I-91 to 1st R.
10.45	L	Somers (Rte 83) to immediate R.			
10.49	R	Rte 140			
14.62	L	Rte 30			
16.60	L	Handel (Pine on R) (dirt road 19.20-19.71) to end	39.56	L	Bridge St. (Rte 140) across bridge to first X
18.65	R	Gulf to 1st L.	39.79	R	R Water St. under I-91
19.81	L	Mountain View to end	41.01	L	Wagner to end
21.45	L	South Rd. (Rte 83)	41.37		into industrial park
22.18	R	Billings to end			

Tobacco barns on Fletcher Road, Enfield

[30] Simsbury – Southwick – Suffield

Meeting Place: *Simsbury, Hopmeadow Street (Route 10), International Skating Center parking just north of Hoskins Rd*
Length: *32 miles*
Lunch: *After leaving Simsbury, there are no eating places except on Congamond Road in Massachusetts, at Route 10 and at Congamond Lake.*
Sights: *Farms, horses, tobacco barns, historic houses, forests, hilltop views, state parks, Congamond Lake (the boundary between Connecticut and Massachusetts), Bradley International Airport, Connecticut Air National Guard, and Walgreens' Northeast Distribution Center.*
Challenge: *easy; with a few rolling hills and paved roads with light traffic.*

This is Connecticut horse and tobacco country, with a dip into the small Massachusetts wedge along the otherwise perfectly straight northern Connecticut border. The roughly circular route starts near the Farmington Canal Greenway Trail in the south, and crosses over it on the Massachusetts side and again just north of the start. There are no towns to speak of on the entire route.

Beginning north of the center of Simsbury on Hopmeadow Street, we head west and north on Hoskins Road, which turns into County Road and quickly out into the farmland past one tobacco drying barn after another. Soon we begin to see large horse farms with extensive complexes of barns, always painted bright red. Barn Door Hills Road heading north becomes Bushy Hill Road, and a short left-right on North Granby Road and then Wells Road takes us past more horse farms and cattle farms. Wells becomes Vining Hill Road and after crossing the Massachusetts border becomes Mort Vining Road all the way to Vining Hill (just a few houses), where a right turn takes us on another Vining Hill Road—if it sounds a little confusing, just keep going, even though street signs are scarce here.

We're now on Route 168, which takes on the name Congamond Road after Route 10 (where there are food markets) and leads us across the Farmington Canal Greenway Trail that ends at Northampton. Shortly, we cross over the huge Congamond Lake that provides the border with Connecticut (on its eastern side—Massachusetts gets the lake), and presumably the excuse for the short hachette chop of Massachusetts into Connecticut's territory. There are a few restaurants here. Continuing over the bridge, the route becomes Mountain Road, past more tobacco barns. At a sharp right-hand bend in the road, the old road continues straight to a dead end, and here we turn left on Warner Town Road, and briefly again into Massachusetts where it becomes South Longyard Road before turning

right onto Rising Corner Road to the little intersection of the same name.

Here we start our long drive south on North Stone Street, then South Stone Street. If there ever were another more beautifully landscaped community, I don't know where. Much of this may be due to the influence of the Robert Baker Nursery, where the view at the Baker home at 1255 N. Stone St. is absolutely breathtaking with its rhododendrons, mixture of woods and groves, hillsides, and wooden bridges. It's easy to miss from the road, with only a small metal address marker, but it's across from a lovely old ramshackle white home. Further on, Route 187, or Sheldon Street (easy to miss with no sign, but it's across from Austin Brook Drive at a triangle), brings more vast farmland strewn with rusty old abandoned farm machinery. Right on South Grand Street takes us past more tobacco farms and then, on Russell Road, abruptly shaking us out of the past, to Bradley International Airport. Here we turn south on Perimeter Road which takes us smack into the Connecticut Air National Guard base, with its display of vintage airplanes out front (which the nice guards at the guard station won't let you come in to photograph, but do it anyway out on the road). Right on Nicholson Road and a quick left takes us on a long tour of Bradley Park Road and International Drive past a mile of industrial buildings and then what must be one of the largest buildings on earth—the very modern and colorfully boxy distribution center for Walgreens. The road continues, becoming Seymour and Hatchet Hill, ending with a right on Route 189. Left on Floydville and Wolcott roads takes us past the Jewish graveyard, nursery hothouses, and the tiny Simsbury Airport where, at any minute, a little single-prop plane is likely to take off right beside us. Just past the airfield we cross the Farmington Canal Greenway Trail again, and then a left on Hopmeadow Street takes us immediately back to the parking lot.

Farm on Hatchet Hill Road, near Tariffville

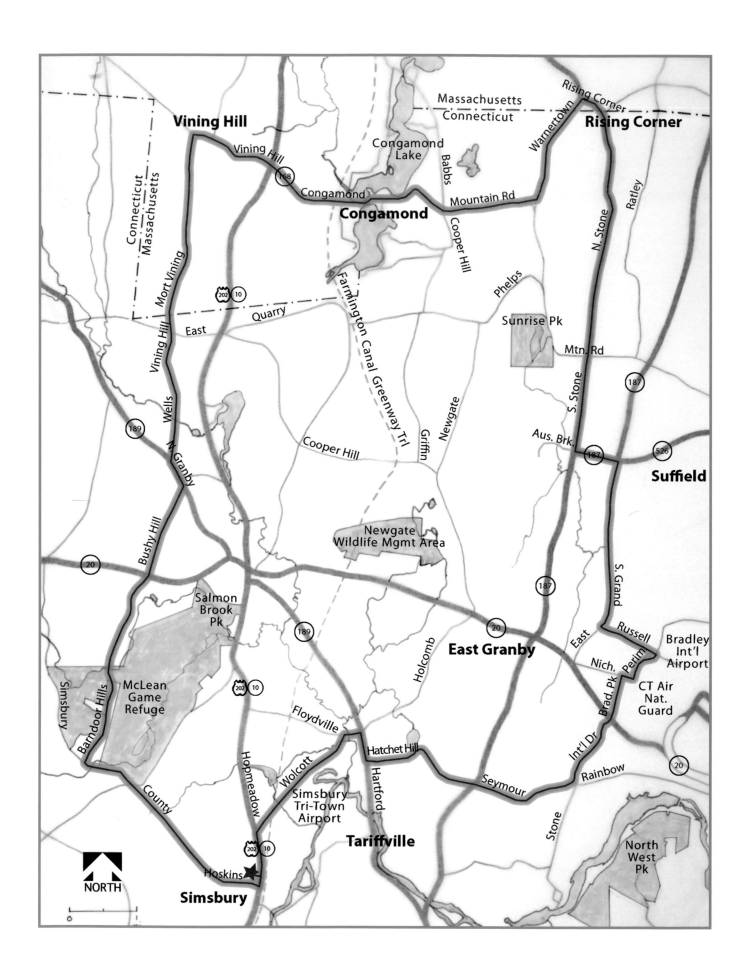

30. Simsbury – Southwick – Suffield
Meet: Simsbury, Hopmeadow Street (Rte 10),
Int'l Skating Center parking just N. of Hoskins Rd

00.00	R	out of parking lot
00.15	R	Hopmeadow (Rte 10) to 2nd R.
00.50	R	Hoskins to Y.
01.15	F	County
03.16	R	Barn Door Hills
03.21	BR	Barn Door Hills → Bushy Hill to end
06.85	L	N. Granby (Rte 189)
07.15	R	Wells → Vining Hill → Mort Vining in MA
11.25	R	Rte 168 (Vining Hill → Congamond—past lake across bridge into Mountain Rd)—at end, a sharp right bend merges on Warner Town Rd, you keep straight to end to turn L.
15.70	L	Warner Town (no sign) → S. Longyard
17.06	R	Rising Corner to end 1st R.
17.42	BR	N. Stone → S. Stone to triangle with Austin Brook on R.
21.66	L	Rte 187 N. (no sign) to 1st X. at Rte. 187 L.
22.17	R	S. Grand (no sign) → East St to 1st L.
24.23	L	Russell to 1st X.
24.95	R	Perimeter to 1st X. at CT Air Nat. Guard
25.38	R	Nicholson to 1st L.
25.45	L	Bradley Park → International Dr → Seymour → Hatchet Hill to end
29.67	R	Rte 189 (Hartford Av) to 1st X.
30.00	L	Floydville to 1st L.
30.20	L	Wolcott to end
31.70	L	Hopmeadow (Rte 10)
32.10	R	into driveway of International Skating Center
32.24	L	into parking lot

Horse farm across the Massachusetts border on Vining Hill Road

[31] Farmington Canal Greenway Trail (North)

Meeting place: Trailhead parking on Brickyard Rd, north of Route 4 in Farmington (Directions from New Haven: 91 North to Exit 20, north on Route 9 to end, 84 West to 1st exit, Route 4 West about 4 miles, right on Brickyard Rd c. 1 mi., to trailhead parking on left.) (From Hartford: 84 West and follow directions above from exit at Route 4.)
Length: 40 miles
Lunch: Bring lunch to enjoy by Cranberry Park, or the Massachusetts border, or stop at an eatery in Simsbury or a small food store further north along the trail.
Sights: A peaceful ride on a very long bike path through the woods with no traffic. This is the northern third of the Farmington Canal Greenway Trail, which will eventually run 60 miles from New Haven to the Massachusetts border.
Challenge: easy; generally flat, paved bike path, some detours on paved streets with little traffic.

This is the northern one-third of what is now labeled the Farmington Canal/Greenway eventually intended to extend continuously from the New Haven Harbor on the Long Island sound to the Massachusetts border and ultimately to Northampton, following the old railroad tracks which have long disappeared in most places. As can be expected, the northern third is the most remote and rural, which makes it a special delight. Like the lower two-thirds, it is a nice, level, paved path even though it goes through some of the hilliest regions of Connecticut. By the fall of 2008, the entire length had been paved, and seems to be completed, except for some detours on the motor roads at the towns of Avon (which seems to be permanent) and Simsbury (although the official website map shows a continuous trail). A detailed map of this section of the East Coast Greenway may be found at the website: http://greenway.org/maps/ECG-CT3.kml.

We begin at Farmington east of the village of Unionville at the parking for the Farmington Canal Greenway Trail on Brickyard Road. From here we head north on the Trail, where we pass forests and swampland and wonderful spreads of wildflowers. At the end of the first trail section, the bike route is well marked, following Security Drive, Darling Drive, under Route 44, through the Avon Town Hall grounds, Ensign Drive, and Fisher Drive, where we connect with the second trail section. In Avon, visit the Living Museum of Avon in a restored nineteenth-century schoolhouse at 8 E. Main Street (Rte. 44), where there are interesting exhibits focusing on the history of the Farmington Canal.

The second trail section continues for 4 miles and is idyllic. The trail section ends rather unceremoniously on Hopmeadow Street, where we can either continue on a rutted, narrow sidewalk or on the street itself. We soon pass the magnificent, white, classical-style Congregational Church high on the hill, where we turn down Drake Hill Road and meet the third trail section immediately on the left. A detour on Hopmeadow would take us into the charming village of Simsbury, with the campus of the Simsbury Historical Society and its eighteenth-century Phelps Tavern Museum and other original buildings, as well as some spectacular nineteenth-century mansions.

The third trail section parallels a street along the town park out into the countryside. At the Imperial Nurseries, for some inexplicable reason, the trail detours for an extra mile around the neat rows of newly-planted trees and bushes, although a clear, wide swath is available straight through the nursery, between the plantings, and should have been cut by eminent domain. I guess the nursery is not called "Imperial" for nothing. On the other side, on Floydville Road is a huge, yellow, abandoned set of buildings now covered with ivy. Further on is the historic Granby Station along the old rail line. A high bridge leaps the river at Cranberry Park, offering grand views to the east and west. At Phelps Road an overpass gives a view of the surrounding farmland, and the Trail continues about a mile past majestic cliffs (best seen by a detour a few hundred yards down Phelps Road), paralleling a little stream to the Massachusetts border. The border (at this writing) is at a decrepit little bridge across an arm of the parallel stream running west and disappearing into a swamp, with a small concrete pylon on the left side of the trail marked Connecticut on the south face and Massachusetts on the north face. The trail is finished all the way to Northampton, Massachusetts, so that would be the next ride. But this ride terminates at the state border. It is an unremarkable border crossing—no visitor center, no brass bands, or waving flags, but we can say we reached it, and return back to Farmington by the same route.

Farmington Valley Greenway, near the Massachusetts border

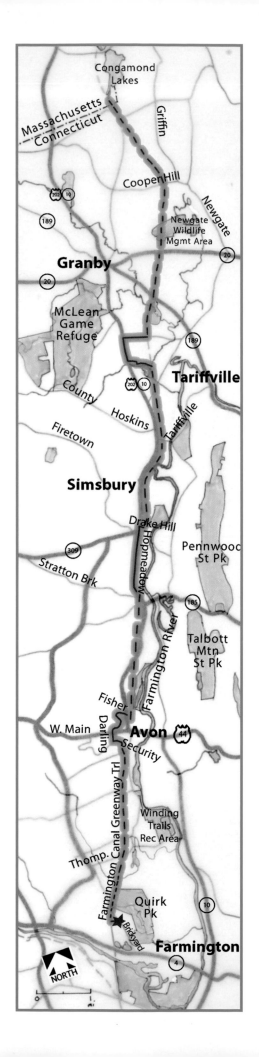

31. Farmington Canal Greenway Trail (North)
Meet: Trailhead parking on Brickyard Rd, N.
of Rte 4 in Farmington

Note: The northern section of the Greenway has been largely finished since 2008, with a few detours on the roadways that seem to be semi-permanent—check Greenway website for updates (although these data sometimes seem to represent wishful thinking rather than the reality at the moment): www.fvgreenway.org.

00.00	R	onto Farmington Canal Greenway Trail to end of 1st section at Avon	20.14		Massachusetts border—return back same Trail to beginning of 3rd section
03.44	F	through parking lot—follow "bike route" signs:	30.85	R	Drake Hill Rd—1 bl to end
			30.96	L	Hopmeadow St
	F	Bike Route on Security Dr to end	31.17	F	Farmington Canal Greenway Trail to beginning of 2nd section (R off trail following "bike route" across Rte 10)
	R	Darling Dr			
	L	under Rte 44, through Avon Town Hall			
	L	Ensign Dr to end	35.19	F	Fisher
	R	Fisher Dr across Rte 10		L	Ensign
05.05	F	onto Farmington Canal Greenway Trail to end of 2nd section at Simsbury		R	through Avon Town Hall & under Rte 44 to end of path
				R	Darling
09.07	F	Hopmeadow St		L	Security Dr to end
09.28	R	Drake Hill Rd—1 bl		F	through parking lot
09.40	L	onto Farmington Canal Greenway Trail past Phelps Rd. to end of 3rd section at little bridge marking the Massachusetts border	36.80	L	"bike route" onto Farmington Canal Greenway Trail to beginning at parking lot
			40.28	L	into parking lot at Brickyard Rd

Escarpment on the Farmington Valley Greenway at Phelps Road, Suffield

[32] Farmington River Trail to Simsbury

Meeting place: Farmington, at the trailhead on Brickyard Rd (between Routes 4 & 167)
Length: 30 miles
Lunch: There are several cafes and restaurants in Collinsville and Simsbury. Or bring lunch to enjoy at the lake at Stratton Brook State Forest or at the Simsbury Pedestrian Bridge or under the Pinchot Sycamore at Weatogue.
Sights: Farmington River, Farmington Canal Greenway, historic homes, state parks, forests, lakes, historic mills and factories, the picturesque villages of Collinsville and Simsbury, Simsbury pedestrian bridge hung with flowers, the immense Pinchot Sycamore, and floral swamp.
Challenge: easy; generally flat, mostly paved bicycle trail, some rural roads and streets with little traffic, and a couple of miles of gravel path. A hybrid bicycle is best, but a road bike can also make it.

Over the river and through the woods, this is a pleasant and placid ride without a car in sight for most of the route. The Farmington River Trail follows the river of the same name on the old New Haven & Northampton Railroad line, opened in 1850 from Farmington to Collinsville.

To start, the parking lot at the Farmington Canal Greenway Trail crossing on Brickyard Road is convenient. Going south, the trail passes over the broad Farmington River, where magnificent views both East and West are worth a stop on the bridge. The Greenway ends at Red Oak Hill Road, and a right turn takes us immediately, at New Britain Avenue, to the beginning of the Farmington River Trail, where we head north. It is first a paved path, turning into dirt after crossing under Route 4, and then stone and eventually a paved bike trail that follows the river into Collinsville. This can be recognized by the old railroad bridge over the complex of the red brick Frederick Humphrey mill and factories of the Collins Company (world-famous for its axe and machete blades) from the nineteenth century. Here is a good place to stop the odometer and tool around the town to see the elegant nineteenth-century homes and the mill, as well as to relax at one of the charming cafes or to watch the kayaks from the river bank.

At the end of the trail along the river, we climb Gildersleeve Avenue and continue on to Dowd Avenue and Route 44 to Lawton Road, Dry Bridge, Notch, and Mountain Roads through a beautiful rural area. Right on Nimrod Road through Massacoe State Forest to Town Forest Road takes us straight into the gravel path through the heavily wooded Stratton Brook State Forest, with its peaceful streams, lakes, and sandy beaches, following the old Connecticut Western Railroad line opened in 1871.

At the end of the dirt path we continue in the same direction on Route 167 to Route 10, passing the magnificent Simsbury Congregational Church high on the hill, with a quick dogleg left-right and onto Drake Hill Road at Simsbury. Here is where the Farmington Canal Greenway Trail begins heading north again. Simsbury is a good place to take a detour north on Route 10 for a few blocks to view the stately nineteenth-century mansions and the campus of the Simsbury Historical Society, with the charming Phelps Tavern Museum from the eighteenth century. From Drake Hill Road (instead of taking the Farmington Canal Greenway Trail south) we take the first right across the spectacular Simsbury Pedestrian Bridge completely hung with glorious flowering plants. The bridge was built in 1892 for the railroad by J. E. Buddington of New Haven, but it was restored in 1995, and the locals hang flowering plants on every available horizontal beam that bloom throughout the spring, summer, and fall. This is a good place to relax and have lunch. Across the bridge, keeping always right on Riverside Road, East Weatogue Street, and Route 185, we meet the Farmington River again at the enormous, historic Pinchot Sycamore, a good place to relax on the grassy lawn by the river. The sycamore, the largest tree in Connecticut, is twenty-four feet in circumference and named in honor of Gifford Pinchot of Simsbury (d. 1946), cofounder of the Yale School of Forestry and first chief of the US Forestry Service.

Right again on Route 10 (Hopmeadow Street) and we come quickly to the continuation again of the Farmington Canal Greenway Trail. There is one further detour where the trail is interrupted at Avon, but the bike route is clearly marked along streets and through the Town Green and the Town Hall, passing under Route 44. At the trailhead parking lot the trail resumes, past beautiful floral wetlands and woods, and takes us straight back several miles to Brickyard Road.

Phelps Tavern Museum, Simsbury

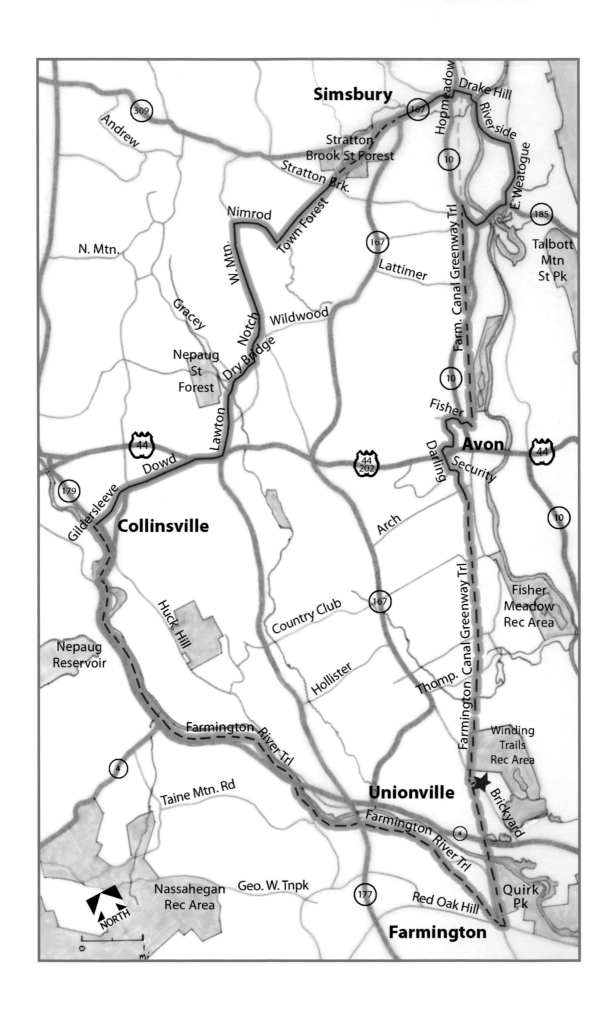

NORTH

32. Farmington River Trail to Simsbury
Meet: Farmington, at the trailhead on Brickyard Rd (between Rtes 4 & 167)

00.00	L	from parking lot onto Farmington Canal Greenway Trail to end
01.82	R	Red Oak Hill Rd. – cross New Britain Av & F on Farmington River Trail to end of 1st section
05.10	F	dirt path
06.90	F	paved Trail continues through Collinsville across Rte 179 twice
10.00	F	Gildersleeve to end
11.00	R	Simonds to end
11.05	RL	dogleg onto Dowd Av to end
11.90	R	Rte 44 to 1st L.
12.30	L	Lawton
13.05	BR	Dry Bridge to end
13.60	L	Notch to end
14.20	F	West Mountain
15.35	R	Nimrod (part dirt) around sharp L to Town Forest
17.05	F	cross Stratton Brook Rd. onto gravel path through Stratton Brook State Park to end

18.35	LR	dogleg F onto Rte 167 (West St)
19.10	L	Rte 10 (Hopmeadow) to 1st R.
19.16	R	Drake Hill, BR across Pedestrian Bridge (festooned with flowers) to end
19.54	R	Riverside to end
20.35	R	East Weatogue to end
21.18	BR	Rte 185 to end
21.66	R	Rte 10 (Hopmeadow) to 1st light
21.88	SL	onto Farmington Canal Greenway Trail
24.45	BR	off main Trail at "Bike Route" sign & F along Fisher Dr to 1st L on Ensign and continue on "Bike Route" to R through Avon Town Hall, through underpass under Rte 44 to L on Security Dr to parking lot at trailhead
26.00	LR	dogleg onto Farmington Canal Greenway Trail
29.30	L	into parking lot at Brickyard Rd

Collins Tool Factory, Collinsville

[33] New Hartford – Hartland – Riverton

Meeting place: Route 44 at 219, New Hartford, parking behind Town Hall
Length: 31 miles
Lunch: Except for restaurants at the starting point in New Hartford, and another restaurant in East Hartland (and no cafes or convenience stores), there is only one deli on the entire ride, toward the end at Riverton. Best to bring lunch to enjoy at one of the reservoirs or brooks.
Sights: Historic homes and churches, state parks, Barkhamstead Reservoir, the Farmington River, quaint little villages, and lots of green forests and mountains.
Challenge: moderate; paved roads with almost no traffic and long hills.

The exceedingly long uphill climbs for the first three-quarters of this ride are quite a challenge, and you'll think you're out in the middle of nowhere for much of the time. But the last quarter of the ride is an easy level route following the Farmington River. The entire ride essentially circles around one long and narrow reservoir. Miles go by without a car in sight. The route goes through thick forests, and passes numerous trailheads for hiking.

We begin in New Hartford, which is worth a little time either at the beginning or the end, with some charming shops, restaurants, the grand North Church Congregational, and historic nineteenth-century houses, all along the Farmington River. Heading north on Route 219, we follow Lake McDonough, a beautiful sight, with a public beach at the northern end. This is worth a stop, following the drive back to the bottom of the gigantic Saville Dam and the picnic area around the sandy beach. Up the road, at the top of the dam we get our first view of the southern end of the enormously long Barkhamsted Reservoir. Continuing north on 219 and forward on 179, we climb slowly past the Tunxis State Forest to the tiny village of East Hartland, with its stately and simple "First Church," eighteenth and nineteenth-century houses, and one nice Italian restaurant. From here we continue north on Route 20, which is a lonely road over several mountain ridges, passing again through the Tunxis State Forest, and crossing several small brooks. Lunchtime might be spent on the rocks at Hubbards Brook, where the short Millstone Road goes a tenth of a mile and stops at the Massachusetts border and a trail continues along the stream. From here your strength will be tested on a very long series of climbs past the upper reaches of the Barkhamsted Reservoir, which stretches far below you in the hollow between the mountain ridges.

The long ride on Route 20 passes the tiny village of West Hartland, with its simple Second Congregational Church, and finally brings us to the village of Riverton, where there are a couple of restaurants and a deli, as well as the sprawling whitewashed buildings of a historic factory, the famous Hitchcock Chair Company, occupying the bank of the Farmington River since 1826. Here we cross the river and head back south on West River Road, closely following the Farmington River, replete with fly fishermen trying their luck, all along the way to the road's end. A left on Route 44 takes us back quickly downhill to New Hartford.

Lake McDonough

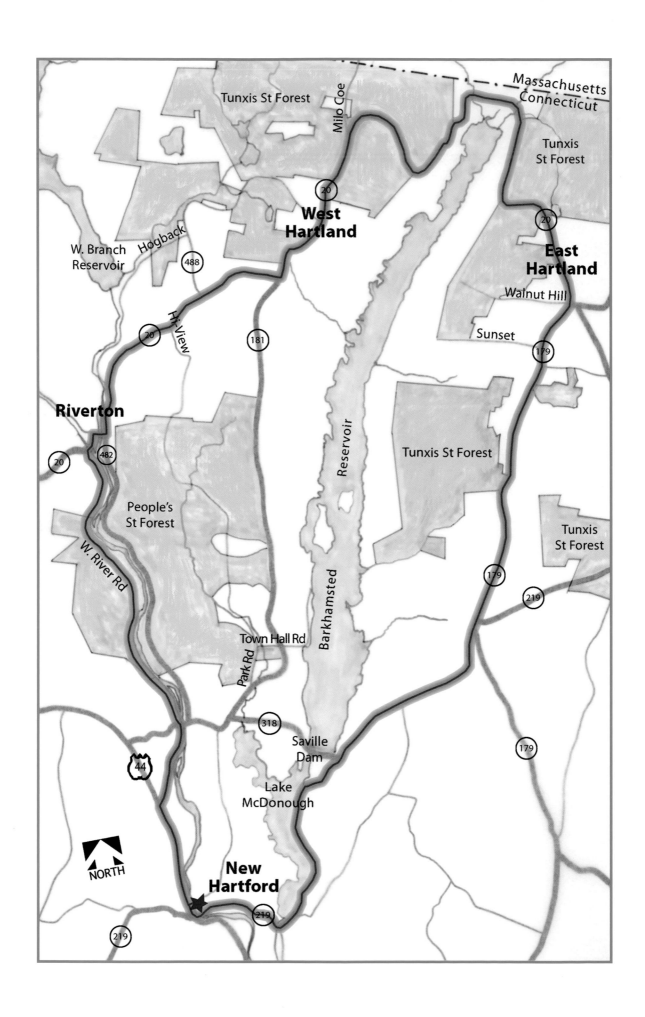

33. New Hartford – Hartland – Riverton
Meet: Rte 44 at 219, New Hartford, parking
behind Town Hall

00.00	S	Rte 44
00.10	L	Rte 219
06.85	F	Rte 179
11.25	F	Rte 20 to Riverton, across river
23.77	L	W. River Rd. → Rte 181 to end
28.83	L	Rte 44
30.76	L	into parking

Main Street, New Hartford

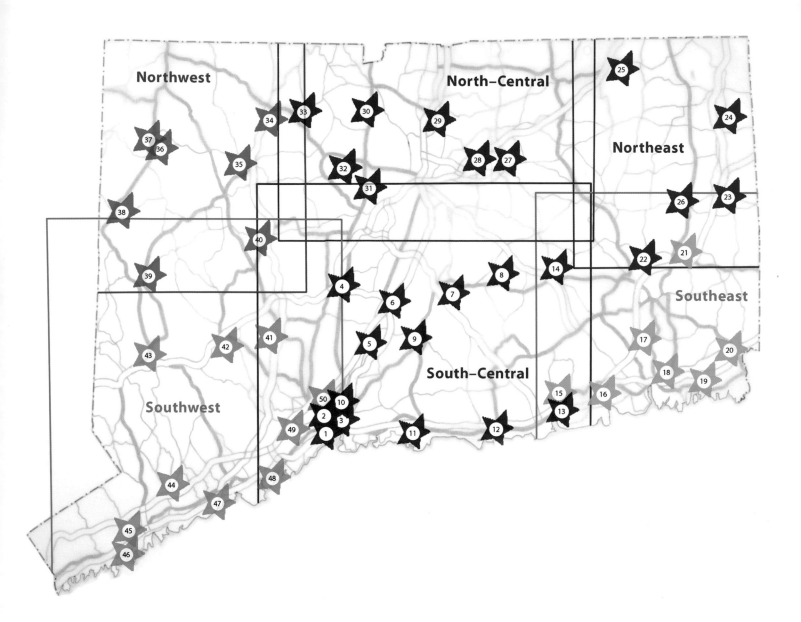

Northwest

Litchfield Hills, The Upper Housatonic to the Berkshires

Fishing on Stillwater Reservoir, Torrington

[34] Burrville – Colebrook – Riverton

Meeting Place: *Burrville, Route 8, Exit 46 at Industrial Park on Pinewoods Rd just east of the exit*
Length: *31 miles*
Lunch: *There are several food markets along the way north, with restaurants in Riverton. Or bring lunch to enjoy along the river, in a state forest, or in a small village.*
Sights: *Farms, historic homes and churches, quaint villages, state forests, bubbling brooks, Highland Lake, and the Farmington River.*
Challenge: *easy to moderate; many long, level stretches with some short steep hills, and paved roads with very little traffic.*

This is a charming little ride in the Berkshires of Connecticut just near the Massachusetts border. For such a hilly area there are surprisingly long stretches of level road because of the many waterways that the roads follow. Nevertheless, the ride begins and ends with some rather steep little hills on the east-west routes, so we keep it short.

There is a convenient starting point at the otherwise unremarkable industrial park at Pinewoods Road, with lots and lots of parking on a weekend. Heading west on Pinewoods, which becomes Highland Lake Road and then Mountain Road, we run smack into the southern tip of Highland Lake. This beautiful body of water, unfortunately for the rider, is completely surrounded by private lakefront homes peopled by rather suspicious owners. We were called on the carpet for just peering over an overlook. Nevertheless, it's a pleasant ride along the waterside up West Wakefield Boulevard for almost two miles to the northern end. Here, zigzagging a block each on West Lake, Woodland, Boyd, and Lake, we come to Route 183 and the town of Winsted, facing the imposing, stone, Romanesque/Renaissance-style Second Congregational Church, built in 1898. For a side trip, turn right on route 183 into the center of Winsted. But our tour goes left, and follows 183 for almost seven miles through the charming little hamlet of Colebrook, founded in 1779. This is a good place to have lunch, and a view of the simple, wooden, Federal-style Congregational Church surrounded by eighteenth and early-nineteenth-century homes and a charming country store. Down the pike at Sandy Brook Road stands a most charming little one-room schoolhouse, The Rock School, built in 1779 and used until 1911, with no electricity or running water, and a tiny little outhouse in the back. Inside, the schoolhouse is still furnished as if the scruffy little urchins were still there.

The ride down Sandy Brook Road follows the bubbling brook of the same name and, for the entire four-and-a-half miles, you can sit back and just gently coast. Along the way is a wonderful scene of wildflowers lining the stream banks. At Route 8 we head southeast, passing the most outrageous antique and boat shop with odds and ends sprawled all over the yard. Following Riverton Road, which merges with Robertsville Road, we arrive in the hamlet of Riverton, where the historic sites are the pristine, white, Congregational Church; Pinney Tavern (1828); the Old Riverton Inn; the Farmington River; and the sprawling Hitchcock Chair Company. Built along the river bank by Lambert Hitchcock in 1826, the company offered "the latest & most approved patterns" according to a large wooden plaque. From Riverton, West River Road takes us for five miles along the meandering Farmington River and the Peoples State Forest, with fly fishing and tubing as the only distractions. At the end, a rural, hilly ride along Old Country, Eddy, East West Hill/Turnbull, West Hill, and a block on Route 183 takes us back to Pinewoods Road and the parking lot.

Hitchcock Chair Company built by Lambert Hitchcock in 1826

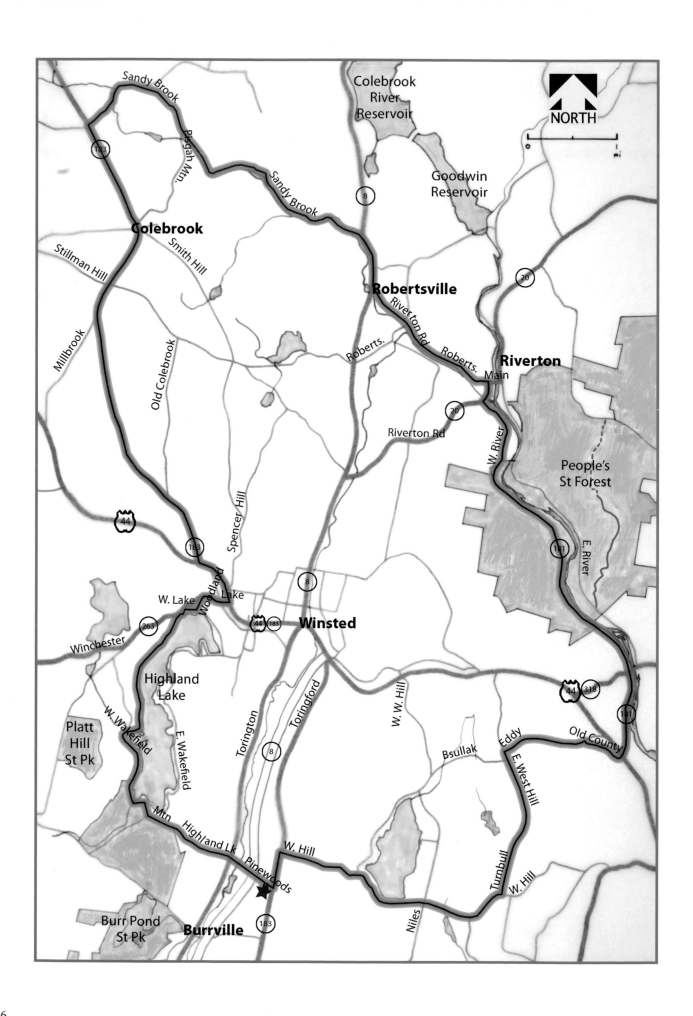

34. Burrville – Colebrook – Riverton
Meet: Burrville, Rte 8, Exit 46 E. on Pinewoods Rd. to the industrial park

00.00	L	Pinewoods
00.47	F	Highland Lake Rd
01.69	BR	Mountain Rd. to lake
01.89	L	W. Wakefield Blvd. to end
04.75	R	West Lake to 1st L.
04.83	L	Woodland to end
05.05	R	Boyd (Rte 263)
05.24	F	Lake (Rte 263 continues) to end
05.39	L	Rte 183 through Colebrook to one-room schoolhouse on R.
12.00	R	Sandy Brook Rd. to end
16.49	R	Rte 8 to 2nd L.
17.15	L	Riverton Rd. → Robertsville Rd. to Riverton at Main
19.03	R	Riverton Rd. (Rte 20) south to 1st L.
19.28	L	W. River Rd
23.40	F	Rte 181 (W. River Rd. continues) to Rte 44
24.40	F	Old County Rd. to end
24.95	L	Eddy to end
25.98	L	E. West Hill → Turnbull
27.80	R	W. Hill to 1 bl to Y
27.88	BL	W. Hill/Brodie Park
30.80	L	Rte 183
31.24	R	Pinewoods to parking
31.35	L	into parking

Antiques shop, Robertsville

[35] Litchfield – Torrington – South Norfolk

Meeting Place: *East Litchfield at Route 8, Exit 42, on Thomaston Rd at Route 118, Park & Ride*
Length: *32 miles*
Lunch: *There are several cafes, restaurants, and convenience stores at Litchfield, toward the end of the ride. Or bring lunch to enjoy at one of the lakes.*
Sights: *Historic homes, state parks, lakes and reservoirs, quaint villages, and lots of green.*
Challenge: *easy to moderate; paved roads with light traffic and some rolling hills.*

This is an amazingly level route despite the fact that we are right in the middle of mountains all around, close to the Berkshires and the Massachusetts border. What makes the effort so imperceptible is that the road north follows streambeds in the hollow between two mountain ridges on an extremely gentle incline until we reach our northern point at South Norfolk. The road back then follows the top of the ridges, with some dips and climbs, but gently taking us on a gradual decline all the way down to Litchfield and then again eastward and mostly downhill to our beginning at East Litchfield.

We begin just off Highway 8 at Route 118 heading north on Thomaston Road through South Main, briefly on Route 202 to cross the bridge over the Naugatuck River and then immediately north for a half block on Main and immediately left on Water Street. This leads through the western edge of Torrington, following the upper reaches of the Naugatuck River, which we cross again on Church Street, and out of Torrington on Riverside to Route 272. This ten-mile stretch takes us past some magnificent rural scenery, including the Stillwater Reservoir, with access for fishermen; the John A. Minetto State Park; Hall Meadow Brook Reservoir; Reuben Hart Reservoir across the road with its deep gorge; the lovely, meandering Meadow Brook; and numerous working farms with charming old barns surrounded by gentle, low

mountains. Finally, a climb to the top takes us past a huge, ramshackle, old sawmill until we reach South Norfolk.

A sharp turnaround back up a sharp incline on Goshen East Street (really a rural mountain road) lands us on top of the ridge we had been following at the bottom of the gully. Here are magnificent views from the top, where we pass wonderful historic farm houses and rolling hills and miles and miles of forest. There is rarely a car in sight. An almost constant, slight downhill coast takes us on East Street North and then past Route 4 on East Street South and Norfolk Road to Route 63 and the mystical old village of Litchfield. Spend some time here to take in a mile of sights leading each way from the intersection of Routes 63, 118, and 202, with grand avenues; service walking paths along the rows of fabulous eighteenth and nineteenth-century homes; a large Green in the center facing the magnificent, classical, First Congregational Church (1829); and charming little shops and restaurants everywhere that beg for a stop to chat with some of the colorful local folk.

Our final, short leg takes us eastward on Route 118 with an initial dip down into a hollow and up again. But our well-deserved reward comes on old East Litchfield Road leading back downhill almost all the way, past historic homes and farms to our beginning just off Highway 8. Just prop your feet up and relax.

A Farm on Route 252, Goshen

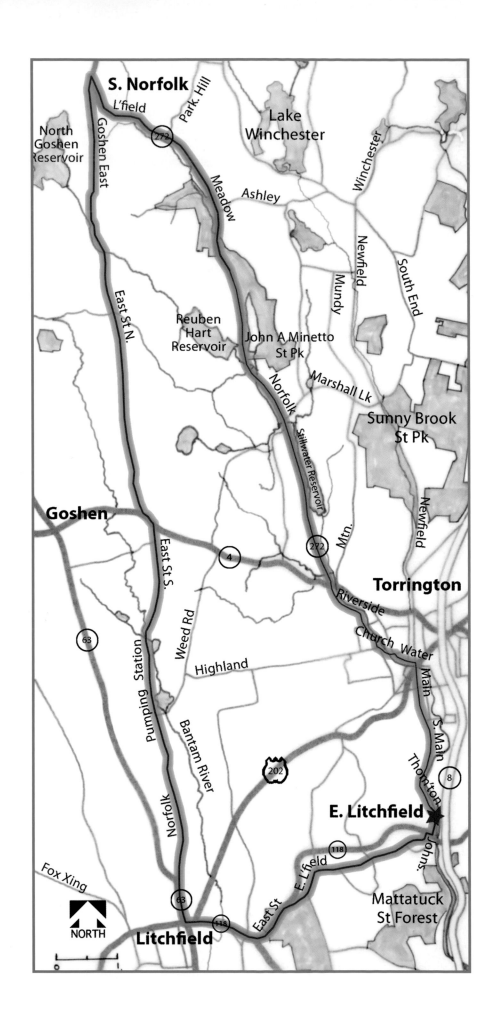

35. Litchfield – Torrington – South Norfolk
**Meet: East Litchfield at Route 8, Exit 42, L. on
Rte 118 and N. on Thomaston Rd. to Park & Ride**

00.00	R	Thomaston → S. Main to end
02.55	BR	Main (Rte 202) across river & immediately BL on Main 1/2 bl to 1st L.
02.60	L	Water
03.00	L	Church across river
03.22	F	Riverside → Rte 272 (Norfolk → Meadow → Litchfield)
13.40	SL	Goshen East → East St-North to end
20.45	L	Rte 4 to 1st R.
20.73	R	East St-South → Pumping Station → Norfolk to end
26.18	F	Rte 63 (North St)
27.00	L	Rte 118 (East St)
28.80	R	East Litchfield
31.42	L	Johnson to 1st R.
31.50	R	Rte 118
31.60	L	Thomaston
31.65	R	into parking

Birthplace of Harriet Beecher Stowe, eighteenth century, Litchfield

[36] West Cornwall – Falls Village – Goshen

Meeting Place: West Cornwall, Route 128 (parking south at river access on Lower River Rd)
Length: 29 miles
Lunch: There are several charming cafes and restaurants in West Cornwall, Falls Village, and Goshen. Or bring lunch to enjoy along the river or in a state forest.
Sights: Farms, historic homes, quaint villages, state forests, lakes, the Housatonic River, and the West Cornwall Covered Bridge.
Challenge: moderate; many very long gradual hills, paved roads with very little traffic, and several miles of dirt road.

For the first six miles this seems to be an easy ride north through nothing but forest to Falls Village in Canaan, but the next twelve miles back down south are almost a continual climb up to the top of a very long hill, upon which sits the village of Goshen. But our hard work is rewarded on the last ten miles back to West Cornwall, which is almost a continual coast with two very steep plunges downhill. For those who like an extreme challenge, try the route in the opposite direction. You'll see why we chose to do this route clockwise. The hills are still there but the inclines are a bit more kind.

We begin at the picturesque little village of West Cornwall at the Covered Bridge across the Housatonic River, built possibly in 1837, but certainly by 1864. Heading north on River Road we go for several miles on packed dirt right beside the river, which then becomes macadam as Lime Rock Road until it hits Route 7. Here we continue north on the same country road, which is labeled, ironically, the Warren Turnpike. At the end, under the railroad and a dog's leg right and left takes us down Main Street in the quaint little village of Canaan known as Falls Village. Here there are a number of charming old buildings such as the Town Hall, an old bank, nineteenth-century houses, an old church totally shingled, the majestic brick Victorian-style library, and, on Route 7, the South Canaan Meetinghouse built in 1804. There is also a delightful cafe.

From here we head southeast on Route 63, which has a little more traffic, and is uphill almost all the way. It's almost entirely farmland and forest, with beautiful houses and small ponds and streams.

A detour is recommended here for the more casual riders, as the second half of this route is a grueling uphill climb all the way to Goshen. At 13 miles, turn right on Route 43, which is Cornwell Hollow Road and is relatively flat, passing through tranquil farmland all the way to the right turn at Route 128.

For those who do follow the uphill Route 63, finally, at the top is the loose assemblage of buildings known as Goshen, among which are a few really interesting ones such as the stately Congregational Church built in 1833, the lesser, but charming, Gothic-style St. Thomas Chapel built in 1876, and two curious buildings with shingled squared cupolas, one of which is the Town Hall, and the other the Goshen Historical Society.

Turning west on Route 4 we head back to West Cornwall, first on rolling hills, mostly downward, and then forward on Route 128, careening almost entirely downhill. If you still have some energy left, take a detour through the Mohawk State Forest, on the left, where there are numerous walking trails, or further on into the smaller subsection of the sprawling Housatonic State Forest. And finally, we get a chance to rest on the grass beside the river at the Covered Bridge, and perhaps take a well-deserved drink across from the Toll House or have a good meal at one of the two country restaurants to end the day.

The old Toll House, West Cornwall

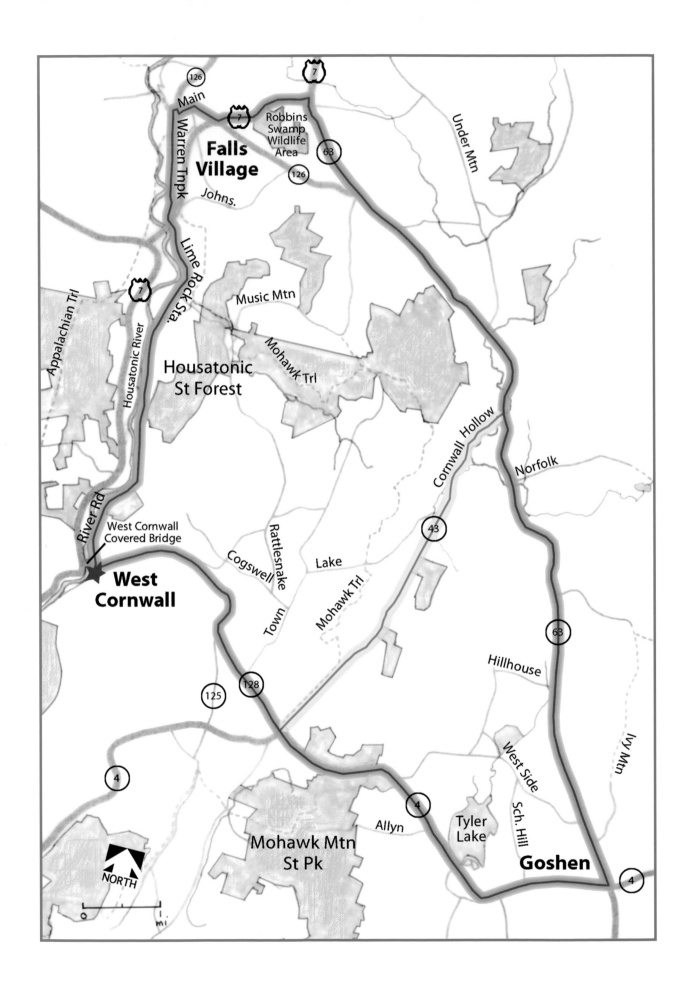

36. W. Cornwall – Falls Village – Goshen
Meet: W. Cornwall, Rte 128 (parking south at river access on Lower River Rd)

00.00	N	River Rd. (mostly dirt road) → Lime Rock Station (across Rte 7)
04.90	F	Warren Tnpk to end
06.40	R	Water under railroad to 1st R.
06.43	R	Railroad to 1st L.
06.48	L	Main
06.75	F	Rte 126 (Main St. continues) to 1st L.
07.05	L	Rte 7 (S. Canaan Rd) to 1st X.
08.33	R	Rte 63 to Goshen (a long strenuous climb)

(Alternate easier route:)

13.09	*R*	*Route 43 (Cornwall Hollow Rd)*
18.13	*R*	*Route 128 to end at West Cornwall (22.23 mi.)*
20.00	R	Rte 4
25.40	F	Rte 128 to end at West Cornwall
29.50		to covered Bridge

The David M. Hunt Library, Falls Village

[37] West Cornwall – Twin Lakes

Meeting place: West Cornwall, Route 128 (parking south at river access on Lower River Rd)
Length: 36 miles
Lunch: There are several charming cafes and restaurants. Or bring lunch to enjoy at the stone wall overlooking Mudge Pond.
Sights: Farms, historic homes, quaint villages, state parks, lakes and rivers, wildlife sanctuaries, forests, and the West Cornwall Covered Bridge.
Challenge: moderate to difficult; rolling hills and a couple of very steep hills, paved roads with very little traffic, and several miles of dirt road.

This route is a challenge from the start, but the rewards come halfway through the ride, with an almost continual decline from the north point back to the south at West Cornwall. Mercifully, it's not too long, and you'll feel great coasting in to finish. We begin at the bright red West Cornwall Covered Bridge. West Cornwall is a charming old village with cafes, restaurants, snack shops, and the old Toll House. Take in the spectacular views of the river and the beauty of the old covered bridge as you cross, keeping right, to Route 7. The bridge is the product of many reconstructions since 1864, when it was plain, unpainted timber, completely overhauled in 1945, painted red in 1957, and reinforced with an interior structure of steel in 1973.

Here's where the fun starts. West Cornwall Road begins here with a steep climb for one mile. Less experienced riders may want to simply walk their bikes and save their energy. After the old cemetery it's easier, and we continue for six miles, passing the Miles Wildlife Sanctuary with the beautiful Miles Pond and Roy Swamp and its marshy flora and fauna. Left on Route 41 we enter the serene village of Sharon with its wide greenway, nineteenth-century homes and the magnificent brick Congregational Church built in 1824. Arriving at the stone clocktower at Route 4, we turn around and take Route 361 out of town. Mudge Pond Road takes us past the vast pond of the same name with its marshes, overlooked by stately farms surrounded by low stone walls. Across the border with Salisbury, the road becomes Indian Mountain Road, which merges into Route 44 (Millerton Road) at the Wononskopomuc Lake (an Indian name) which passes through the village of Lakeville

and then Salisbury, both with magnificent nineteenth-century homes and vast gardens. The Federal-style, white clapboard Salisbury Congregational Church, with its elegant cupola and Palladian windows, was built in 1800. Classical, Federal-style, and Gothic houses make this town a feast for the eyes.

Our final stretch north is on the relatively easy Under Mountain Road past bucolic farms and old cemeteries to the Mount Riga State Park Scenic Reserve, where we need to keep an eye out for the Beaver Dam Road on the right. This takes us immediately past the privately owned Fisher Pond, with its island in the center, then north on Taconic Road to the first right, passing several curious old stone cottages. Twin Lakes Road circles around the Washinee and Washining Lakes (again, Indian names) surrounded by private vacation homes with a big public boat launch.

Crossing the upper reaches of the Housatonic River (now just a creek) we turn right on Route 126, which winds down through Robbins Swamp Wildlife Management Area and takes a sharp left between two gorgeous Federal-style homes on Point of Rocks Road (still Route 126) bypassing Falls Village. Here we turn right on Route 7, and a mile and a half later, just before the bridge back over the Housatonic River, we turn left onto Lime Rock Station Road, which follows the old Housatonic Railroad to become the packed-dirt River Road over the border of Cornwall. This takes us through the Housatonic State Forest on a general slight decline and ends back at the village of West Cornwall and the Covered Bridge. The charming old restaurants and shops there beg for an extended visit to relax before heading home.

The Congregational Church of Salisbury, 1800

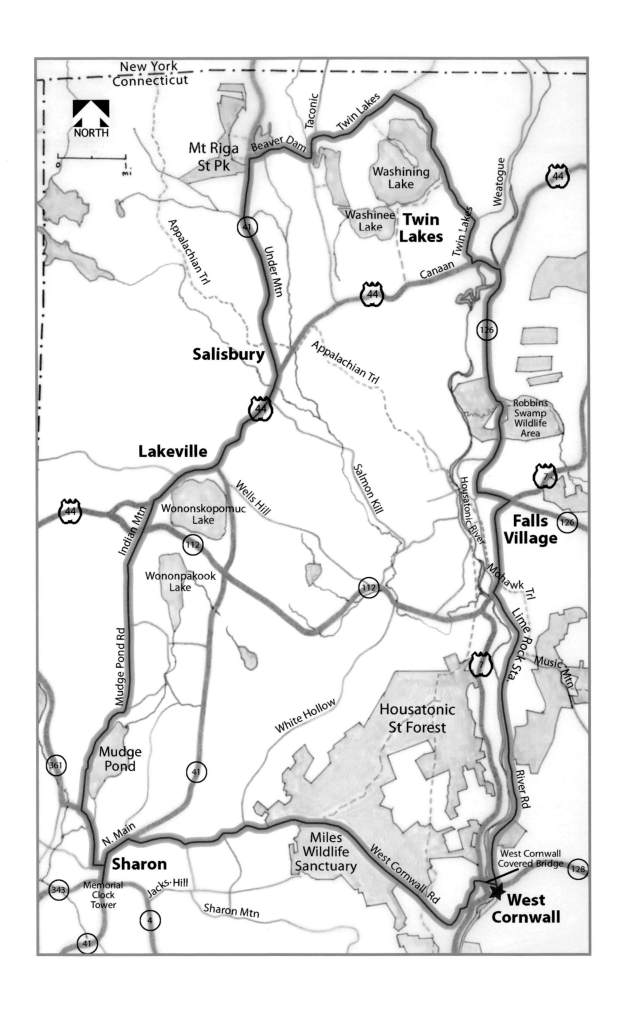

37. W. Cornwall – Twin Lakes
Meet: W. Cornwall, Rte 128 (parking south at river access on Lower River Rd)

00.00	W	through the Covered Bridge, bearing right to Rte 7
00.10	F	West Cornwall Rd. (a punishing uphill ride for 1 mile) to end
06.10	L	N. Main (Rte 41) thru Sharon to tower at Rte 4
06.25		Return on Main 1 bl
06.40	L	Rte 361 past cemetery
07.38	R	Mudge Pond Rd. → Indian Mountain Rd. to end
13.70	R	Rte 44 (Millerton Rd)
15.20	BL	Rte 41 (Under Mountain Rd) past 2 cemeteries
18.67	R	Beaver Dam Rd. to end
19.70	L	Taconic Rd. to 1st R.
22.10	R	Twin Lakes Rd.—several right turns
24.94	F	Canaan Rd. (Rte 44) across bridge
26.28	R	Rte 126—several turns
29.50	R	Rte 7 to just before 1st river bridge (if you see Rte 112 you've gone too far)
31.20	L	Lime Rock Station Rd— becomes River Rd. (dirt) in Cornwall—to end
36.00	R	to Covered Bridge

West Cornwall Covered Bridge, 1864, across the Housatonic River

[38] Kent – West Cornwall Covered Bridge – Falls Village

Meeting Place: *Kent Shopping Village, Routes 7 & 341*
Length: *38 miles*
Lunch: *Bring lunch to enjoy at West Cornwall Covered Bridge, in one of several state parks, or along the Housatonic River. Or enjoy the cafes at Falls Village, West Cornwall, or back at Kent.*
Sights: *Kent cafes and shops, Sloane Stanley Museum, Kent Furnace, the Housatonic River (the entire way), the waterfall at Kent Falls State Park, Housatonic Meadows State Park, West Cornwall Covered Bridge, mountains and f orests, quaint villages, and historic churches and homes.*
Challenge: *easy; flat to rolling hills, paved roads with light traffic, and a 3-mile stretch of dirt road. A hybrid bike is recommended, although a road bike can make it.*

Beginning at Kent village, with its many cafes and shops patronized heavily by tourists from New York City, we ride for nearly twenty miles north on Route 7—all the way to Falls Village in Canaan. For more on this beautiful scenic route into Massachusetts, see *Along Route 7: A Journey through Western New England*, by Stephen G. Donaldson (Atglen, PA: Schiffer, 2010). Although the cafe and art crowd at Kent is all City, with an intermingling of schoolboys from the private Kent School, a lot of local flavor comes by too.

A few miles out of Kent, the traffic subsides and it becomes a very pleasant, easy ride following the imperceptibly slight upward grade of the upper Housatonic River and the Housatonic Railroad side by side. Along the way, it's worth a stop at the Kent Falls State Park with its cascading waterfall and the wading pool at the bottom, very popular with the folks from Kent. Further up the road is Housatonic Meadow State Park, with broad grassy lawns and access to the river, where boaters float past in their bright kayaks. From here we pass through several miles of the Housatonic State Forest, where there is a camp ground. At West Cornwall, the lovely red covered bridge is down below us at the river, but we'll be passing through this on our way back. Just after crossing the river for the second time, we reach the tiny Falls Village, in Canaan, by way of Beebe Hill Road and Main Street. Here there is some interesting nineteenth-century architecture in the plain little Congregational Church; the Community Center, in an old, completely shingled, gray church; the imposing Romanesque stone library; The Falls Village Inn; the town hall; and many others. A tiny little cafe here on Main Street is the only watering hole at the northern end of this loop.

The way back is on Railroad and Water Streets, under the railroad, and south on Warren Turnpike, a lonely country road. Crossing Route 7, we continue on Lime Rock Station Road, which becomes River Road, and meanders for five miles back and forth across the railroad and follows the river, becoming a dirt road for three miles. This stretch is very sparsely inhabited, with rarely a car in sight. Lots of spots along the river are nice to relax. At West Cornwall, the little road ends, and we turn west on Route 128 through the Covered Bridge (alternating one-way traffic pattern). Along the banks of the river, here are picnic areas, and a couple of charming eateries worth a stop. Immediately after the bridge, we head south on Route 7 again all the way back to Kent on an easy ride, with a few low hills, following the Housatonic as it descends.

For those experienced riders who are still bursting with energy, an alternative return route would be to turn right on Route 4 at Cornwall Bridge and follow Northrup, Ellsworth, Modley, and Skiff Mountain Roads over the very challenging inclines of picturesque Skiff Mountain. For most of the first seven miles it's a grueling climb, partly on dirt road, with finally a four-mile descent back to Route 341 at Kent School.

Back at Kent, the cafes close up early, especially on Sunday, when the tourists head back to the city, so expect to relax there for a drink or some of their famous chocolate only if your ride ends before 5 P.M.

River Road, Cornwall, with the Housatonic River and the Housatonic Railroad

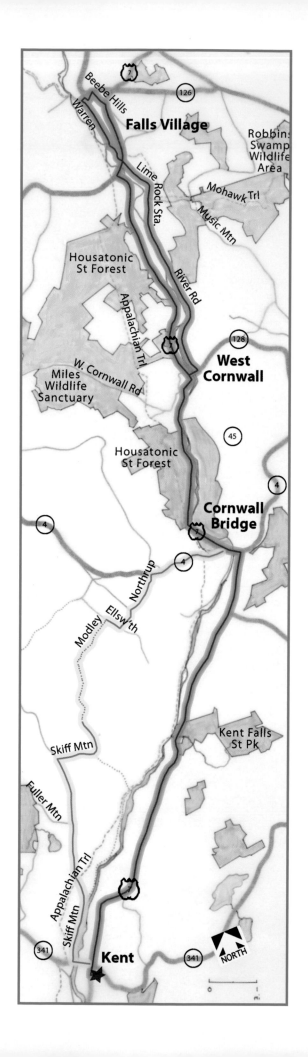

38. Kent – W. Cornwall Covered Bridge – Falls Village
Meet: Kent Shopping Village, Rtes 7 & 341

00.00	R	Rte 7 (N. Main St) to Falls Village
19.63	L	Beebe Hills Rd. to Congregational Church on L.
19.90	L	Main (just before Rte 126) to end
20.12	R	Railroad St
20.17	L	Water under RR to 1st L.
20.20	L	Warren
21.66	F	Lime Rock Station Rd
22.14	BL	River Rd. across RR (dirt road 22.95-25.95)
26.46	R	Rte 128 (Sharon-Goshen Tpke) through covered bridge
26.63	L	Rte 7
40.10	L	Rte 341 and into parking

For the extremely energetic, an alternative to the return route on Highway 7:

30.70	*R*	*Rte 4 W (steep uphill)*
32.31	*L*	*Northrup to end (steep uphill)*
33.57	*R*	*S. Ellsworth to 1st L.*
33.83	*L*	*Modley (dirt road to 36.05)* → *Skiff Mt Rd*
37.72	*L*	*Skiff Mt Rd to end (all downhill)*
41.72	*L*	*Rte 341*
42.03	*L*	*at Rte 7 in Kent into parking*

Kent Falls State Park

[39] New Milford – Lake Waramaug – Kent – Bulls Bridge

Meeting place: New Milford: Route 202 to parking along the Housatonic River
Length: 42 miles
Lunch: Bring lunch to enjoy at Lake Waramaug or Bulls Bridge. Or enjoy the cafes at New Preston or Kent.
Sights: Lake Waramaug, Kent, Sloane Stanley Museum, Kent Furnace, Kent School, Schaghticoke Indian Reservation, Bulls Bridge, Housatonic River (almost half the way), quaint towns and villages, and historic churches and homes.
Challenge: moderate; rolling hills, paved streets with some traffic, and one long stretch of dirt road.

Water, water, water, and more water characterizes this ride, including some of the most idyllic woodsy scenes, folksy common villages, as well as places where the super rich play. We begin the ride at New Milford, a charming town with a little bit of both folksy and rich, where we park along a stretch of weeping willows lining the Housatonic River. Following Route 202 (a detour through the picturesque heart of town on Main Street and right on Elm takes us the same direction), we head straight on a rather well-trafficked road all the way to New Preston (for those masochists in the group, a foray either east or west of this route will find some of the most vertical hills in Connecticut, such as Route 109 to Washington Depot). Main Street in New Preston, just off our route, has some charming cafes and other shops. From here, Route 45 takes us north quickly to the beginning of Lake Waramaug, where the long ride on West Shore Road ambles around almost the entirety of the undulating coastline of the Lake and back to continue north on Route 45 (those in a hurry can simply skip the west shore and keep on Route 45, which is also pleasant, following the east shore). At the northwestern tip of the Lake is the Lake Waramaug State Park with picnic tables and a small beach, and a great view of the grand homes across the shore. North 45 joins Route 341, where the magnificent Warren Congregational Church stands high on a grassy incline, from which we travel up and down manageable hills with a good shoulder all the way to the town of Kent.

Kent is probably the most overrated tourist attraction in the state, drawing the rich and famous from around the country (Henry Kissinger, Oscar de la Renta, and Patti LuPone have homes here). Whatever historic charm this little crossroads once had has now dissipated in the profusion of commercialism, with little "shoppes" everywhere, all developed since the late 1980s. If chocolate shoppes, ice cream shoppes, fancy consignment shoppes, little dress shoppes, little designer art galleries, and little antique shoppes are your cup of tea, then you'll love a stop here. A better bet is to buy a sandwich at the gas station that dominates the central crossroads, and take it to enjoy along the river, where you'll spend your next fifteen miles. A few side trips are worth the visit—the Appalachian Trail just across the river, the old Congregational Cemetery, the old railroad station, and The Sloane-Stanley Museum, with its collection of early American tools and the ruins of the Kent Iron Furnace dating to 1826. Passing the charming little stone St. Andrews Church, also built in 1826, we reach the Kent School, which is worth the amble through it with visions of neo-Georgian and neo-Gothic architecture and fresh-faced prep school boys playing lacrosse on the manicured lawns. Go straight through the campus to the end on the walks if it's summer; otherwise take the riverside drive to its exit.

Heading south from the campus, we spend more than an hour cruising imperceptibly downhill, first along Schaghticoke Road, which takes us through the Indian Reservation of the same name (only sparsely populated, and not a tourist destination, although an ancestral shrine can be seen along the road). Idyllic scenes along the river make this ride extremely pleasant, with glimpses of eighteenth-century homes on the opposite bank. At the end is the 1842 Bulls Bridge, an unpainted covered bridge reincarnated from earlier bridges built in 1811 and 1760 across the Housatonic River. An absolute must is climbing down the rocks to the waterfall just before the bridge, where little eddies have carved out skull-like boulders and rocks on the shore. Hiking trails through the woods provide a retreat. After a short ride south from here on Route 7, a left at the quaint little village of Gaylordsville on Riverview Road and then River Road (entirely dirt for four miles following the edge of the river), followed by Boardman Road takes us back to our starting point. The long length of the river has various viewing points with the odd fisherman or two, good for an occasional rest stop.

Warren Congregational Church, early nineteenth century

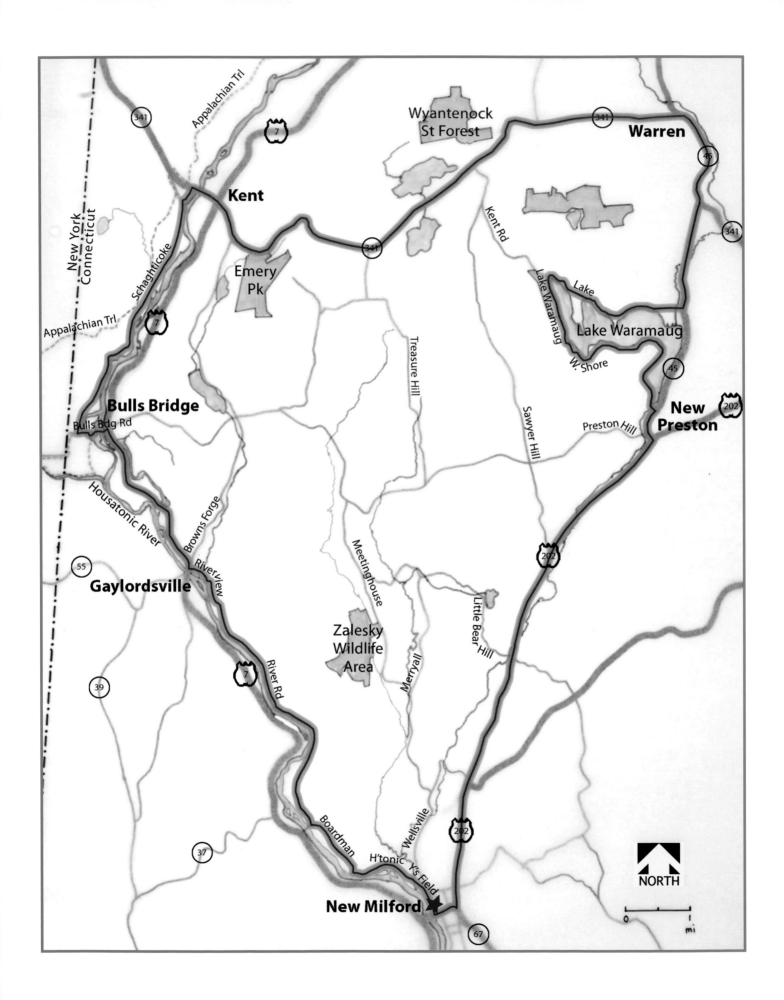

39. New Milford – Lake Waramaug – Kent – Bulls Bridge
Meet: New Milford: Rte 202 to parking along the east bank of the Housatonic River

00.00	L	Rte 202 to bend		27.15	L	Schaghticoke thru Indian Reservation to end
00.40	L	Rte 202 (continue)		31.08	L	Bulls Bridge Rd. thru Covered Bridge
07.90	L	Rte 45 to Lake Waramaug				
08.50	L	W. Shore Rd. → Lake Waramaug → Lake Rd. around Lake to end		31.60	R	Rte 7 to just before river crossing at Gaylordsville
14.60	L	Rte 45 (Lake Rd) to Warren		34.13	L	Riverview
16.20	L	Rte 341 (Kent Rd) through Kent, across Housatonic River to Kent School		34.45	F	River (becomes dirt road) to end
				38.80	L	Boardman → Housatonic → Young's Field
26.65	L	through Kent School along river to end of campus		41.50	R	into parking lot

Bulls Bridge, 1842, across the Housatonic River

[40] Black Rock – Bantam Lake

Meeting place: *Parking lot at Subway, Reynolds Bridge. Take Route 8 to Exit 38, west to Route 6 and into parking lot at southbound ramp.*
Length: *30 miles (shortcuts are possible)*
Lunch: *There are several small cafes and food stores, including a delicious chocolate shop. Or bring lunch to enjoy at the lake.*
Sights: *Historic homes, quaint villages, lots of green, Black Rock State Park, Bantam Lake, and the White Memorial Foundation and Conservation Center*
Challenge: *moderate; paved roads with light traffic and rolling hills.*

This is a wonderful, peaceful ride through farmland and tiny villages, with lots of forested mileage. The route is modified from the Connecticut Bicycle Map. Traced in a figure 8, the route allows the rider to opt for a shorter ride of twenty miles or an even shorter ride of ten miles at the northern end.

We begin at the village of Reynolds Bridge in Thomaston, just at Route 8 on Route 6 and head west, immediately branching off on Route 109. It's an almost steady uphill climb for nine miles, passing Black Rock State Park, the Black Rock Lake (a reservoir), and the small crossroad towns of East Morris and Morris with its simple Congregational Church, an early schoolhouse, and the Old Town Hall built in 1861. Morris dates to the 1720s and it is a charming little town. The climb continues until we reach the South Bay of the natural Bantam Lake on Route 209. Here is one beautiful view after another, with a relatively level route all around the west side of the lake. Bantam is taken from the name of a Native American tribe, a division of the Pootatuck. Around the north side, an uvula-shaped peninsula juts out from North Shore Road, operated as a wildlife sanctuary by the White Memorial Foundation, a private institution that owns vast areas of land north of the lake. It's worth riding out on the gravel path all the way to the end for a magnificent 360° view of the lake and its opposite shores. Further on, Route 202 takes us to Bissell Road, and the home of the White Memorial Foundation and Conservation Center, with its Nature Center and Museum. Vast holdings of forest are crisscrossed by walking paths, which are well used by hikers. Kayakers can be seen on the Bantam River. The museum is open daily for a small fee, and it highlights the flora and fauna of the region.

Heading south on Whites Wood Road and Route 61, we pass back through Morris and the Old Town Hall, heading toward Bethlehem. Our path stops short of Bethlehem and cuts across Kasson, Old Watertown, and Judd Farm Roads (continuous). But for a diversion, Bethlehem is only one mile south, and worth a visit to the 1754 Bellamy-Ferriday House and Garden, especially during its Fall Festival in October. Indulge in a hay ride, pumpkin bowling, bobbing for apples, and cheese sampling, as well as exhibitions of antique tools and birds of prey. Our route takes us to Route 63 South to Watertown, which is worth exploring. The central square (or actually a rectangle) is bounded by a magnificent First Congregational Church high on the hill, the old Town Hall with its tower, and the expansive United Methodist Church, with a modified rose window. Route 6 takes us over hill and dale with one nice long descent back to Reynolds Bridge and our starting point.

White Memorial Sanctuary, Point Folly, off North Shore Road, Bantam Lake

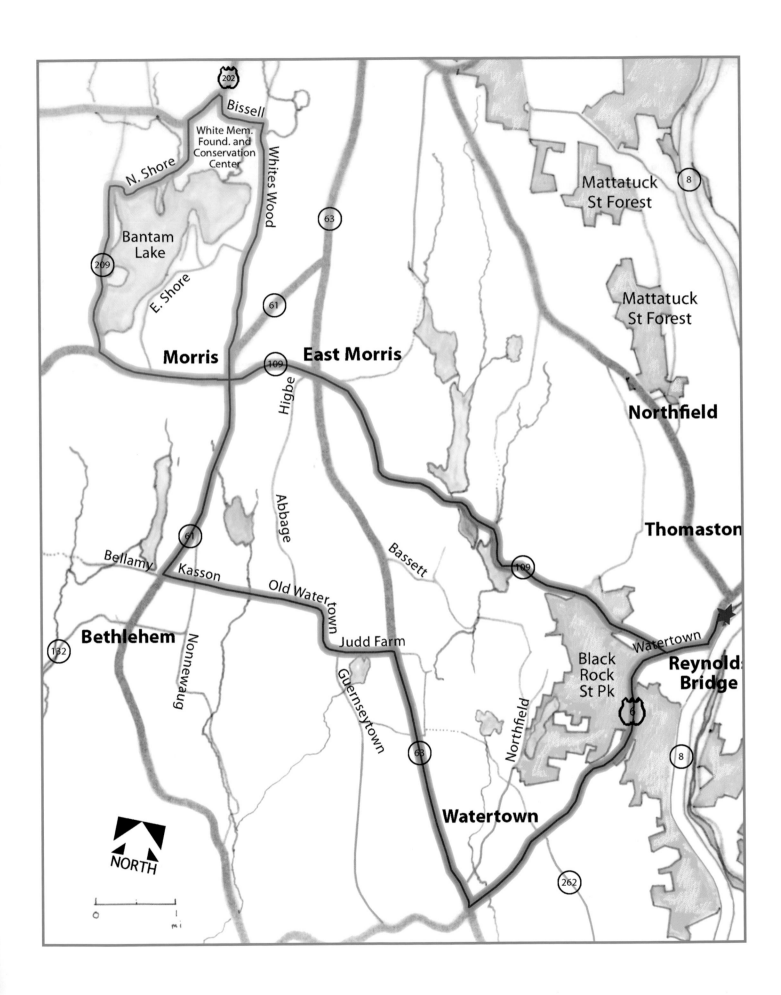

40. Black Rock – Bantam Lake

Meet: Parking lot at Subway, Reynolds Bridge. Take Rte 8 to Exit 38, west to Rte 6 and into parking lot at southbound ramp.

00.00	W	Rte 6 (Watertown Rd) to 1st X.	16.75	F	Rte 61 (South St → N. Main)
00.50	BR	Rte 109	19.45	L	Kasson → Old Watertown→ Judd Farm to end
09.06	BR	Rte 209 (Bantam Lake)			
11.00	R	North Shore to end	22.70	R	Rte 63 (Litchfield Rd)
12.65	R	Rte 202 (Main) to 1st R.	25.85	L	Rte 6 to Rte 109
13.15	R	Bissell to end	30.00	F	Watertown Rd. to end
13.95	R	Whites Wood to end	30.50	L-R	into parking lot at Thomaston

First Congregational Church, early nineteenth century, Watertown

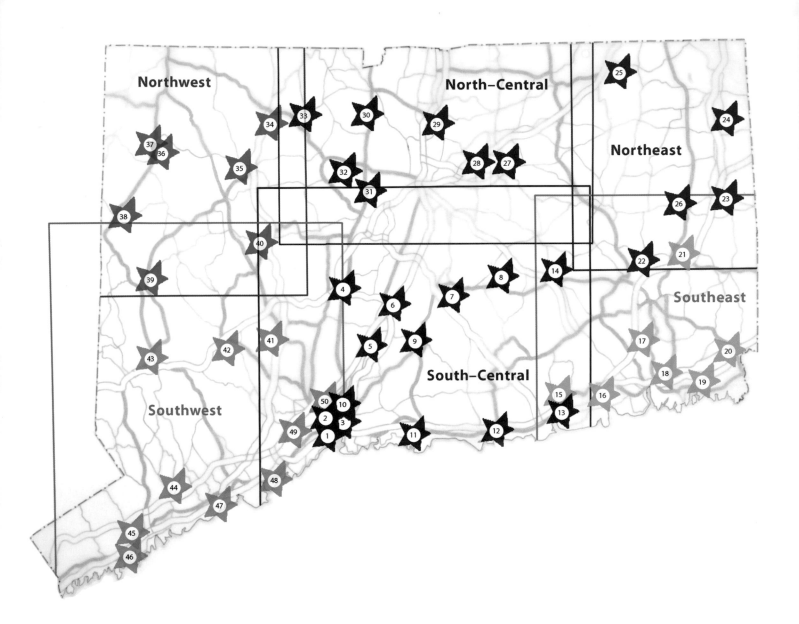

Southwest

From Long Island Sound to Candlewood and Black Rock Lakes

The Long Island Sound from Shore Road, Greenwich

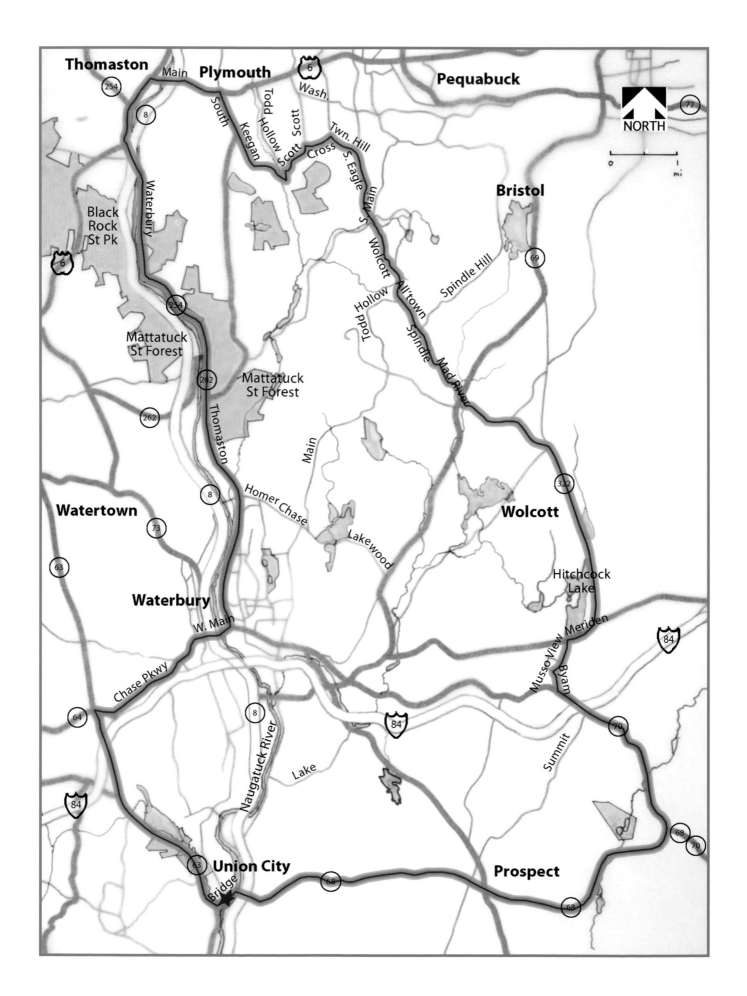

41. Union City – Thomaston
Meet: Union City, parking on Rte 68, W. of Naugatuck River bridge (Exit 28 off Rte 8)

00.00	R	Rte 68 E across river
07.46	L	Rte 70 under Rte 84
10.28	R	Byam to 1st R.
10.60	R	Musso View to end
11.10	R	Meriden to Y.
11.56	BL	Rte 322 N (to R. just before 69)
15.80	R	Mad River Road
16.50	BR	Spindle Hill
17.06	F	Allentown → Wolcott → S. Main
19.06	L	South Eagle
19.10	L	Town Hill
20.62	L	Cross
20.98	L	Scott to end
21.50	L	Todd Hollow to quick end
21.60	R	Keegan
22.75	F	South St
23.40	L	Rte 6 (Main) to center of Thomaston
24.50	L	Rte 6 (Main)
25.00	F	Waterbury (Rte 254 S) to bridge on R. (don't cross)
29.40	F	Rte 262 S
26.00	F	Thomaston Av to end
33.60	R	W. Main → Chase Pkwy to end
35.75	R	Rte 64 to 1st X.
36.05	L	Rte 63
39.70	L	Bridge St. (Rte 68)
39.95	R	into parking

Wolcott Green and Congregational Church, early ninteenth century

[42] Southbury – Washington

Meeting Place: *Park & Ride, Route 84, Exit 14*
Length: *38 miles*
Lunch: *There are no cafes, restaurants, or convenience stores, except for a country store near the beginning at South Britain. Best to bring lunch to enjoy at one of the brooks or farms.*
Sights: *Historic homes and churches, brooks and ponds, the Housatonic River, quaint little hamlets, lots of large farms, green forests, and mountains.*
Challenge: *moderate to difficult; paved roads with almost no traffic and some short and long hills at the northernmost and southernmost points.*

What you won't see on this trip is easier to describe than what you will. There are no great historic sites or towns or beaches or large state parks. This is pretty much open country, thank God, and it is what farmers see. Enjoy the quiet and unremarkable expanses. This is a route with one pre-Revolutionary war home after another.

Beginning on South Britain Road at Route 84, we continue for exactly seven miles without a turn, passing the village of South Britain, which is about the biggest grouping of houses you'll see along this route. The stately, classical Congregational Church, built in 1825, is across from an establishment called the Country Store, painted red with verandas all around, probably good for sitting on a rocker and putting up your feet. Opposite is the extremely simple old Methodist Church, now abandoned. Here is a mix of early eighteenth and early nineteenth-century houses, all lovingly maintained. So far it's been an easy, relatively level ride. More wonderful historic houses await us on West Side and Westwood Roads. Jack's Bridge Road branches off at a beautifully pristine eighteenth-century home, and then links us to Route 47 North with the (blink and you'll miss it) hamlet of Hotchkissville and then on toward Washington.

The village of Washington, high on a hill, is worth the climb to see more historic homes, the magnificent 1801 Congregational Church, and the grand Tudor-style buildings of The Gunnery, a private high school established in 1850, high on a bluff surrounded by a forbidding stone wall.

Returning back on Route 47 and heading south on Painter Ridge Road, we pass some luxurious views of the vast countryside with multiple ridges on the horizon, and pristine red barns with silos. The hills here can be challenging. Painter Hill Road and then Route 317 take us into the little hamlet of Roxbury, with first a classical, white early-nineteenth-century Congregational Church and then at the center, the petite, and later, simple, neo-Gothic Christ Church Episcopal. From here we head south again on South Street and Purchase Brook Road to meet the lower Housatonic River at River Road, across from the waterside playgrounds of Shady Rest. This takes us along the river, passing the little, grassy Southbury Park, and across Route 84 to Fish Rock Road and some steep little hills. Lakeside Road (I didn't see a lake) and George's Hill Road take us back under Route 84 to the starting point.

Old abandoned Methodist Church, South Britain

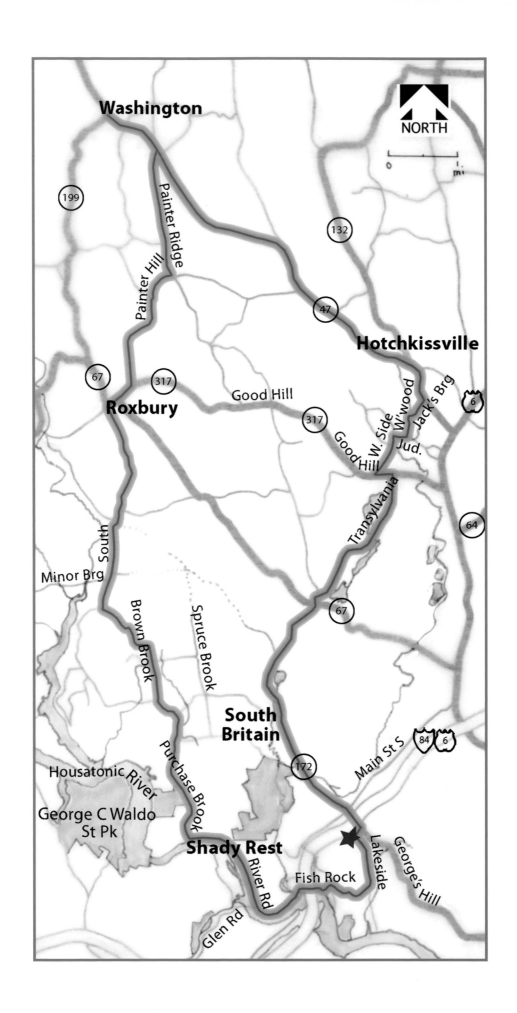

NORTH

Washington

199

132

Painter Ridge

Painter Hill

47

Hotchkissville

67

317

Roxbury

Good Hill

317

W'wood

Jack's Brg

Good Hill

W. Side

Jud.

6

Transylvania

64

South

67

Minor Brg

Brown Brook

Spruce Brook

South
Britain

84   6

172

Main St S

Housatonic River

Purchase Brook

Lakeside

George's Hill

George C Waldo
St Pk

Shady Rest

Fish Rock

River Rd

Glen Rd

42. Southbury – Washington
Meet: Park & Ride, Rte 84, Exit 14, at Lakeside & Main

00.00	N	Rte 172 (Lakeside/S. Britain) to cross Rte 67
04.20	F	Transylvania to end
07.00	L	Good Hill (Rte 317) to 1st R.
07.26	R	West Side to 2nd L. at Judson
08.10	L	Westwood to 1st R.
08.45	BR	Jack's Bridge to end
08.82	L	Rte 47 (Washington → Woodbury → Green Hill) to Washington at Congregational Church
17.58	L	Kirby
17.60	L	(in front of church to Rte 47)
17.62	R	Rte 47 (Green Hill → Woodbury)
18.88	R	Painter Ridge
21.04	R	Painter Hill to end
23.28	R	Rte 317 (Church St) to center of Roxbury
23.80	L	South St. → Brown Brook Rd
28.60	BR	Purchase Brook
29.73	BR	Continue on Purchase Brook to end
32.96	L	River Rd. to cross Rte 84 to 1st R.
35.94	R	Fish Rock to end
37.17	L	Lakeside
38.17	F	George's Hill
38.35		into the Park & Ride at Exit 14

Country store, Route 84, South Britain

[43] Lake Candlewood

Meeting Place: Route 84, Exit 6, East Hayestown Rd, the parking lot of Hatters Community Park, Hayestown, immediately south of southern tip of Lake Candlewood
Length: 34 miles
Lunch: There are many cafes and convenience stores on the west side of the lake, but few on the return trip on the east side.
Sights: Lake Candlewood!
Challenge: moderate; hilly, on paved roads with continuous traffic on the route north on the west side but little traffic on the return south on the east side of the lake.

This is a ride to do in the fall, winter, or spring, but not in the summer when the lake traffic—trucks hauling boats on trailers on narrow two-lane roads—is horrendous. A lot of people live here because of its proximity, via Route 84, to New York. Another reason to do it closer to winter is that during most of the year the shoreline of the lakes is shielded from view from the road by a thick line of woods, but when the leaves fall, the view is unobstructed. In October there is probably no more spectacular display of brilliant reds and yellows in all of Connecticut. The entire route encircles the very long and jagged edge of Lake Candlewood, with a few other smaller lakes and ponds thrown in. The route is modified from Cue #2 on the Connecticut Bicycle Map.

Beginning at Doyles Pond in Hatters Community Park, Hayestown, East Hayestown Road takes us immediately to the very southern tip of the lake, where we get a spectacular view from the waterside. North on Pembroke Road follows the eastern shore of Margerie Lake Reservoir, but the thick woods along the entire length hide the lake from view. Routes 37 at this point, and especially on 39 further on, have one storm drain after another, often projecting nearly halfway into the lane, and always with the grill turned the wrong way, which makes them hazardous for bicycle tires—a situation the state needs to fix since it designates this a specially recommended "Loop Ride Route." Since the road is narrow and heavily traveled in this section, with no shoulder, extreme caution is advised. Finally, we cross over to the western shore of Lake Candlewood, with wonderful views at the New Fairfield Marina. Further on, there are great views at the Lake Candlewood Marina on the right and Squantz Pond State Park on the left just before crossing the bridge to the east side of the Pond. Here again, heavy woods obscure the view through to our meeting up again with Route 37.

The village of Sherman is the only eighteenth-century settlement on the route, and it is cute as can be, with its Historical Society in an old red barn and the Playhouse operating in the spiky old Congregational Church. After Sherman, the traffic thins, but there is a grueling uphill grind, at the top of which is a winery for those who just want to call it quits here and spend the rest of the day with a bottle of blackberry wine and pick berries in the open fields. But for the stalwart who push on, from the Litchfield line to the end of Route 37 is a glorious, winding, downhill rush through thickly wooded terrain. This is the midpoint where we head south again on Route 7.

After a couple of miles along the Housatonic River, a right on Candlewood Lake Road goes straight up for one mile to the top. It continues on a roller coaster ride along the New Milford Bay to Old Town Park Road, and a right on Sullivan takes us on a winding ride south on Candlewood Lake South. A right on Forty Acre Mountain Road and another on Hawthorne Cove leads us around the peninsula of Hawthorne Terrace—on Shore and Pocono Point Roads—with its gorgeous homes overlooking two fingers of the lake. This continues as Forty Acre Mountain Road again, and after turning right we pass the state boat launch at Lattins Cove for another great view of the lake. Stadley Rough Road then leads us south to Hawley, Great Plain, and Hayestown Roads, past Candlewood Park, with its vast expanse of lawn overlooking the very southernmost tip of the lake, especially spectacular on a late afternoon in October with the sun raking the flaming wooded splendor across the water.

Farm on Route 37, Sherman

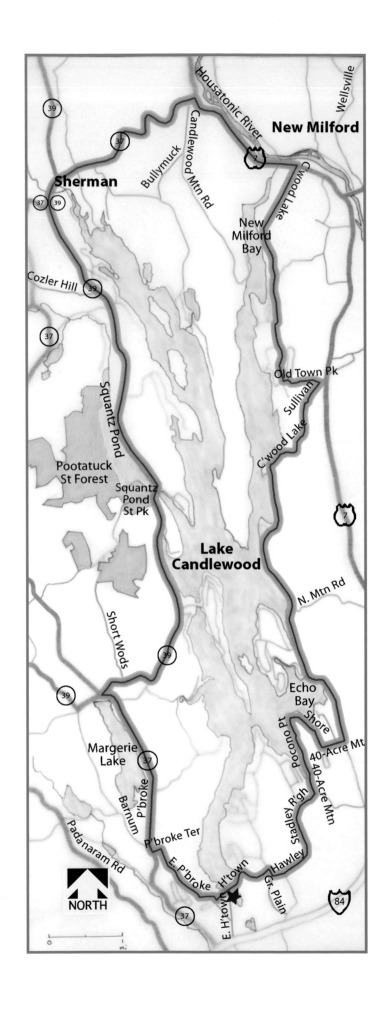

New Milford

Housatonic River

Wellsville

39

37

Sherman

Bullymuck

Candlewood Mtn Rd

7

C'wood Lake

New Milford Bay

37 39

Cozler Hill

39

37

Old Town Pk

Sullivan

C'wood Lake

Squantz Pond

Pootatuck St Forest

Squantz Pond St Pk

Lake Candlewood

7

N. Mtn Rd

Short Wods

39

39

Echo Bay

Shore

40-Acre Mt

Pocono Pt

40-Acre Mtn

Margerie Lake

37

P'broke

Barnum

Stapley R'gh

Padanaram Rd

P'broke Ter

E. P'broke

Hawley

H'town

Gr. Plain

84

NORTH

37

E. H'town

0   1   3:

194

43. Lake Candlewood
Meet: Rte 84, Exit 6, E. Hayestown Rd, at Hatters Community Park, Hayestown, immediately S. of southern tip of Lake Candlewood

00.00	R	E. Hayestown Rd
00.13	L	Hayestown Rd
00.34	R	E. Pembroke Rd. to end
01.55	L	Pembroke Ter 1 bl to end
01.60	R	Pembroke Rd. (Rte 37)
04.30	R	Rte 39
13.05	F	Rtes 39 & 37
13.50	F	Rte 37 to end
16.52	R	Rte 7
18.32	R	Candlewood Lake Rd. to end at Skyview
21.85	L	Old Town Park Rd. to end
22.40	R	Sullivan to 3-pronged fork
23.21	F	Candlewood Lake S. past Echo Bay Marina to 1st X.
28.65	R	Forty Acre Mountain Rd. to end
29.00	R	Hathorne Cove
29.27	L	Shore Rd. to end
29.63	L-R	dogleg on Park onto Pocono Point Rd. → Forty Acre Mountain Rd
30.95	R	Forty Acre Mountain Rd. to end
31.25	L	Stadley Rough Rd
32.15	F	Hawley to end
32.65	R	Great Plain Rd. to 2nd L.
32.75	L	Hayestown Rd
33.60	L	E. Hayestown Rd
33.75	L	into parking

Lake Candlewood, Hayestown

[44] Sherwood Island to Saugatuck Reservoir

Meeting place: Westport, at the Park & Ride off Merritt Pkwy, Exit 42
Length: 42 miles
Lunch: There are cafes and restaurants. Or bring lunch to enjoy waterside.
Sights: Long Island Sound, Sherwood Island State Park, beaches, Saugatuck Reservoir, harbors, seventeenth and eighteenth-century houses, seaside mansions, and historic churches.
Challenge: easy to moderate; rolling hills, some flat stretches, and paved streets with some traffic.

Take a ride to the sandy coves of Sherwood Island, passing the pristine and beautiful Saugatuck Reservoir in Redding and the lavish mansions of Southport. The route is modified from Cue #1 on the Connecticut Bicycle Map. We begin the ride at the Park & Ride at Exit 42 on Merritt Parkway in Westport. Turning left on Weston Road, we soon make a right on Lyons Plains Road and go for several miles to the end at three diverging roads. We take the center on Valley Forge Road, following it to the end along Saugatuck Reservoir, far below us on the right. Turning right on the Newtown Turnpike we continue all around the Saugatuck Reservoir, an absolutely pristine lake surrounded by forest that, with a little imagination, could be in the wilds of Alberta. Anywhere along here is a good place to take a path down to the rocky coastline to sit down for lunch.

After leaving the reservoir for some miles, we turn right on a small road oddly named Cross Highway, which leads, after one block, to the village of Redding Ridge, where we turn right again on Route 58 (Black Rock Turnpike). We take this for about six miles past the Aspetuck Reservoir on the left. At the small Aspetuck River, look carefully for the cemeteries on the left and Toth Park on the right where we bear right (do not continue on Route 58) on Redding Road.

After passing Route 136, the second left takes us on North Street, then to the triangle, and right on Congress. At the intersection climbing a small hill, we turn right on Hillside Road to the next intersection, where we turn right on Bronson Road, passing the magnificent, white,

Congregational Church set on the green. After passing the historic eighteenth-century Ogden House Museum and Gardens on the left we follow the houses along Mill Pond and their famous dogwood trees (to be seen in the spring). At the end of Bronson Road, we dip down under Route 95, then do a quick zigzag left on Mill Hill Road, over the railroad tracks, and right on Pequot, dipping left under Route 1. This takes us to a left on Main Street and into the incredibly charming village of Southport, with its Boat Basin, the beautiful stone Episcopalian Church, and exquisite nineteenth-century homes. Following Harbor Road, then Old South Road, we turn left again on Pequot and forward on Beachside Avenue and its magnificent waterfront mansions and their vast gardens.

Just over Route 95, we turn left on Greens Farm Road and then left again on the Sherwood Island Connector into the State Park. Just after entering the park, take the bike path to the right, following it around the perimeter of the park, into the circle around the woods at the western end, and back along the water. Here are two beautiful beaches, very under-used, with a cluster of fishermen angling off Sherwood Point. Return back on the connector, crossing over Route 95 again, and continue left again on Greens Farm Road. The next right on Prospect, another right on Hillspoint, crossing Route 1 and continuing on Roseville takes us through some lovely residential areas. At the end, a left on Cross Highway (actually just a two-lane street) and a quick right on Weston takes us back under the Merritt Parkway (Route 15) and left into the Park & Ride where we began.

Trinity Episcopal Church, 1862, Southport

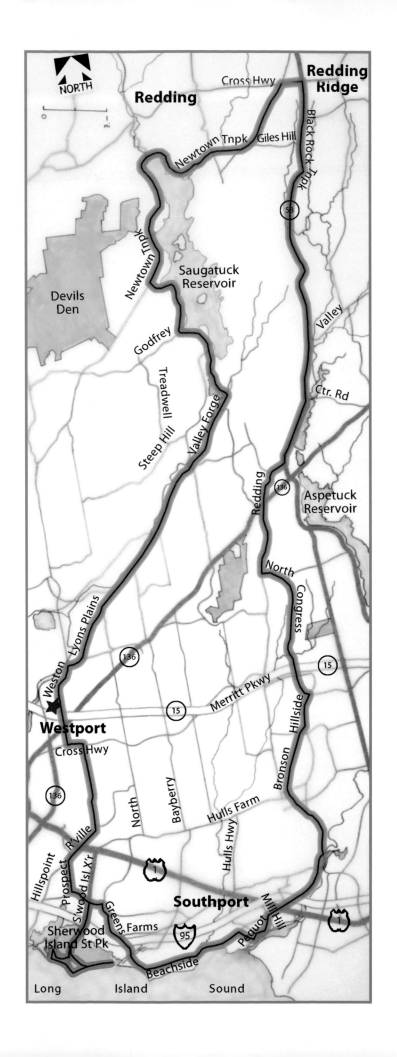

44. Sherwood Island to Saugatuck Reservoir
Meet: Westport, at the Park & Ride off Merritt Pkwy, Exit 42

00.00	L	Weston	28.70	BL	Main to end
00.70	R	Lyons Plains to 3-way split	29.90	R	Harbor Rd—2 bls
04.50	BL	Valley Forge—follows Reservoir	30.10	R	Old South to end
08.30	R	Newtown Tnpk around Saugatuck Reservoir	30.40	L	Pequot → Beachside
			33.00	BL	Greens Farms Road
10.90	R	Cross Hwy—1 bl	35.10	L	Sherwood Island Connector
14.40	R	Rte 58 (Black Rock Tnpk)—pass Aspetuck Reservoir on left to cemeteries on left at Aspetuck River, Toth Park on right (watch for fork in road)	36.20	BR	bike path—follow path around edge of park, circle through woods at western end, and follow along beach to eastern end, then exit park
20.80	BR	Redding	39.00	F	Sherwood Island Connector
22.50	L	North St.	39.40	L	Greens Farms Road—1 bl
22.90	R	Congress—cross Merritt Pkwy	39.70	R	Prospect—1 bl
24.80	R	Hillside	40.10	R	Hillspoint—cross Route 1 and forward on Roseville to end
25.30	R	Bronson—under Rte 95 to end			
28.30	L	Mill Hill—over railroad to 1st right	41.60	L	Cross—1 bl
			41.80	R	Weston under Merritt Parkway
28.40	R	Pequot—under Route 1 to 1st left	42.20	L	into Park & Ride

The beach at Sherwood Island

[45] Darien – Ridgefield – Norwalk

Meeting Place: *Darien Station (Metro-North)—I-95 to Exit 11, north on Boston Post Rd to West Ave*
Length: *55 miles*
Lunch: *There are several small cafes and restaurants in Darien, Ridgefield, and Norwalk. Or bring lunch to enjoy at Compo Beach or Calf Pasture Beach.*
Sights: *Long Island Sound, Compo Beach, Calf Pasture Beach, historic homes and churches, small villages, and the New York border.*
Challenge: *easy to moderate; from flat along the coast to rolling hills inland, all paved streets and roads with some traffic.*

This ride takes us through some of the poshest areas of Connecticut and also through some of the most depressed. It cuts through the southwestern panhandle of Connecticut into the corner of New York State, and concludes with a long ride along the Long Island shore line.

We begin in the upscale community of Darien at the train station and head north on Route 124 for eighteen miles into New York State. The route through the busy town of New Canaan, just north of Darien, takes us near the famous Glass House designed by Philip Johnson and built in 1949, which is now open to the public, along with its painting and sculpture galleries and 47 meticulously landscaped acres (worth a diversion). It's a left on Elm Street in the center of town where Route 124 makes a detour, just across from the train station. Our route passes the beautiful Federal-style Congregational Church, built in 1843, with its Doric pilasters and hexagonal belltower under the tall spire.

Across the state line are the more remote New York villages of Pound Ridge and South Salem, where it is extremely rural. Pound Ridge takes its name from the original Algonquian Indian "pound" or enclosure for game that was on one of the area's many "ridges." The English originally settled here in the 1640s in part of a tract of land purchased from the Algonquians by Captain Nathanial Turner, and it was officially incorporated in 1788. After industry declined in the early twentieth century, the town began to attract actors, writers, artists, and musicians in the 1930s and many of the historic houses were restored. Benny Goodman was one of the first of these residents, and he composed a melody entitled "Pound Ridge." Turning east on Route 35 at South Salem, we re-enter Connecticut and come to the most interesting town of Ridgefield, with its Romanesque revival church built in 1888 with Ridgefield granite and modeled after a small village church in Italy by the architect J. Cleveland Cady, rows of stately eighteenth and nineteenth-century homes, and the Historic Keeler Tavern. Listed on the National Register of Historic Places, the Keeler Tavern Museum, built in 1713 first as a home for Benjamin Hoyt, has been a farmhouse; tavern (by 1862 run by Phillis Dubois, a free black woman); stagecoach stop; post office; hotel for travelers; and, by 1907, home of Cass Gilbert, architect of the US Supreme Court. Now decorated with period furnishings and changing exhibits, costumed guides lead tours through room settings that portray life in rural Connecticut from the early eighteenth century to the mid-twentieth century. Back on our bikes, Routes 102 and 57 take us on a thirteen-mile ride south ending at Westport.

Reaching the coast, we explore all the nooks and crannies of the Long Island sound from the beautiful Compo Beach to the mouth of the Saugatuck River, Calf Pasture Point, with its City Park and beach. With time to kill, a nice long afternoon on Compo or Calf Pasture Beach would be a nice respite before heading back to Darien. Otherwise, moving on, we cross the Norwalk Harbor, and pass through the rather gritty town of Norwalk on Route 136, zigzagging on streets with many different names (but always just follow the signs for Route 136) down to Pine Point, passing the ultra-modern United Church of Royawton. Since the roads down to the Point are private, we continue meandering on Route 136, which takes us all the way back to the Darien Station.

Wilson Cove Yacht Club on the Long Island Sound, Rowayton

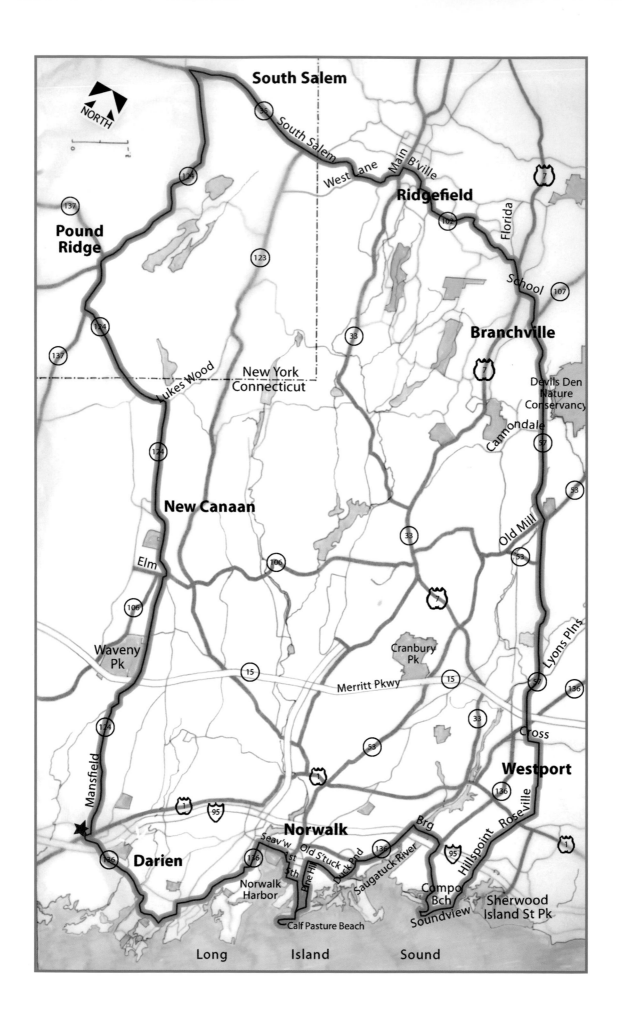

NORTH

South Salem

Ridgefield

Pound Ridge

Branchville

Devils Den Nature Conservancy

New Canaan

Cranbury Pk

Westport

Waveny Pk

Merritt Pkwy

Norwalk

Darien

Norwalk Harbor

Calf Pasture Beach

Compo Bch

Sherwood Island St Pk

Soundview

Long   Island   Sound

45. Darien – Ridgefield – Norwalk
Meet: Darien Station (Metro-North)—I-95 to Exit 11, north on Boston Post Rd to West Ave

00.00	L	North on Mansfield (Rte 124) into NY to South Salem (merges w Rte 137 briefly at Pound Ridge)
17.90	R	South Salem → West Lane → Main (Rte 35)
22.20	R	Branchville (Rte 102)
25.80	R	Rte 7
26.80	L	School St. to Rte 57
27.00	R	Rte 57—cross Merritt Pkwy (Rte 15) to end
35.50	L	Cross—1 bl
35.75	R	Roseville → Hillspoint over Rte 95 to beach
39.70	L	Soundview to end at Compo Beach
40.00	L	into Compo Beach
40.25	R	(around waterside and exit parking lot)
40.80	L	Compo Beach Rd. to end
41.30	L	Compo Rd. South just under Rte 95
42.25	L	Greens Farms → Bridge St. (Rte 136) across Saugatuck R.
42.75	L	Rte 136 (then R-L)
44.20	L	Duck Pond → Old Saugatuck
45.35	L	Pine Hill to end
45.90	R	Canfield to end
46.60	L	Calf Pasture Beach into Park(Circle around Park and exit on Calf Pasture Beach to end)
48.20	L	Marvin → Fifth St. to end
48.50	R	Cove Av to end
48.75	L	First St—1/2 bl to end
48.80	R	Seaview to end
49.25	L	Fort Point (Rte 136) across Norwalk R. to end
44.45	L	Rte 136 (continual turns & street name changes—just follow Rte 136 signs) to Darien
55.00		into parking lot

Keeler Tavern, 1713, Ridgefield

[46] East Coast Greenway: Stamford – Greenwich – New York State

Meeting Place: *parking lot at Dyke Park, Stamford South End (I-95, Exit 7, S. on Washington to end)*
Length: *27 miles*
Lunch: *There are cafes, restaurants, and convenience stores in Old Greenwich, Cos Cob, Greenwich, Byram, and Port Chester.*
Sights: *Dyke Park, marinas and boats, mansions, mansions, and more mansions.*
Challenge: *easy; almost entirely flat, paved streets with little traffic south of the I-95 corridor, but moderate traffic on main city streets north of I-95.*

Note: Watch for "private road" changes, which may require deviation from this route.

The route is given here because it is the westernmost extension of the "East Coast Greenway" bicycle route leading into New York State—a detailed map may be found at the website: http://greenway.org/maps/ECG-CT3.kml.

This is the most frustrating route, however, in the entire state of Connecticut for a bicycle rider. Between Stamford and the New York border, including Old Greenwich, Riverside, Cos Cob, and Greenwich, with probably a hundred miles of meandering coastline on the Long Island Sound and its inlets and harbors, I could not find a single street that leads to the waterside (except under I-95 and just a few miserable little parks)—every access indicated on the map was marked private and off-limits to the public! When I rode this route a few years ago, there was still one beautiful access point across a narrow causeway called Tods Driftway to Greenwich Point Park, with wonderful views of Greenwich Cove and the Long Island Sound, within sight of the faint, jagged skyline of New York City far in the distance, and a long sandy beach. But now you need to show a residents' pass (May 1 through October 31), and all others, including bicyclists, must go into the town of Old Greenwich to the Civic Center 3 miles away to buy entrance tickets. Protest—make your voices heard to the Greenwich Parks and Recreation Department and the Board of Selectmen.

What you will see on this ride are mostly the new mansions of the super rich. A very few of the homes are actually interesting architecture, some historic, especially in Old Greenwich. But if you like touring multimillion dollar estates, this ride is for you. And an advantage to bicyclists is that there is little traffic on these coastal roads, thanks to the exclusivity.

We begin at the small, but truly lovely, Dyke Park on a peninsula jutting out into the Stamford Harbor, with walking paths and picnic areas, and fishermen, overlooking the boat docks on the east and west branches of the Rippowam River. Heading out of the park on Dyke Lane and Washington Boulevard, we cross the River on Pulaski Street and head south on Southfield Avenue toward Dolphin Cove, but

this is all private ("No Trespassing" signs all about), so we head west on Top Gallant and then southwest on Fairfield and Shore Road. Here is where we would have taken the causeway to Greenwich Point Park if it were not for the new discriminatory ruling (off-season, November through April, continue to Tods Driftway into the Park to the end and then return—c. 4 miles additional).

Instead, we head north on Sound Beach Avenue into Riverside, with an excursion into the next peninsula on West End, Riverside, Marks, Willow. Indian Head Road would take us to Indian Point on the Cos Cob Harbor if it were not for more barricades and "no trespassing" signs along the way, so we turn north on Indian Head and Riverside Avenue, passing private roads all the way barring access to the river, until we reach Route 1 or East Putnam Avenue, across the Mianus River Pond, leading to the main shopping area of Greenwich. But we turn left here on River Road. Here is worth a stop at a marina overlooking boat docks and the soaring I-95 bridge. Further on, meandering along Strickland, Sound Shore, and Indian Field Roads, our hopes are dashed, once again by "private road" signs, to reach the end of the peninsula to see the islands, so we turn right on Davis and find ourselves in Bruce Park, with a circle around a muddy pond, but worth relaxing on a park bench to have lunch under one of the few trees in this rather bleak landscape. Circling out and west again, we cross the Indian Harbor on Davis, Indian Harbor, and Museum Drives. If time permits, here would be worth a visit to the Bruce Museum high on the wooded hill, with its impressive collections of modern painting and sculpture.

Continuing forward on Arch Street, just in the shadow of I-95, we pass the Steamboat Harbor with its promenades, waterside restaurants, and excursion boats. Left on Horseneck and south again on Shore Road would take us to (what must be the lovely) Belle Haven Peninsula, but again, "private road" signs send us back north on Field Point Road under I-95, and under the railroad to Prospect, and then west on Old Field Point, which becomes Hamilton and then Ritch. Heading south on Byram Shore Road, we are

Steamboat Harbor, Arch Street (alongside I-95), Greenwich

obstructed again from reaching the end of the peninsula at what would be the southernmost point of Connecticut, so we head north on River Road, under I-95 again, by Mead and South Water to Mill Street, which takes us over a little bridge crossing the grimy Byram River into New York State at Port Chester. Although the immediate area looks a little worse for the wear, one could explore a little further and find some wonderful restaurants.

The return follows what is called (rather optimistically) the "East Coast Greenway." Although one is hard-pressed to find either "coast" or "green," it is a "way" to get back east quickly, following the gritty underbelly of I-95 and the New York, New Haven, and Hartford Railroad, back to our starting point at Dyke Park, where we can probably catch a game of the local Little League.

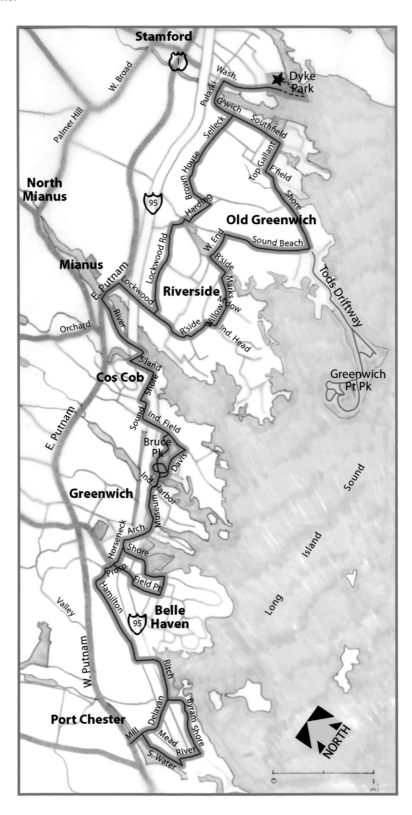

[47] East Coast Greenway: Southport – Stamford

Meeting Place: *Southport Station Parking lot on Center St at Pequot (off I-95, Exit 19, continue past several stops, left on Center under railroad)*
Length: *45 miles*
Lunch: *There are several cafes and restaurants as well as many convenience stores. Or bring lunch to enjoy on the beach.*
Sights: *Long Island Sound, beaches and beach houses, harbors, lighthouse, historic villages, homes and churches, modern architecture, Sherwood Island State Park, and many other waterside diversions.*
Challenge: *easy; almost entirely flat, paved streets with little traffic along the coastline but moderate traffic on the city streets.*

This route takes us through more of the poshest areas of Connecticut, with continual views of the Long Island Sound and the many bays, rivers, and harbors that create this jagged coast and beg for constant diversions from the main route. Along the way there are also small pockets of just plain folks and some deterioration, especially in the larger cities. But here is also where the super wealthy live on grand estates, and there is one eye popper after another. The route west is a modification of the East Coast Greenway trail, with a few detours down to the waterside. A detailed map of this section of the East Coast Greenway may be found at the website: http://greenway.org/maps/ECG-CT3.kml.

Southport is one of the most charming towns in Connecticut, and here is where we begin, just opposite the elegant Episcopalian Church on Pequot at Center Street. Heading west for several miles, to Beachside and Greens Farms Road, we pass magnificent nineteenth-century homes, and the most spectacular waterfront mansions. At the Sherwood Island Connector, we go forward, but if you have some time to kill (and you've started this bike ride early in the day) a detour left, down to Sherwood Island State Park, is exceedingly rewarding, with picnic areas, walks through the woods, and a mile of beautiful beach. Otherwise, we continue on to a left at Hills Point Road to a tour around the coastline, where there are magnificent views of the sound along Soundview and Compo Beach. Again, this is a great place to stop, and even take a dip.

Heading north again on Compo Road South, we cross the Saugatuck River on Bridge Street and here we follow Route 136 (which zigzags along various street names) all the way across the East Norwalk peninsula (Here, also, there would be nice diversions south on Harbor Road to the end of Saugatuck and back; and further on Old Saugatuck Road, a left on Pine Hill heading south would take us a mile down to Calf Pasture Beach, a big sprawling green space surrounded almost completely by water, with more sandy beach—but we do visit that in Ride 45). We continue on Route 136 by Fort Point Street across the Norwalk Harbor by the Washington Street Bridge and south again always following the signs for Route 136 (again, going by many street names), with beautiful views of the sound from a promontory along Wilson Avenue, and another after a left on Bluff Street, to visit the Rowayton Peninsula at South Beach, with its big stretch of sand following the periphery. Rowayton Avenue becomes Cudlipp and Tokeneke, following the coastline, passing a startling, modern architectural wonder, The United Church of Rowayton, with its sweeping and soaring roof peaks, designed by Joseph Salerno in 1962, evoking a billowing sail or spiralling shell.

Locust Hill Road leads to Old Kings Highway (another excellent detour south on Goodwives River Road leads two miles to the beautiful Pear Tree Point Beach and then to Long Neck Point, the entire way designated a "Bike Route"). Our route becomes Boston Post Road (Route 1) (where another detour south on Nearwater Lane would lead to the beautiful Weed Beach Park), then we head south on Weed Avenue along Holly Pond. At the end of Weed Avenue is the lovely Cove Island Park with a wraparound beach and fantastic views of the Sound. We then head straight west on Cove Road through the rather nondescript and industrial coast of southeastern Stamford, where we come to a rather austere end on Jefferson, Dock, Pacific, and Washington Boulevard, where the neglected neighborhoods and industrial parks at this writing are being transformed into upscale neighborhoods with art galleries and design shops. At the end we enter by a gravel path through Dyke Park, with a beautiful promontory jutting out between two large marinas on either side.

The return takes us under the elevated I-95 through Stamford, where we pass by the railroad station and left to South State Street, continuing on the more direct route indicated on the official map of the East Coast Greenway, back to our start at Southport.

The Long Island Sound from Dyke Park, Stamford

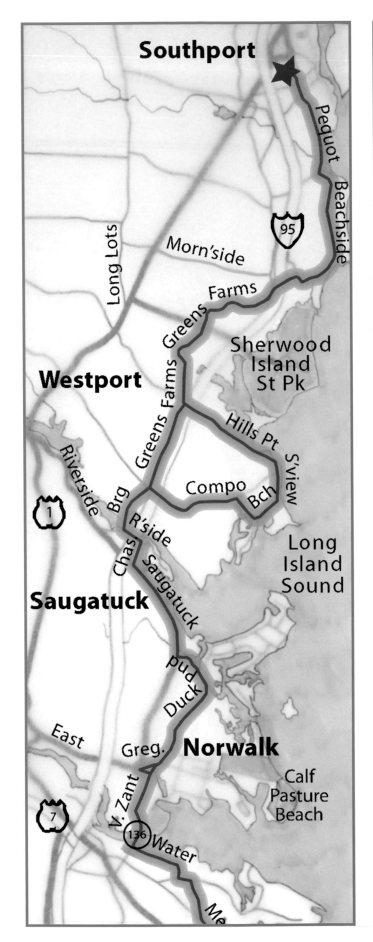

Southport

Pequot

Beachside

95

Morn'side

Long Lots

Greens Farms

Westport

Greens Farms

Sherwood
Island
St Pk

Greens Farms

Hills Pt

S'view

Riverside

Brg

Compo

Bch

1

R'side

Long
Island
Sound

Chas.

Saugatuck

Saugatuck

pud

Duck

East

Greg.

Norwalk

V. Zant

7

Calf
Pasture
Beach

136

Water

Me

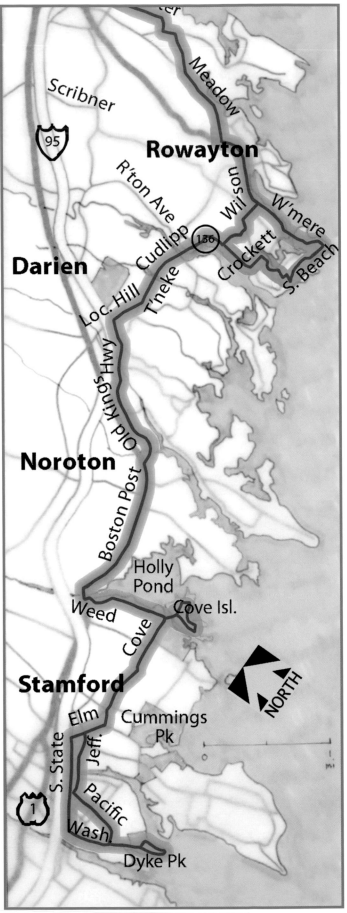

95

Scribner

Meadow

Rowayton

R'ton Ave

Wil'son

Darien

Cudlipp

136

Crockett

W'mere

Loc. Hill

T'neke

S. Beach

Old Kings Hwy

Noroton

Boston Post

Holly
Pond

Cove Isl.

Weed

Cove

Stamford

NORTH

Elm

Cummings
Pk

1

S. State

Jeff.

Pacific

Wash.

Dyke Pk

210

47. East Coast Greenway: Southport – Stamford
Meet: Southport Station Parking lot on Center St at Pequot (off I-95, Exit 19, continue past several stops, left on Center under RR)

00.00	R	Pequot
00.75	F	Beachside
02.20	F	Greens Farms
03.50	L	Hills Point → Soudview → Compo Beach (zig-zags)
06.90	BL	Compo South—under railroad and I-95 to immediate L.
07.10	L	Bridge St. across bridge to 1st L.
07.60	L	Riverside
07.70	R	Charles → Park
07.90	L	Saugatuck
08.90	L	Duck Pond Rd. → Old Saugatuck to end
10.23	BR	Gregory to 1st L.
10.35	SL	East Ave.
10.45	R	Rte 136 (follow signs with name changes: Van Zant → Fort Pt. St. across bridge to 1st L. → Water → Burritt → Woodward → Meadow → Wilson)
13.85	L	Bluff → Westmere
14.53	F	Parkview
14.63	R	Rocky Point
14.70	F	S. Beach → Crescent Beach Rd. to end
14.92	R	Ensign to 1st L.
14.95	R	Gull to 1st R.
14.97	L	Pine Point
15.35	R	Roton to 2nd L.
15.58	L	Crockett to end
15.80	R	Rte 136 (Rowayton → Cudlipp → Tokeneke)
17.10	L	Old Farm to immediate R
17.11	R	Locust Hill to just before I-95
17.66	F	Old Kings Hwy
18.75	L	Boston Post Rd. (Rte 1) across bridge to 1st L in Stamford
20.20	L	Weed to end into Cove Island Park across bridge and around perimeter road to exit back at Weed
22.07	L	Cove to end
23.20	R	Elm to 2nd L
23.40	L	Jefferson
23.86	F	Dock
24.00	L	Pacific
24.50	L	Dyke Park into the park and around to the right on the gravel path

Return by the East Coast Greenway official route:

25.00		Return by the gravel path out of the park on Dyke Park Ln → Washington
25.52	R	South State
26.05	R	Elm
26.40	L	Cove
27.55	L	Weed
28.42	R	Boston Post Rd. (Rte 1)
29.80	BR	Old Kings Hwy
30.70	F	Locust Hill
31.50	F	Tokeneke → Cudlipp → Rowayton
32.76	L	Wilson
33.12	L	Rte 136 (Wilson)
34.50	L	S. Main
35.80	R	Washington across bridge
35.90	F	Rte 136 (Washington St. → Fort Point → R on Van Zant → Gregory around R to 1st L on Old Saugatuck → Duck Pond → R on Saugatuck → R on Park → Charles → L on Riverside → R on Bridge St.) —cross Saugatuck River
39.80	F	Greens Farms
42.60	F	Beachside
44.10	F	Pequot
45.00	L	Center St. into parking lot

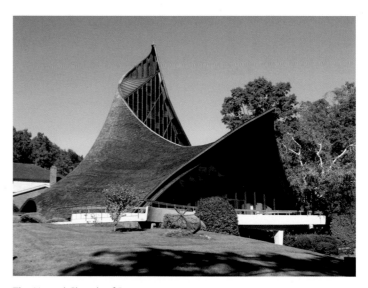

The United Church of Rowayton, 1962

[48] East Coast Greenway: Milford – Southport

Meeting Place: *Connecticut Audubon Coastal Center, end of Milford Point Road, Milford (I-95, Exit 34)*
Length: *43 miles*
Lunch: *There are many cafes, restaurants, and convenience stores. Or bring lunch to enjoy on the beach.*
Sights: *Long Island Sound, beaches and beach houses, harbors, historic homes and churches, Connecticut Audubon Coastal Center, Wildlife Refuge and Bird Sanctuary, Seaside Park, and Barnum Lighthouse.*
Challenge: *easy; generally flat, paved streets with little traffic along the coastline but moderate traffic on the city streets.*

This is the central stretch of the East Coast Greenway Trail from the New York border to New Haven, where it connects with the Farmington Canal Greenway. Like the others, it meanders in and out of coastal peninsulas, with magnificent views of the Long Island Sound, with beach house after beach house, and some of the most extravagant old mansions on the Connecticut coast. Many of the beaches are privately owned, but there are state and city parks where the public has access. The ride described here follows the direct official Greenway Trail on the route westward from Milford, more of a "brownway," especially when it cuts through the heart of Bridgeport, but it gets us rather quickly to our destination at Southport. A detailed map of this section of the East Coast Greenway may be found at the website: http://greenway.org/maps/ECG-CT3.kml. The return departs from the official trail on the way back (eastward from Southport), looping down to the coast whenever possible for a more picturesque view.

We depart from the beautiful Charles E. Wheeler Wildlife Management Area, which should be visited either at the beginning or the end of the ride. Riding northward to Route 1, we then cross the bridge over the Housatonic River into Stratford. This takes us, via Ferry Boulevard, Stratford, and Connecticut Avenues past the tiny, jewel-like St. Nicholas Russian Orthodox Church in Stratford through to some unavoidable derelict areas of East Bridgeport full of once-lovely houses that we hope someday will be restored. At the most unattractive intersection of Stratford Ave., I-95, and the Peqonnock River, there is a view of the Bridgeport-Port Jefferson ferry amidst immense power houses and smokestacks, charming in its own right.

Exiting the rather nondescript several miles of Bridgeport and Black Rock, it is with some relief that we cross the little bridge over Ash Creek on Post Road into a different world. A slight detour on Riverside Drive and South Benson Street delivers us to Old Post Road and into the heart of historic Fairfield, with its great stone Romanesque-style First Church Congregational and the splendid white colonial Town Hall (rebuilt in 1791 after being burned to the ground by the British—it houses documents dating from 1648) across from each other. The Burr Homestead of 1790 is one of many eighteenth-century homes along this street.

Continuing on Old Field Road to Sasco Hill and then Harbor Road takes us into the absolutely exquisite nineteenth-century town of Southport with its glassy streams bounded by weeping willows, a serene Trinity Episcopal Church mirrored across a pond, the harbor with its yachts, and some of the most spectacular neo-Gothic and neo-classical homes.

We return from here eastward on the same route directly through Fairfield, now deviating at Black Rock from the East Coast Greenway as we turn south on Gilman Street along the lovely Ash Creek and on to Grovers Street which follows the coastline with a long promenade and sandy beach. Across Cedar Creek from some of the most extraordinary mansions facing the sea appears the long spit of land ending in the Barnum lighthouse. Zigzagging along the coast and up Ellsworth Avenue we return to Fairfield Avenue, and then, at the elevated railroad, head east on a very industrial and potted Railroad Avenue to reach Iranistan Avenue back under the I-95 overpass, then South Avenue to Barnum Dyke and gratefully down to the sea. A bike path leads out to the end of a long spit of land called Seaside Park, lined with a very busy beach, at the point of which is an isolated rocky point with the simple white Barnum lighthouse crowning the end, worth a short walk. The view from here is magnificent, with tugboats pulling barges from the port of Bridgeport on Burr Creek. Returning by the same bike path, we enter Sound View, with a long promenade and a rather impressive monument to Christopher Columbus. Here we can catch a glimpse of the Bridgeport-Port Jefferson Ferry crossing the Sound. (For the more adventuresome, take the 45-minute ferry ride across to Port Jefferson and bicycle across Long Island to the ferries at Sayville crossing to Fire Island—c. 20 miles each way).

Broad Street takes us north to Cesar Batalla Street and smack into the looming red brick neo-Romanesque home of the Barnum Institute of Science and History in Bridgeport. Water Street north meets Fairfield Avenue, which takes us across the bridge to Stratford Avenue and again across the no man's land of I-95 overpasses; but after the second bridge we turn south on Seaview, which runs along an industrial but colorful coastline. Back up Central Avenue and right on Orange, we head out on Hollister Avenue and then Lordship

The lighthouse at Seaside Park, Bridgeport

Boulevard across a vast marshland full of long-necked stalking birds, with the faint horizon of the smokestacks of Bridgeport way in the distance. Zigzagging through the town of Lordship to skirt several blocks of private beachfront, then following the coast on Park, Cove Prospect, Riverdale, and finally Short Beach Road, we cut through on a short bike path to Main Street and past the Igor Sikorsky Memorial Airport. Main Street, Stratford, is lined with charming eighteenth-century homes, one of which belonged to William Samuel Johnson, one of the framers of the US Constitution. East on Stratford Avenue and then Ferry Boulevard returns us across the Housatonic River and back down to the Wildlife Management Area. Here, a stroll out on the beach to view the expansive marsh grass and then up the tower to see the sun low on the horizon over the mud flats is a must.

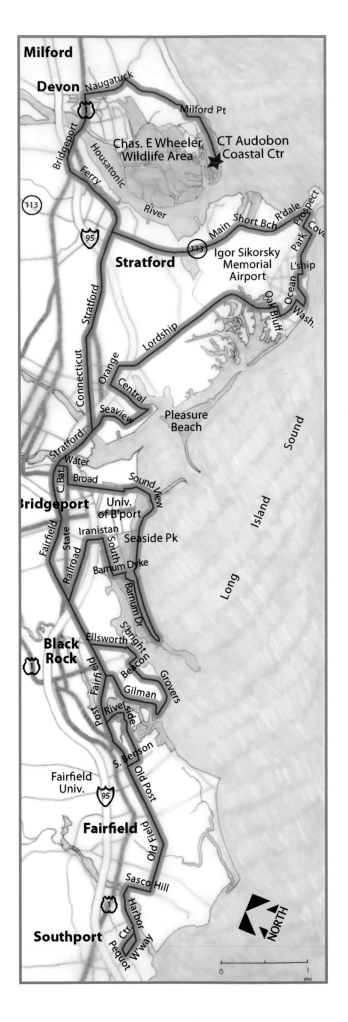

48. East Coast Greenway: Milford – Southport

Meet: CT Audubon Coastal Center, Milford (I-95, Exit 34, R on Rte 1, L on Naugatuck, R on Milford Point to end)

[Out route follows the official CT East Coast Greenway Trail]

00.00	F	Milford Point to Seaview
00.35	L	Milford Point
01.53	L	Naugatuck
02.10	L	Rte 1 (Bridgeport Av) across bridge & under I-95 to 1st L.
02.75	BL	Ferry Blvd. (Rte 130), keep L under I-95 again, to end
04.00	BR	Stratford under I-95 → Connecticut under I-95 → Stratford across bridge, under I-95 & across 2nd bridge → Fairfield under Rte 8 & I-95 → Post Rd. across small bridge to 1st L.
10.81	L	Riverside around bend to end
11.71	R	S. Benson 1 bl
11.89	L	Old Post
12.40	F	Old Field to end
13.61	R	Sasco Hill to 1st L.
13.95	R	Harbor Rd. across bridge to 1st L.
14.08	L	Harbor Rd. thru Southport
14.66	R	Westway 1 bl

[Return route deviates from the official CT East Coast Greenway Trail around shoreline]
[If starting here, park at the Southport RR Station parking lot]

14.95	R	Pequot 1 bl
15.05	R	Center to end
15.16	L	Harbor Rd.
15.83	R	Harbor Rd. across bridge
15.96	R	Sasco Hill to 2nd L.
16.30	L	Old Field → Old Post → Post Rd. → Fairfield
19.24	R	Gilman → Grovers along sea
21.25	R	Beacon to end
21.38	L	Seabright to end, dogleg L/R on Brewster:
21.58	R	Ellsworth
22.05	R	Fairfield Av under I-95 to 1st R. before RR
22.22	R	Railroad Av to just before I-95 overpass
23.42	R	Iranistan Av under I-95 to 2nd R.
23.56	R	South Av to end
24.07	L	Barnum Dyke to end
24.33	R	bike path along beach & Barnum Dr into Seaside Park to end at lighthouse jetty
25.30		Return by bike path along beach → Sound View Dr to end of park
27.72	L	University to 1st R.
27.76	R	Broad under I-95 to 1st R.
28.42	R	Cesar Batalla 1 bl to end
28.50	L	Water
28.74	R	Fairfield → Stratford over 2 bridges to I-95E
29.60	R	Seaview
30.40	L	Central under I-95 to 1st R.
30.96	R	Orange
31.23	R	Hollister under I-95 → Lordship Blvd.
31.35	BR	Lordship Blvd. (Rte 113) across marsh to 1st X.
33.58	R	Oak Bluff to 1st L.
33.74	L	Ocean
34.02	R	Washington to end
34.16	L	Beach Dr to 1st R.
34.41	R	Ocean to 1st R.
34.60	R	Lordship Rd. 1 bl to end
34.64	L	Park to end
35.00	L	Cove to end
35.37	R	Prospect to 1st L.
35.59	L	Riverdale to end
36.06	R	Lighthouse 1 bl to end
36.09	L	Short Beach
36.46	F	bike path 1 bl to road
36.51	F	Main (Rte 113) past Sikorski Airport
38.42	R	Stratford 1 bl
38.54	BL	Ferry Blvd.
39.75	BR	Bridgeport Av (Rte 1) across Housatonic R. bridge
40.44	R	Naugatuck
41.84	R	Milford Point to end
42.55	F	into parking

Town Hall, Colonial, rebuilt 1791, Fairfield

[49] Housatonic River: Long Island Sound – Ansonia

Meeting Place: Route 15, Exit 53, Route 110 South to Park & Ride
Length: 45 miles
Lunch: There are many cafes, restaurants, and convenience stores. Or bring lunch to enjoy along the river.
Sights: Housatonic River, Naugatuck River, Long Island Sound, beaches and beach houses, wetlands, historic homes and churches, and Boothe Memorial Park.
Challenge: mostly easy; with flat, paved streets and roads with little traffic along the coastline but moderate traffic on the city streets and on Routes 34 and 110. Moderate difficulty on the Great Hill west of Ansonia.

The centerpiece of this ride is the crossing high above the Housatonic River on the bike trail alongside the Merritt Parkway Bridge, Route 15. This is the beginning of a planned trail to parallel the Merritt Parkway for 37.5 miles all the way to the New York border, as a part of the great dream for a continuous East Coast Greenway.

We begin our ride at the entrance to the bridge trail, but first, we travel for six miles north on Route 110 under the Merritt Parkway, past Sikorsky Aircraft, along the west side of the Housatonic River, riding high on a bluff past the Beacon Point Marina far below, through Sunnyside, under Route 8, to Shelton. Here we cross the bridge over the Housatonic and immediately plunge down the opposite bank and onto the Derby Greenway Trail, which curves around under the Conrail Bridge (an optional right turn takes a detour through the fields and back to the main path) and under Route 34, where it zigzags up to an elevated trail along the Naugatuck River. Two miles later we reach the end and cross the Naugatuck on Division Street. Now Route 115 turns into 334, which takes us almost six miles to the northernmost point of our ride, taking us back over the Naugatuck at Ansonia, where there is a great view of the old industrial town, with smokestacks and rusted metal warehouses blocking the view of the huge Gothic stone church on the hill. After crossing Route 8, Fountain Lake Road continues on a steady, steep incline to 11.65 miles, where the road makes a sharp bend to the right, becoming Great Hill Road, appropriately named, at which we continue uphill until we finally reach the top at 12.50 miles. This is the only moderately difficult section of the entire ride. But the reward is one continuous thrill ride downhill all the way to the end at 13.70 miles. After turning left on Route 188, we are rewarded further with another cruise downhill.

Here we find ourselves back at the Housatonic River, with gorgeous views of the water, motorboats and water skiers, Yale University's Gilder Boathouse, waterfront homes, and fishermen along the shores, all the way for four miles back to Derby, where we continue on Route 34 back across the Naugatuck again and southward. After Mount St. Peter's Cemetery, south on Derby Milford Road and then Wheelers Farms Road takes us to Wellington and the entrance to the bike path. After a loop we find ourselves hurtling down the protected path alongside the Merritt Parkway and suddenly sailing high above the Housatonic, with motorboats passing far below and a wonderful view of the river stretching north and south. Signs at the end of the path direct us south on Route 110, which we take for 3 1/2 miles along the river again to the I-95 overpass.

This is Stratford, where Ferry Boulevard, Elm Street, and Main follow the Housatonic shoreline all the way to Short Beach, past the Igor Sikorsky Memorial Airport. Following the streets on the peninsula facing the Long Island Sound (Lighthouse, Riverdale, Prospect, Cove, Park, Lordship, Ocean, and Oak Bluff), we get beautiful views of the beaches on the sound. Lordship Boulevard now takes us across the magnificent expanse of marshes, "The Great Meadow," extending all the way to Bridgeport, after which we ride to the west on Route 113. Surf Avenue takes us back under I-95 past the St. Michael's Cemetery and the exquisite, tiny, gold-domed St. Nicholas Russian Orthodox Church. Stratford Avenue east and Route 113 North lead through the heart of Stratford, with its beautiful old homes and historic churches. At the country club, we detour on Cutspring and Whippoorwill to head north on Main Street through Putney, where we encounter one of the most curious places, the Boothe Memorial Park, with its historic Boothe Homestead and outbuildings in eccentric styles, along with an original Merritt Parkway Toll Booth plunked down in the middle of a field. The park would be a great place to lounge a bit, listening to live music (if the time is right) before continuing on to Route 110 and back to the parking lot.

Boothe Homestead, Boothe Memorial Park Museum

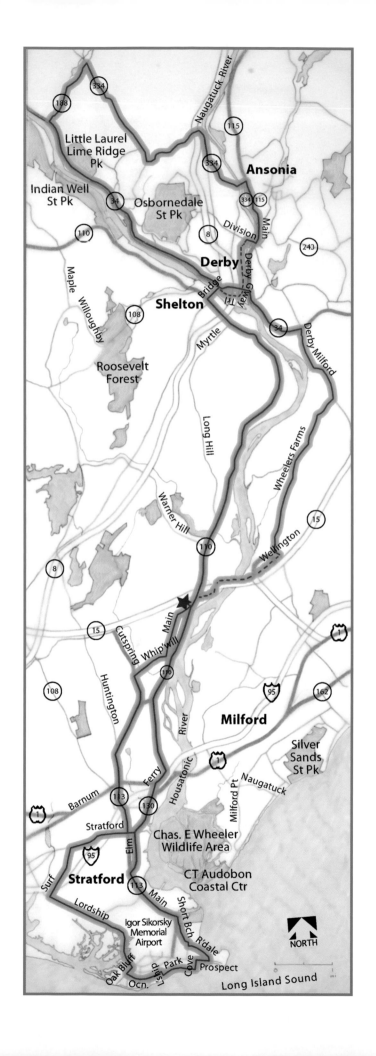

NORTH

Long Island Sound

49. Housatonic River: Long Island Sound – Ansonia
Meet: Rte 15, Exit 53, Rte 110 S. to Park & Ride

00.00	L	Rte 110 under Rte 15 to Shelton
06.00	R	Bridge St. across Housatonic R. bridge
06.22	R	Derby Greenway Trail bikepath (6.64 L on trail, 6.84 L again—optional R at 6.64 loops around and rejoins the main trail)
07.95	R	Division across Naugatuck R.
08.15	L	Main (Rte 115)
09.29	L	Rte 334 (Maple → Franklin to end)
10.05	R	Rte 334 (Waklee across Rte 8)
10.57	L	Rte 334 (Fountain Lake → Great Hill Rd)
13.70	L	Rte 188 (Squantuck) to end
14.95	L	Rte 34 through Derby, under Rte 8 and across the Naugatuck R., then south
21.05	R	Derby Milford
22.45	R	Wheelers Farms Rd
25.50	R	Wellington
25.64	L	on to bike trail following Rte 15 over Housatonic R. to end of bridge
26.76	R	on bike trail to 110 S.
27.30	L	Rte 110 (River Rd)
29.59	L	Rte 110 (E. Main) to end at Rte 95
30.85	R	Rte 130 (Ferry Blvd.) straight (don't BR) under I-95 to end at Stratford Av
32.05	L	Elm
32.78	L	Main (Rte 113) past Sikorski Airport
34.05	L	Dorne to 1st R.
34.10	R	Short Beach
34.47	R	Lighthouse to 1st L.
34.50	L	Riverdale to end
34.97	R	Prospect to 1st L.
35.20	L	Cove to end
35.35	R	Park along L. I. Sound to end
35.90	R	Lordship Rd. to 1st L.
35.95	L	Ocean to end
36.58	R	Oak Bluff to 1st L.
36.68	L	Lordship Blvd.
37.92	L	Lordship Blvd. (Rte 113)
38.82	R	Surf
39.77	R	Rte 130 (Stratford Av)
40.07	BL	Rte 130 (Stratford Av)
40.67	L	Rte 113 (Main) to country club
43.02	L	Cutspring to 1st R.
43.50	R	Whippoorwill to end
44.14	L	Main to end
45.22	L	Rte 110 (River Rd) to parking
45.40	L	into parking

The Housatonic River at Shelton

[50] New Haven – Seymour – Ansonia – Southbury

Meeting Place: Edgewood Park at Whalley & Fitch (car entrance on Edgewood Av)
Length: 53 miles, 36 miles, or 29 miles
Lunch: There are several small cafes. Or bring lunch to enjoy by the river.
Sights: Historic homes, churches and public buildings, state parks, quaint villages, forests, farms, lots of green, lakes, Housatonic River, Naugatuck River, and Southford Falls State Park.
Challenge: moderate to difficult; paved roads with light to moderate traffic, continuous long hills, and several miles of dirt road.

To the average rider, this very hilly ride to the northwest from New Haven may seem punishing at times, but the experienced rider will chew it up and spit it out. From Westville in New Haven, Route 243 takes us out of the city, and a right on Route 313 takes us on a steady climb past the tranquil Peat Swamp Reservoir all the way to Seymour, with its stately nineteenth-century buildings along the Naugatuck River. The busy freeway, Route 8, has spoiled this town with its giant overpass cutting right through the middle, but there's still plenty of charm on either side. We make a sharp left to climb up Church Street, passing some charming eighteenth and nineteenth-century homes and the Trinity Episcopal Church built in 1857, with its mix of Federal portico, Victorian ornamentation, and Romanesque window, and then on to Botsford, turning right on Canfield, then a dogleg left-right onto Cemetery Road. A left on Holbrook, continuing straight after the circle (here's where inexperienced riders might want to turn left and head back home on Route 334 to 243) takes us on a downhill ride to the Housatonic River. Route 34 North along the river offers panoramic views and a little restaurant to relax and take in the scene. Just before this heavily trafficked road crosses the river, we exit on Loughlin Road for some more climbing through a wooded area, meandering north on Good Hill Road and O'Neill Road. (*Here, at the end at Route 188, some riders may want to take a right and head back home, to make the ride 36 miles.*)

Continuing on, the route is another short figure 8 of seventeen miles (*So, again, the fainthearted can cut out at midpoint, but they would be missing some treats*). We turn left on Route 188, and immediately at the Y in the road, we bear left on Edmonds Road, which becomes Jeremy Swamp Road, part of the way a dirt road passing through glorious forests with an occasional home here and there, and crossing Route 67 to the end. At Community House Road, a left takes us back to Route 67, where we cross again and head south on Kettletown Road, where it's almost all downhill, past some elegant farms. This merges into Mapletree Hill Road, and shortly thereafter we go to the left on Laborde and Pisgah Roads and another left on Thompson, which becomes Hulls Hill Road for several uneventful miles north through rural residences. A right on Diamond Match Road ends at Route 188 at the beautiful Southford Falls State Park, where, at somewhere around the midpoint in our ride, a rest by the falls would be nice.

Continuing north on Quaker Farms Road, we turn right on Route 67. (You can detour on the Old State Road [No. 2 and No. 1] wherever it veers off to the left giving a respite from the traffic on this main road.) Three-quarters of a mile on the right is a must-stop for the most heavenly home-made ice cream at Rich Farm. You'll need the energy, turning right on Hogsback Road, for the next half-mile that seems straight up. It's more like a camel's back. The reward comes with a nice mile and a half downhill (although it would be more pleasant if they kept this road repaired).

At the end we turn left on Route 188, past the Posypanko Recreational Park, mostly woods, and through the nineteenth-century village of Quaker Farms, a delight with its early Victorian home of 1857, several classical homes, and the stately Congregational Church with its mix of Federal-style architecture with Gothic windows. From here we travel all the way back down to the circle we crossed before, and continue straight on Route 334 to the town of Ansonia. After crossing over Route 8 (this time sunk into the ground) and then the Naugatuck River again, we turn right on Route 115 through the commercial area of the town. A left on Route 243, go sharply uphill past some wonderful eighteenth-century and nineteenth-century homes. Here we are following the route from Ansonia to New Haven taken by the inventor of the bicycle, Pierre Lallement, on his first ride in April 1866. After a few miles we are rewarded with a couple of long, glorious, downhill stretches where you can even exceed the posted speed limit if you're brave. This takes us to Whalley Avenue and our start at Edgewood Park, where a nice long rest on the grass along the West River would be relaxing.

Southford Falls State Park, Southford

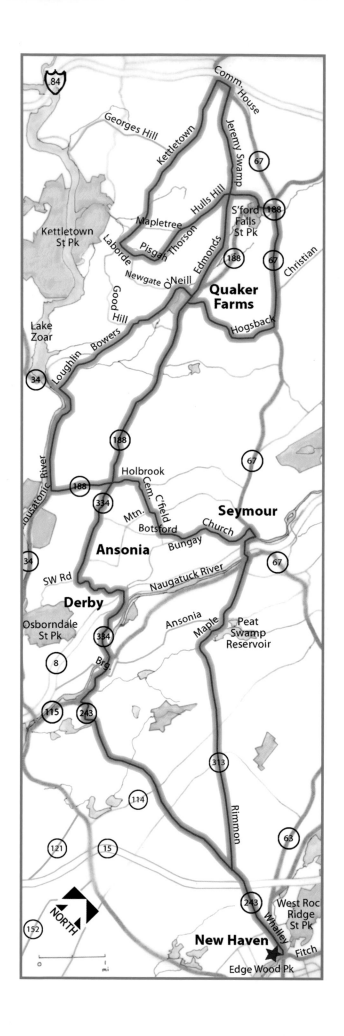

50. New Haven – Seymour – Southbury
Meet: New Haven—Edgewood Park at Whalley & Fitch (car entrance on Edgewood Av)

00.00	L	Whalley Av—west
00.10	BL	Rte 243 (Fountain → Ansonia Rd) under Rte 15
02.00	BR	Rte 313 (Rimmon → Maple → Broad → River) across river, under Rte 8 to end
08.90	L	Rte 67 (Bank) across creek to 1st L.
09.00	SL	Church → Bungay
10.60	BR	Botsford to first X
11.00	R	Canfield to end
11.35	L	Mountain to 1st R.
11.43	R	Cemetery to end
12.05	L	Holbrook to circle

(Tired? Go to 40.04—L.)

12.60	F	Rte 188 (Squantuck) to end
13.80	R	Rte 34 along river past curve L
15.83	R	Loughlin → Bowers to end
17.88	R	Good Hill to end at Y
18.18	BL	O'Neill to end

(Tired? Go to 36.13—L.)

19.33	L	Rte 188 (Quaker Farms Rd)
19.45	BL	Edmonds → Jeremy Swamp Rd. (becomes a dirt road between Plaster House & Hulls Hill Rds)

(Tired yet? R. on Hulls Hill instead—go to 31.16)

Continue across Rte 67 to end

23.78	L	Community House Rd. 1 bl to end
24.00	L	Kettletown to end at merge with Mapletree
27.38	F	Mapletree Hill to 2nd L.
27.88	L	Laborde to 1st L.
28.18	R	Pisgah to 2nd L.
28.53	L	Thorson → Hulls Hill past Jeremy Swamp Rd. to 1st R.
31.16	R	Diamond Match to end
31.36	L	Rte 188 (Quaker Farms) past Southford Falls St. Pk to end
31.98	R	Rte 67 (Oxford Rd)

35.03	R	Hogsback to end (tough climb)
36.13	L	188 (Quaker Farms) to circle
40.04	F	Rte 334 (Great Hill) to Y
43.09	BR	Rte 334 (Wakelee Av) across bridge over Rte 8
43.63	BL	Rte 334 (Franklin)
44.33	L	Rte 334 (Maple) across bridge over river
44.45	R	Rte 115 (Main)
45.60	L	Rte 243 (Elm → Prindle → Pulaski Hwy → Ansonia → Fountain)
52.30	BR	Whalley to 2nd light
52.40	R	into Edgewood Park

A farm in Southbury